FOCUS ON JESUS

FOCUS ON ISSUE

FOCUS ON JESUS
Essays in Christology and Soteriology

by

Gerald O'Collins, SJ, and Daniel Kendall, SJ

Gracewing.

First published in 1996

Gracewing
Fowler Wright Books
2 Southern Ave, Leominster
Herefordshire HR6 0QF

ISBN 0 85244 360 9

Typesetting by
Action Typesetting Ltd, Gloucester, GL1 1SP

Printed by Cromwell Press
Broughton Gifford, Wiltshire, SN12 8PH

Contents

An asterisk indicates that an article was co-authored by Daniel Kendall and Gerald O'Collins.

Introduction

In *Interpreting Jesus* and *Christology*,[1] one of us (Gerald O'Collins) developed two full-length studies on the person and redemptive work of Jesus Christ. Despite their differences in overall content and specific concerns, both books centred on the Easter mystery – a choice supported by both the historical origins and the liturgical traditions of Christianity.

Nevertheless, for the convenience of the reader, this present work will not begin with the essays on the crucifixion and resurrection, but will take the 'mysteries' of Christ as they unfold sequentially: from the incarnation, through the public ministry, the crucifixion and the resurrection, and on to the mediation of salvation for the human race. This whole sequence will be introduced by a critical survey of current trends and will be followed by a review of several major themes in Christology. The central aim of this collection is to fill out and add to what *Interpreting Jesus* and *Christology* have already proposed.

The titles of the articles (which were originally published between 1971 and 1995) have, with one exception, not been changed. A few necessary corrections have been made. The pieces are all reprinted here with permission.

Some of the articles have a popular and 'spiritual' tone. We include them, however, without any embarrassment. Increasing contacts with Eastern Christians – 'Eastern' in the sense of their being Asian and/or members of 'Oriental' Christian Churches – have helped to convince us that theology must also be expressed in more accessible (that is to say, more narrative, spiritual and liturgical) ways.

In the table of contents an asterisk indicates the articles which were originally co-authored by both of us. One of us (Daniel Kendall) prepared the index of names. This book is dedicated to Loretto Kendall and appears also in memory of Robert D. Kendall (d. 1993). As regards the Bible, we generally follow the RSV (Revised Standard Version) translation.

Gerald O'Collins, SJ, 31 July 1995.
Gregorian University (Rome);
Daniel Kendall, SJ,
University of San Francisco.

1

What they are saying about Jesus now

Christology, as Walter Kasper and others (including myself) have argued, should centre on the death and resurrection of Christ. Taking their stand at the paschal mystery, theologians, like the Christian liturgy itself, should look forwards to the *eschaton* and backwards to the pre-existence of the Logos 'before' creation. Nevertheless, this critical evaluation of some tendencies and debates in current Christology will follow an easier pedagogical order: from the eternal life of the Trinity, through the incarnation and paschal mystery, to the role of Christ as universal Saviour and coming Lord. It is obviously impossible to report everything and everybody. The present chapter will select a number of significant themes and mention a few relevant authors.

I

Pre-existence, incarnation and virginal conception indicate a first batch of Christological controversies and, one must also say, aberrations. In his *Christology in the Making*[1] James Dunn argued a double thesis: first, that there are no demonstrable antecedents in Jewish and Gentile thought that could account for the fully personal pre-existence of Jesus as the eternal Son of God and Logos who came into our world; second, that it was only with John's gospel and letters that we clearly find this doctrine of pre-existence. Dunn's first thesis seems sound: the particular Christian doctrine of the Son of God's personal pre-existence and incarnation has no genuine parallels in earlier religious beliefs from which it could have been derived. The second thesis has been widely criticized and rejected. Even if Christ's divine pre-existence is 'only' the point of departure for the apostle's argument, it is affirmed as early as Paul (2 Cor 8:9) and some older traditions he quotes (e.g. Phil 2:6–11).

Dunn's book had the merit of stirring up a considerable biblical and theological debate. One limitation in that controversy – a limitation that is more regrettable on the part of the theologians who entered in the debate – was the widespread lack of interest in what philosophers of religion had been saying about time and eternity in the aftermath of a 1981 article by Eleonore Stump and Norman Kretzmann.[2] Karl-Josef Kuschel's 664-page work, *Born Before All Time?* (German original 1990),[3] illustrates how theologians have often failed to be in sufficient dialogue with their philosophical colleagues. The book diligently gathers data from the Scriptures and a wide range of religious writings but largely ignores the relevant issues explored by philosophers. Any serious theological study of Christ's pre-existence demands, it seems to me, a careful philosophical analysis of time and eternity.

Some recent revisionist Christologies (if one may call them Christologies rather than 'Jesuologies') have been chipping away at the central belief that is very closely connected with Christ's pre-existence: namely the incarnation of his divine person. The objections are manifold.

(a)   During his ministry Jesus did not teach this about himself.

(b)   The doctrine of the incarnation gradually evolved – in a kind of apotheosis of Jesus, which

(c)   was promoted by common thought-forms in the ancient world and reached its climax in 325 when the Council of Nicea declared him to be 'of one being' with God the Father.

(d)   It is logically incoherent for one person to be simultaneously divine and human.

(e)   The traditional doctrine of the two natures, besides being inexplicable, leaves Christ's humanity depersonalized and turns Jesus the man into a non-person.

(f)   The revisionists encourage us to talk of the incarnation as 'merely' metaphorical and accept Jesus simply as someone through whom God acted decisively and who embodied the divine purposes and ideals for us.

John Hick's 1993 work, *The Metaphor of God Incarnate*,[4] exemplifies this kind of case against traditional belief in Jesus Christ as one divine person in two natures. Does this case stand up?

As regards (a), two items call for mention. Hick and others who take this revisionist line seem to assume tacitly that anything that Jesus did not say of himself in so many words does not really count. This is to minimalize the force of implicit claims; not to make blatantly explicit claims about oneself is not necessarily the same thing as making no claims at all. When Jesus asserted his personal right to decide about the divine law, the divine place (the Jerusalem temple) and the divine day (the sabbath), he lifted himself above the prophets and laid claim to an authority on a par with God's. What are we to make of his using the self-designation of 'the Son of man' to arrogate to himself the divine prerogative of future and final judgement over all people? A further consistent feature in the argument coming from those who press point (a) is that they quietly presume that God's revelation stops with the life of Jesus. How do they know that subsequently (that is to say, after Jesus' death and resurrection) God did not and/or could not disclose to the apostolic generation anything essential about the person and work of Jesus? Why must the revelation of Jesus himself and his role be limited to the period of his earthly life?

Point (b) simply flies in the face of the evidence from the first Christian writer. In his earliest letter (1 Thessalonians, from around 50) Paul refers the divine title 'Lord' 24 times to Jesus. In a subsequent letter he ascribes to the 'one Lord, Jesus Christ' the divine work of creation (1 Cor 8:6). He applies to Christ several texts which the Old Testament uses of Yahweh: for instance, 'Whoever calls upon the name of the Lord will be saved' (Rom 10:13). In his first letter Paul writes of Christ's role as eschatological judge (1 Thess 2:19; 3:13), an eminently divine function. It is clear that the apostle is not introducing a novelty by attributing divinity to Christ. Certain key passages that bear on the issue come out of the pre-Pauline tradition like the liturgical formula (in Aramaic), 'Come, Lord Jesus' (1 Cor 16:22), and the hymn that not only confesses the exalted Jesus as the divine 'Lord' to whom belongs 'the name which is above every name' (= God's name) but also applies to him Old Testament language used for divine worship (Phil 2:9–11; see Isa 45:23).

While debates over such issues as justification not coming through the works of the law turn up repeatedly in the Pauline correspondence, nowhere do we find hints of any controversy stirred up by Paul's Christological monotheism. His readers do not object to what the apostle writes about Jesus: as Lord and Son of God, being acknowledged alongside 'God our Father', deserving adoration, and being the divine source of human salvation. If Paul was responsible for promoting a startling new doctrine, the apotheosis of Jesus, why was no voice raised against him in angry protest – especially from the earliest Christians who had been raised in strict Jewish monotheism?

What of (c), the assertion that people in the ancient Mediterranean world were readily disposed to believe in a pre-existent divine person entering our world? We have already noted the serious case James Dunn has brought against this claim. We might also recall how alien belief in incarnation was to several major philosophies around at the time Christianity emerged: Epicureanism, Stoicism and developed forms of Platonism. Despite some possibilities for dialogue which Christians developed from the time of Justin Martyr, the genuine incarnation of the pre-existent Son of God was quite alien to Stoic pantheism and Platonic idealism. They resisted rather than supported any move to believe in such an incarnation. As many have argued, instead of representing a capitulation to Platonism in particular, the Council of Nicea opposed a heresy (Arianism) that was encouraged by Platonic doctrine. With its teaching about the gods living in intercosmic spaces and paying no heed to our world, Epicurean thought was in practice atheistic and lent no support to Christian belief in incarnation. Epicureans, no less than Stoics and Platonists, did not encourage such a belief. In any case, here as elsewhere, cultural and philosophical causes that might have encouraged a new belief must always be distinguished from reasons for and against its being true.

Then there is argument (d): the 'incarnation' is logically incoherent since this belief puts together properties that are incompatible. How can one person, Jesus Christ as the God-man, be simultaneously finite and infinite – that is to say, mortal and limited (since he is man) and immortal and unlimited (since he is God)? It seems like proposing a contradiction in terms such as calling someone a married bachelor. A clear contradiction in terms arises, however, only when mutually exclusive properties are being attributed to the same subject, at the same time and *within the same field of reference* (or under the same aspect). The last condition saves belief in incarnation from the charge of being a blatant contradiction in terms: Jesus Christ is infinite within one field of reference (his divinity) and finite within another (his humanity). One may not be able to establish positively the logical coherence of the incarnation. But the revisionists can assert its incoherence only by slipping over one element in the principle of contradiction.

What of the claim that belief in the incarnation, by acknowledging only his divine personhood, credits Christ with a depersonalized and radically deficient humanity (e)? Something essential seems to have been left out: his human personhood. This difficulty rests, however, on a confusion between nature, whether human or divine, (which one 'has') and person (which one does not 'have' but 'is'). Christ had and has a complete human nature – that is to say, all the essential properties required to make up a full human being. The person or subject acting through this (perfect) human nature was/is that of the divine Logos and not an individual human personhood that in all other cases corresponds to an existing human nature. In this way Christ's humanity, so far from being depersonalized, belonged and belongs to a person who eternally is.

Revisionists, when interpreting Jesus, reach for the language of action and try to steer clear of ontology or categories of being (f). They highlight the way Jesus functioned and functions as embodying the divine will for us and perfectly representing God among us. But could Jesus function perfectly in that way without being a divine 'Insider' – that is to say, without being ontologically divine himself? Functions do not hang in the air, so to speak, but are exercised by persons. Talk about what Jesus did and does for us cannot evade the question: who and what is he? Can he function in a divine way without actually being divine?

A devastating problem for many revisionists is that their assertions about Jesus exemplifying in a special, even unique, manner the divine purposes for us sits very uneasily with their deism. The deist God, after launching the world through creation, keeps it in existence but otherwise leaves it alone and does not intervene in any new way. If deist-style revisionists opt for such a closed history of the universe, in which God never intervenes but leaves everything and everyone to act in accord with the laws of the original creation, how can they then acknowledge Jesus as truly revealing in a *special* way God's purposes for us? If we think of God after creation as having simply left the universe on automatic pilot, we cannot then turn around and recognize Jesus (or anyone else for that matter) as someone through whom God deals with us in new and special ways.

The deist option eliminates more than the incarnation: it excludes all such special interactions of God with the world as the unique call of the Jewish people, the sending of Old Testament prophets, the resurrection of Christ, the charism to write inspired scriptures, personal providence for every individual and, of course, any miracles. This means, for example, denying the virginal conception of Jesus or at least 'explaining' what Matthew and Luke intend to say about Jesus' human origins in such a way as to leave out any special intervention of God.

At times, authors who are not, or are not clearly, deists allow only for an alternative when they come to the question of the virginal conception: Matthew and Luke intend *either* to impart some revealed truth *or* to make some factual claim about God's miraculous intervention when they write of Jesus' conception. The latter possibility is then ruled out, and we are left with 'a truth of revelation' (Edward Schillebeeckx), a 'primal symbol' (Hans Küng) or 'a theme of Christian pneumatology' (Jürgen Moltmann) – not with 'new informative data' (Schillebeeckx), 'a report of a biological fact' (Küng) or 'a question of gynaecology' (Moltmann). But why not both – namely, the report of a miraculous fact which is also revelatory, symbolic and concerned with the

Holy Spirit? Like some others, from the outset these three authors narrow the choice to an either/or which they fail to justify.

Apropos of Christ's virginal conception, the *Catechism of the Catholic Church* (nn. 496, 498, 505)[5] tries to bolster up the New Testament testimony by following a few fathers of the Church such as Irenaeus and Tertullian who read a key verb of John 1:13 in the singular, instead of the plural ('who was born' rather than 'who were born'). The verse refers then to Jesus' being miraculously conceived by the will of God and not to the new life of grace given to believers. However, the Greek manuscripts of John's gospel read the verb in the singular. It is regrettable to find the virginal conception being defended by an appeal to a minor patristic tradition that textual criticism of the New Testament cannot honestly follow.

II

A whole batch of current debates concerns our knowledge of Jesus' history. From the time of Justin Martyr in the second century and Origen in the third, Christian apologists, while aware of the way their faith was and is peculiarly vulnerable to historical criticism, have refused to give up claims about history necessarily involved in the personal continuity between the pre-existing Logos and the man Jesus who lived and died in Palestine. The confession of faith in Jesus Christ has always involved historical risk, but it is like the risk involved in accepting that 'this man and this woman' are our parents and relying on many other such lived certitudes in our daily existence. It is logically possible that we may have been deluded but we are confident that it is not so.

Contemporary issues about the earthly Jesus include (A) such general questions as *our sources for his life and the right methodology for appropriating his history*, and (B) *such specific questions as Jesus' use of 'Abba' and 'Son of man', his sinlessness and a certain feminine aspect to him*. Any full list of general and specific matters being currently debated would be much longer. But let us at least sample what is going on.

As regards (A), the media have made a great deal of the

work of the Jesus Seminar, theories about Q (a lost collection of Jesus' sayings used by Matthew and Luke) and attempts to assign early dates to such apocryphal, non-canonical documents as the Gospel of Thomas and the Gospel of Peter.

In 1993 the North American and European scholars who make up the Jesus Seminar published the results of their research into the 1,500 sayings of Jesus found in the four canonical gospels and the non-canonical Gospel of Thomas as *The Five Gospels: What Did Jesus Really Say?*[6] They judged only 18 per cent of the words attributed to Jesus to have been spoken by him. A colour-coded analysis of his sayings uses red if the seminar thinks that Jesus made the statement, black if it judges the statement to have been created by the early Christian editors, pink and grey if they place it somewhere in between. The members of the seminar want the public to perceive them as hardheaded, scientific scholars, free from the subjective prejudices of traditional faith. Seeds of doubt about any such claim to 'scientific objectivity' had already begun to grow in my mind after they published *The Gospel of Mark: Red Letter Edition* (1991)[7] and listed only one out of 111 sayings as absolutely authentic: 'Render to Caesar the things that are Caesar's and to God the things that are God's' (Mark 12:17). Why single out for top historical marks this statement and not rate as highly any of the other numerous sayings in Mark's gospel that commentators normally consider to go back to the earthly Jesus? Am I being overly suspicious in thinking that subjective convictions about Church-state separation and related political matters just might have encouraged the seminar members to assign to this particular verse the highest grade of authenticity?

One is left puzzled over what the members of the Jesus Seminar are finally trying to do. Are they systematically evading the religious purposes for which the gospels were written? We would only shake our heads in sorrow over experts who use their painstaking archaeological excavations at Troy as an excuse for never reading Homer's *Iliad* for what it is: a simply wonderful epic poem. What would we make of those who prattle on about passages from Holinshed's *Chronicles* chosen and adapted by Shakespeare for his historical plays but refuse to face the great drama and poetry of *Henry V* and *Richard II*? The work of the Jesus Seminar seems like a game in which entire texts get split up into fragments and are left on the ground as if they were items from a dismembered jigsaw puzzle. After being tagged ('Jesus undoubtedly said something like this'; 'probably from Jesus'; 'doubtful'; or 'Jesus never said this'), the fragments are put back together. Even then the color-coding gets in the way of reading the complete text, which any case is not the same as our canonical gospels.

The four gospels are literary wholes, which testify to the life, death and resurrection of Jesus with a spiritual power that has changed and shaped the lives of millions of people. The primary point of these texts is to invite a religious response, not to serve as raw material for dissection in an historical laboratory. Are the members of the Jesus Seminar just a little like those who want to use the *Iliad* simply as a source book for archaeology and Shakespeare's historical plays as background material on the rise of the Tudor dynasty? In short, does the approach of the Jesus Seminar reveal a reader-response that methodically does violence to the texts under scrutiny?

In defence of what he and his colleagues have been doing, the founder of the seminar, Robert Funk, pleads that 'Jesus should have his say in the religion that bears his name'. If Jesus had wanted to have a direct, personal say, however, he would have left us material in writing. We still have nearly a thousand letters from one near-contemporary of his, Cicero (d. 43 BC) and ten books from another reporting the wars he won, Julius Caesar (d. 44 BC). Instead of following suit, Jesus founded a community that produced four gospel portraits of him. These can be classified as representational and concerned with portraying historical detail (Mark, Matthew and Luke) or more theologically impressionistic and concerned with characteristic effects produced by Jesus (John). Jesus has had his say, but he has mediated it all through the committed witness of those foundational witnesses, the four evangelists, and the other New Testament authors.

Two of the gospel-writers (Matthew and Luke) apparently used as their major sources Mark, and a collection of sayings now lost (Q) which scholars have at least partially reconstructed from the reports of Jesus' sayings in Matthew and Luke. It is one thing to join the majority of mainline scholars in endorsing this two-source theory: it is quite another to accept Burton

Mack's ingenious and often arbitrary reconstruction of various stages in the composition of Q that correspond, he claims, to different periods in the history of a hypothetical Q community. As Mack tells (or should we say makes up?) the story of that imaginary community in *The Lost Gospel* (1993),[8] they changed from a loose table-fellowship in Galilee who recalled Jesus' quips which challenged the conventional values of his society to become an apocalyptic sect concerned with judgement to come. Along the way they transformed the original Jesus, a Hellenistic Cynic sage, into a Jewish, apocalyptic prophet. In reaching these conclusions, Mack suppresses evidence from the first Christian writer, Paul (as well as from the pre-Pauline material embedded in the apostle's letters), reruns the hypothesis of Jesus as a Cynic-style philosopher (an hypothesis discredited long ago and recently blown out of the water by Hans-Dieter Betz), and 'describes' a primitive Jesus movement that seems to have very little to do with religious faith and everything to do with counter-cultural criticism. Luke Timothy Johnson was not exaggerating when he wrote 'Mack shows how bad biblical scholarship can get and yet be published'.[9]

John Dominic Crossan offers a further example of such bad biblical scholarship, hyped up into a marketing success. In his 1991 *The Historical Jesus* (followed up in 1993 by *Jesus: A Revolutionary Biography*),[10] he 'reconstructs' Jesus as a Cynic peasant, akin to a magician, who practised free healing, common eating and radical egalitarianism in the service of the kingdom of God. Jesus' 'resurrection' is reduced to his continuing impact on his community and symbolic assertions about leaders and leadership groups. Neither talk of resurrection nor any of the Son of man sayings (except for the one about his 'having nowhere to lay his head') make it to the thirteen pages which are allowed to derive from the historical Jesus. The book is fundamentally flawed by assuming that a number of non-canonical gospels (in particular, the Gospel of Thomas, a so-called Egerton Gospel, a hypothetical Cross Gospel and the so-called Secret Gospel of Mark) originated substantially in the earliest period of Christianity (AD 30–60) and hence antedate all of our canonical gospels. The problem, however, is that we have only fragments for the 'Egerton Gospel', whose composition is generally dated to the second century, and none at all for the 'Cross Gospel', which Crossan argues is now embedded in the mid-second-century apocryphal Gospel of Peter. A very early date for the Gospel of Thomas and its independence from our New Testament gospels are maverick claims endorsed by hardly any reputable scholars. As regards the 'Secret Gospel of Mark', many scholars doubt its very existence and some wonder whether it was a hoax perpetrated by the late Morton Smith.

As regards (B), any list of particular issues being currently discussed about the earthly Jesus would have to include *his filial consciousness, his self-presentation as the coming Son of man, his sinlessness and some feminine aspects to him.*

Mark's gospel twice reports Jesus as indirectly referring to himself as 'the Son' (Mark 12:1–12; 13:32). In a passage from Q (Matt 11:27 = Luke 10:21–22) Jesus claims a unique and exclusive knowledge of God as 'the Father' possessed by 'the Son' who is tacitly identified as 'me'. In Mark's gospel Jesus calls God 'Father' at least four times and once addresses God as 'Abba' – an Aramaic term which seems to lie behind a number of passages in Matthew and Luke where God is named as 'Father'. James Barr and others have rightly corrected the view that 'Abba' was baby-talk, a way of speaking about or to God as 'Daddy'. Nevertheless, while 'Abba' was not simply a child's address to its male parent, this familiar way of speaking to God was highly unusual, if not unique, in the Palestinian Judaism of that day. 'Abba' was a significantly distinctive feature of Jesus' prayer life. His example encouraged his followers to pray to God in that way (Gal 4:6; Rom 8:15).

A few scholars have argued against tracing back to Jesus the use of 'Abba' or 'Father' of God or in prayer to God. In doing so, they find it significant that 'Father' occurs 'only' nine times in Q and 'only' four times in Mark. After all, the canonical Old Testament calls (or addresses) God as 'Father' fifteen times. The Qumran documents have yielded at least three cases of God being addressed as 'Father' or 'my Father', and there is one such case from the non-canonical 3 Maccabees. This argument, however, slips over a crucial point about the comparative length of the literature being examined: the Old Testament and the other texts of pre-Christian Judaism from which the cases are drawn constitute a corpus of writing (A) that is at least forty times longer than Mark and Q combined (B). That fact makes the thirteen references to God as 'Father' in (B) look distinctive over against the nineteen references in the ever-so-much-longer (A). Add too that God is called 'Father' at least 254 times in the whole of the New Testament, a body of texts which is no more than 20 per cent of the size of (A). The nineteen examples from (A) then begin to look insignificant when compared with the cases of God being called or addressed as 'Father' found in the New Testament and to be traced back to Jesus himself. His teaching and the example of his own prayer prompted the personal sense of God's fatherhood typical of early Christianity.

Debates continue to swirl around what the Synoptic gospels report about Jesus' use of the 'Son of man' language: in particular, his repeated (implicit) references to himself as the Son of man who will come to judge all people at the end. This claim to come in heavenly glory and act with sovereign power at the final judgement is nothing less than an assertion of personal divine authority. God and only God has the prerogative of judging everyone at the end, as the Old Testament expectation of the future 'day of the Lord' makes clear. Some scholars continue to doubt whether Jesus made reference to himself as the 'Son of man' to come in judgement. One of their major reasons is that they find it 'problematic' to imagine Jesus casting himself in the unique, divine role of eschatological Judge.

A further question which deserves singling out from the many contemporary issues about the historical Jesus touches his sinlessness. Was he not merely (a) *de facto* free from sin but also (b) *de iure* immune from the possibility of sin? If we answer yes to (b), how can we reconcile such an absolute intrinsic impeccability with Christ's complete humanity – and, specifically, with his genuine human freedom? If he could not have been bad, was he truly human?

The issues here are complex and obviously involve our notion of what human freedom is or should be like. I devote pages to the issue of Christ's sinlessness in my *Christology*.[11] Here let me simply note that one cannot hold that being human and being incapable of sin are incompatible properties. Otherwise I would have to say that the two-weeks-old Francesco I baptized recently is not truly human, because here and now he is incapable of sin.

In this forthcoming book I tackle a related question: that of the faith exercised by the earthly Jesus. It is regrettable that several commonly used translations of the New Testament are still reluctant about rendering Hebrews 12:2 as it stands: the perfect climax of those who have run the race of faith (Heb 11:1–12:2), Jesus is 'the pioneer and perfecter of faith'. Commentators on Hebrews have long ago made their peace with the fact that the author is speaking of Jesus' own faith. Some contemporary translators do not seem to be in dialogue with the commentators. They continue to add to the original (Greek) text an 'our' and turn Jesus into 'pioneer and perfecter of our faith'. Of course, he is also that, but Hebrews is primarily presenting his life as the supreme example of how to run the race of faith. From the time of St Thomas Aquinas Catholics normally held that, right from his conception, the human mind of Jesus enjoyed the beatific vision. The result of such a gift was to rule out the possibility of his exercising faith during his earthly existence; he lived by sight. Leading Catholic theologians, the International Theological Commission and now the *Catechism of the Catholic Church* have quietly dropped talk of the beatific vision in the human mind of Jesus during his earthly pilgrimage. That makes it more of a pity that the *Catechism* did not follow the Letter to the Hebrews and raise the question of Jesus' faith.

The *Catechism* does quote two key New Testament passages (Matt 23:27 in no. 558 and 1 Cor 1:24 in no. 271) that bear on Jesus' feminine qualities. In the first he himself evokes an Old Testament picture of God as a protecting eagle, but gives the images a homely twist by presenting himself as a farmyard hen who gathers and protects her chickens under her wings. In the second passage Paul begins (or lends support to?) the tradition of applying to Jesus an Old Testament feminine personification of the divine activity by calling Jesus 'the Wisdom of God'.

III

Apropos of the death and resurrection of Jesus, a vigorous biblical (and to some extent theological) debate about the intentions with which Jesus faced death has quietened down. Almost a

Catholic monopoly during the seventies and eighties, this debate saw notable contributions coming from Guillet, Hengel, Kasper, Kessler, Küng, Léon-Dufour, Moltmann, Pesch, Schillebeeckx, Schürmann, Vögtle and others. In his *The Death of the Messiah* Raymond Brown documents and evaluates, at least on the exegetical side, the points that came up in that debate.[12] What was largely missing in the debate, however, was a sense of the need to go further and explore what constitutes the moral and religious value of a human action. (After all, the issue under examination is what Jesus intended humanly when confronted with death.) What, for instance, was the object of Jesus' decision and action in Gethsemane? Struggling with this question matters, if we wish to avoid saying that he directly willed his death and saved us by an act of suicide. Once we allow that a calculus of ends and means properly enters into mature decision-making, how might we apply this to Jesus on Holy Thursday (and before)? Beyond doubt, any full and certain answers will evade us. Nevertheless, an adequate reflection on his human intentionality must at least raise such questions. We need also to ask: Could/did Jesus' action enjoy a plus-value that went beyond his conscious intentions? This question wins support from a fact of experience: other agents and particular circumstances can enhance the value of a good human action beyond, even far beyond, what the agent ever intended or imagined.

Some authors continue to give fresh currency to claims about Jesus in his passion being a scapegoat, being cursed by God and suffering the pains of the damned. Here I can do no more than deplore such a theology which, from the time of the Reformation, has enjoyed its supporters among Catholics and other Christians but which rests on a false exegesis of Paul and other biblical authors. In my *Interpreting Jesus* (Chapter 5) I offered a detailed rebuttal of such views of Jesus' death.[13] Volume One of Bernard Sesboüé's *Jésus-Christ l'unique médiateur* (1988)[14] presents and critiques the sad story of those who have misrepresented the crucifixion as if Jesus were a penal substitute who suffers on the cross the full power of divine anger and punishment.

Issues on Christ's resurrection, some of which have been around for many centuries, retain much of their vitality.

(a) What did the New Testament witnesses mean by announcing Jesus' resurrection?

(b) What should we make of the two signs to which they point: the Easter appearances and the discovery of the empty tomb (in that order, please, and not reversed as unfortunately happens in the *Catechism of the Catholic Church*)?

(c) How and why can we believe the resurrection message?

As regards (a), reductionist theories would have it that nothing happened to the dead Jesus himself; it was rather his cause which continued. In his *Risen Indeed. Making Sense of the Resurrection* (1993) Stephen Davis criticizes trenchantly and very effectively such theories.[15] They turn the New Testament writers either into 'obtuse communicators' who were unable to express their intended meaning or into 'deceptive communicators who hid their intended meaning behind the words they used'. With admirable clarity Davis also deals with difficulties raised about (b) and (c), producing one of the best books on the resurrection for years.

IV

Through his resurrection from the dead and the gift of the Holy Spirit, Christ became the effective Saviour of (a) all humanity and (b) the whole cosmos. Both claims call for some attention.

With regard to (a), the resurrection lifted Jesus beyond historical limits to become *the* effective way to God for every man and woman. The faith of the New Testament and of later Christians, even if not articulated in these terms, clearly holds that 'outside Christ there is no salvation'. He is the light of the world who enlightens everyone, the one name under heaven through which we can be saved, the unique mediator between human beings and God.

Some such as John Hick argue that this Christocentric attitude, even if based squarely on the New Testament, should be dropped in favour of a theocentric approach that would tolerantly accommodate different religious responses to God. By requiring not only Christianity but also all major faiths to abandon their particular, absolute claims, Hick is trying to impose his own new form of absolutism – a classic example of the absolutism at the heart of 'liberal' views. If Hick simply wants to 'propose a view', it can then, of course, be disregarded as only an opinion.

Others such as Karl Rahner, Jacques Dupuis and Gavin D'Costa have refused to let their proper respect for the values of non-Christian religions quietly erode their faith in Christ as the unique and universal Saviour. No one can expect here an utterly clear solution to what is after all the mystery of God's redeeming activity, deployed through Christ for all past, present and future human beings. The most satisfactory approach will be to explore the anonymous but effective presence of Christ as the universal Wisdom and Logos. Some push here the contribution of a so-called 'Spirit Christology'. But it seems to me that such a Christology frequently attenuates the distinction between the second and the third person of the Trinity to the point of amalgamating them.

With regard to (b), the ecological crisis, with its growing sense of the delicately balanced and extremely vulnerable life-systems of our planet, has given fresh urgency to the questions: How does the risen Christ show himself to be the dynamic power at the heart of the cosmic process? What should our faith in him produce in terms of active respect for the integrity of creation? Can we connect the scientific findings and theories about our evolving universe with the figure of the cosmic Christ?

This chapter bears the title 'What they are saying about Jesus now'. The set of questions in the last paragraph suggest that this piece could be finally retitled: 'What are they asking about Jesus now?' or 'What should they be asking about Jesus now?' In Christology as elsewhere, wisdom and insight reveal themselves as much or even more by asking the right questions rather than rushing straight to allegedly correct answers. We saw above the need for more philosophical stringency in exploring such issues as the eternal pre-existence of the Logos, the incarnation and some of its implications like sinlessness. Fortunately, philosophers such as Stephen Davis are on hand to help theologians correct and clarify their Christological questions.

2

Christ today

No one – and, specifically, no theologian – has ever managed to describe fully, let alone explain comprehensively, the personal identity and saving 'work' of Jesus Christ: for the simple reason that it cannot be done. In his first encyclical, *Redemptor Hominis*, Pope John Paul II applied the term 'mystery' to Christ about fifty times: a forceful reminder that in our pilgrimage of faith we must be content with glimpses, parables and partial insights. We can never dare to claim, 'Now I really know who Jesus Christ is and what he has done for us'. The fascinating and awesome mystery of the One who is Son of God and Saviour will remain with us all the days of our life.

Nevertheless, there are ways of giving more adequate shape to what we do experience and know of Jesus. Ultimately it is a matter of remembering, observing and cherishing the 'whole Christ', the one whom we will find not only throughout Christian tradition and at the origins of Christianity, but also in every human being, at the heart of the material cosmos, through all our senses, and in all the Christological mysteries – from the creation to the *eschaton*. This chapter can do no more than outline what is entailed in such attention to the 'whole Christ', 'the First and the Last' (Rev 1:17) and 'the same yesterday, today and forever' (Heb 13:8).

The total Christian tradition

No other traditional document on Christ has ever enjoyed the status and success which the Council of Chalcedon (AD 451) won for its teaching on his two natures and one person. At the climax of two centuries of controversy about the right way to interpret and express who (that is, the person) and what (that is, the natures) Jesus Christ was and is, this Council declared:

> Therefore, following the holy fathers, we all with one accord teach others to acknowledge one and the same Son, our Lord Jesus Christ, at once complete in Godhead and complete in humanity, truly God and truly man, consisting also of a rational soul and body; of one substance with the Father as regards his Godhead, and at the same time of one substance with us as regards his humanity; like us in all respects, apart from sin; as regards his Godhead, begotten of the Father before the ages, but yet as regards his humanity, begotten for us and for our salvation, of Mary the Virgin, the God-bearer; one and the same Christ, Son, Lord, Only-begotten, to be recognized in two natures, without confusion, without change, without division, without separation; the distinction of natures being in no way annulled by the union, but rather the characteristics of each nature being preserved and coming together to form one person and subsistence, not as parted or separated into two persons, but one and the same Son and Only-begotten God the Word, Lord Jesus Christ; even as the prophets from earliest times spoke of him, and our Lord Jesus Christ himself taught us, and the creed of the fathers had handed down to us.

I have quoted this classic text at length, because – despite its being probably the most important piece of official Church teaching in post-apostolic times – it indicates how we dare not at this point take a reduced view of the Church's past and sell short the 'whole Christ' of the Christian tradition.

Certain limitations show up at once in the definition of Chalcedon. First, the text is a piece of teaching ('we all with one accord teach'), and is not as such a creed to be used in Christian worship. It records the teaching, not the praying, Church of the past. Second, the definition says nothing about

Jesus' crucifixion and resurrection, while his ministry gets the merest nod ('our Lord Jesus Christ himself taught us'). To put the matter in an extreme form: everything that Chalcedon affirms could still be valid if Jesus had been miraculously snatched away from this world and never died on Calvary. At best, his death is only hinted at in phrases like 'truly man' and 'like us in all respects, apart from sin'. Third, the Council acknowledges his divine and human characteristics in a variety of ways ('complete in Godhead and complete in humanity, truly God and truly man' and so forth) *before* it introduces its own special contribution ('recognized in two natures, without confusion' and so on). In other words, the definition notes the way in which earlier Christian tradition had already elaborated diverse expressions for the being human and the being divine in Christ. Presumably, later Church teachers and writers would produce further ways of speaking about him. Nowhere does Chalcedon impose its 'two-natures' terminology as the *only* language to be used henceforth by all Christians of all times.

Further, we would absurdly limit what we can learn of Jesus Christ from Christian tradition if we ignored the rich range of ways in which his followers have transmitted their experiences of him. To begin with, they have left us hymns, poems, sermons, liturgical texts, scripture commentaries and other writings that centre on him. For example, many who today sing the very personal and deeply-felt prayer 'Godhead here in hiding whom I do adore' – the Hopkins' translation of the hymn to the Eucharistic Lord, *Adoro te devote*, commonly attributed to St Thomas Aquinas – will never have read a page of the latter's theology, nor probably even have heard of the Chalcedonian definition. Yet the Christian tradition continues to speak to them from other, more devotional sources such as the moving chapter from the *Imitation of Christ* (II, 8) on familiar friendship with Jesus; 'To be without Jesus is a grievous hell; to be with Jesus is a sweet paradise.'

Again, there are figures from the Christian past, such as Francis of Assisi, Teresa of Avila or Charles de Foucauld, who were driven by their experience of Jesus to found, reform or inspire religious families and movements which are still with us today; so that when we encounter a Franciscan, a Carmelite or a Little Brother or Sister of Jesus, we can expect to learn something of the special ways in which the Lord was active and experienced by those great Christians in the past whom their modern descendants recall.

Very soon after the foundation of Christianity, other believers began to express their faith and feelings through art: from the simple, tender frescoes in Roman catacombs to the vast bronze statue of the risen Christ in the main audience hall at the Vatican, from the carvings on Chartres cathedral to Rembrandt's treatments of the Emmaus scene, and from the mosaics in Ravenna to Georges Rouault's 'The Holy Face'. As the novelist Iris Murdoch has written in *The Black Prince*: 'Art ... is the telling of truth, and is the only available method for the telling of certain truths.' Admittedly, art has not been the only available method for telling the truth about Christ. Otherwise the gospel writers, for example, would never have been inspired by the Holy Spirit to set down in writing what Jesus's followers had 'heard with their ears, seen with their eyes, looked upon and touched with their hands' (1 John 1:1). Nevertheless, Christian art has consistently mirrored with a peculiar intensity the essence of faith in the Word made flesh. It has attempted to represent the whole person of Jesus Christ, his character and universal significance as Son of God and Saviour. Of course, this art has varied and continue to vary from sublime masterpieces to the much-criticized mass-productions in oleograph, plaster or even modern-day plastic. Yet the fact remains that in all these ways it has told the truth about Jesus with stunning power. I have never heard of anyone, even the most brilliant theologian, wanting to hold a copy of the Chalcedonian definition on his death-bed. But I do know many people who wish to hold a crucifix when dying. And I also know an old ex-prison chaplain who, during thirty years of service, attended fifty-eight hangings. The condemned men found great comfort from the conventional picture of the Sacred Heart which he gave them to kiss and then to grasp in their hand, as the noose went round their neck and the trap-door was sprung open. That picture, with the devotion it expresses, is yet another item which has come to us from our total Christian tradition about Jesus Christ. It, too, has told us something of the truth about him.

The origins of Christianity

Later Christians have always looked back through their traditions to find Jesus there at the origins of Christianity. Through the incarnation, ministry, crucifixion, resurrection, and sending of the Holy Spirit, he did not communicate to the founding fathers and founding mothers of the Church some organized body of revealed truths. Rather he left them wrestling with the mystery of his person and his saving function. Some of them encountered the risen Christ in the period following the first Easter; all of them knew themselves to be permanently incorporated into him through baptism, and all of them had received his Holy Spirit. Their total experience of Christ generated richly varied ways of expressing and proclaiming him. Thus when they thought of his unique relationship with the Father for the salvation of the world, they called him 'Son of God' (Rom 1: 3ff; Gal 4:4–7). When they spoke of him as they experienced him in the worshipping community, they named him 'Lord' (1 Cor 12:3).

If we wish to trace the whole story of New Testament faith, both chronologically and in order of importance, *the end* is where we start – with Christ's saving death and resurrection. Christian faith in Jesus of Nazareth began with his resurrection and the Easter appearances, which brought the disciples to know and believe that the crucified Jesus had been raised and exalted as 'the Son of God in power according to the Spirit of holiness by his resurrection from the dead, Jesus Christ our Lord' (Rom 1:4).

The paschal mystery was the centre for Paul, who wrote his letters during the period between 48 or 49 and the early 60s of the first century. When he composed his gospel around AD 65, St Mark took matters back to Christ's baptism, and left us a work which has often been described as a passion story with a long introduction. In a thoroughly Pauline way, Good Friday and Easter Sunday brood over this gospel, which includes neither nativity nor incarnation narratives. When they wrote later with Mark's gospel in front of them, Matthew and Luke decided to begin with accounts of Jesus's birth and childhood. Finally, towards the close of the first century, St John began his gospel with the sublime announcement: 'In the beginning was the Word, and the Word was with God, and the Word was

God ... And the Word became flesh and dwelt amongst us.'
The movement from Paul through the first three gospels to John
represented an increasing concern to clarify and express Jesus'
origins. This movement continued beyond the age of the apostles to culminate in Chalcedon's confession that Christ was one
person in two natures.

We could decide that our own pondering on the Christ presented by the New Testament should follow the same direction which Christian faith and writing originally took. We
would begin then with the Easter Jesus, not with the
Christmas Jesus. Well and good, provided we do two things.
First, the whole range of the New Testament's confession of
Christ should be respected in its entirety. Here what comes
later chronologically, remains no less valuable than what took
place earlier. Second, those first Christians who stood behind
and wrote our scriptures were driven to praise their Lord and
Saviour in rich and varied ways. I know no better way to
evoke and to enter this full chorus of worship than the
following 'Hymn to God Incarnate':

> You are the radiant light of God's glory; you are the perfect
> copy of his nature (Heb 1:3).
> You are the revelation of a mystery kept secret for endless
> ages (Rom 16: 25); you are the power and the wisdom of
> God (1 Cor 1:24).
> You are the head by whom the whole body is fitted and joined
> together (Eph 4: 16); you are the peace between us (Eph 2:
> 13).
> You are Lord to the glory of the Father (Phil 1:11); you are
> the Son that he loves (Col 1:14).
> You are the fulness of him who fills the whole of creation (Eph
> 1: 23); you are our wisdom and our virtue and our holiness
> and our freedom (1 Cor 1:30).
> You are the beginning, the first-born from the dead (Col 1:18);
> you are the mystery among us, our hope of glory (Col 1:27).
> You are God's secret in whom all the jewels of wisdom and
> knowledge are hidden (Col 2:3); you are head of every
> sovereignty and power (Col 2:10).
> You are the word who is life (1 John 1:1); you are the word
> made flesh (John 1:14).

You are the mediator who brings a new covenant (Heb 12: 24); you are a consuming fire (Heb 12:29).
You are the only Son of the Father, full of grace and truth (John 1:14).
You are the light of the world (John 8:12).
You are the Saviour we are waiting for, the Lord Jesus Christ (Phil 3: 20); you are the Holy One of God (John 6: 69).
You are a light to enlighten the gentiles (Luke 2:32); you are the glory of your people Israel (Luke 2:32).
You are the way, the truth, and the life (John 14:6); yes, you are a king (John 18:37).
You are the living bread which has come down from heaven (John 6:51); you are the only Son who is nearest to the Father's heart, who has made him known (John1:18).
You are God's Son, the Beloved; his favour rests on you (Lk 3:22); you are the Lamb of God (John 1:29).
You are the kindness and love of God our Saviour (Titus 3: 4); you are Emmanuel, God-with-us (Isa 7:14).[1]

Present experience

The Christ of our Christian origins and our Church tradition is also the Christ of our present experience. To begin with, that means his presence in worship. In a now classic passage, the Second Vatican Council spelled out the various liturgical presences of Christ:

> Christ is always present in his Church, especially in her liturgical celebrations. He is present in the Sacrifice of the Mass not only in the person of his minister ... but especially in the Eucharistic species. By his power he is present in the sacraments, so that when anyone baptizes it is really Christ himself who baptizes. He is present in his word, since it is he himself who speaks when the holy scriptures are read in the Church. Lastly, he is present when the Church prays and sings, for he has promised, 'where two or three are gathered together in my name there am I in the midst of them'. (*Sacrosanctum Concilium*, 7)

Here, the Constitution on the Sacred Liturgy spoke affirmatively of Christ's presence in worship, without any intention of denying or discarding his 'extra-liturgical' presences. We would not do justice to the 'whole Christ' of present experience if we passed over those other presences.

In Our Lady of the Dunes, a church on the coast of Belgium, the tabernacle is covered with images of human faces, male and female, young and old, serene and suffering: images that display the whole range of human emotions. That tabernacle brilliantly conveys the sense that we must look for Christ in *all* our brothers and sisters: in the gunman who did the killing as well as in Archbishop Oscar Romero lying bloodstained in his vestments, in the selfish rich as well as in the angry poor, in the awkward curate in a suburban parish as well as in the recklessly generous sister on mission on the Amazon.

Jesus' words about the last judgement (Matt 25:31–46) can always be carried further. They remain beautifully open-ended:

I was an Arab putting up the oil prices, and you recognized
that I was questioning your selfish life-style.
I was a Soviet pilot bombing an Afghan village, and you
prayed for me as well as for my victims.
I was a Vietnamese refugee, and you gave me a chance.
I was an illegitimate and handicapped child, and you opened
to me your home.
I was a terrorist occupying an embassy, and you wondered
what pain had driven me to that end.
I was an underpaid and badly-housed worker, and you tried
to get me justice.
I mattered to no one and was about to take my life, when I
felt the power of your concern and compassion.
I ran an abortion clinic, and you did not condemn me as
beyond redemption.
I was simply the cantankerous neighbour, and you showed
me much love.

He identifies with all those who in their various needs have a claim on our practical love. Through all their different needs, our brothers and sisters bring us Christ's presence. In *Redemptor Hominis*, John Paul II wrote of the mystery of Jesus Christ, 'in which each one of the four thousand million human beings living on our planet has become a sharer from the moment he is conceived beneath the heart of his mother' (13). The Lord comes to us now behind those four thousand million faces; they are all signs and sacraments of his presence.

Living in Rome in the late 70s, I became sadly conscious of the senseless and cruel killings carried out by members of the Red Brigade, the First Line and other terrorist organizations. At the same time, the funeral services of their victims over and over again revealed the presence of the risen Lord, who through his Holy Spirit gives to grief-stricken men and women the power to believe, to forgive and to hope in ways profoundly Christian.

On 30 May 1980, at the funeral of Walter Tobagi, a young journalist assassinated by the Red Brigade in revenge for what he had written about them, Archbishop Carlo Martini of Milan spoke of a 'mystery of meaninglessness and madness', But then he reminded the congregation of that great 'certainty' to be found in the New Testament: 'What is meaningless can gain a meaning'. The prayers of the faithful which followed Archbishop Martini's homily showed most movingly how the crucified and risen Lord can bring those in terrible sorrow to see and affirm meaning in what they experience. Stella Tobagi, left widowed with her two little children, had written this first prayer, and sat with her arms around her son and daughter whilst her sister read it:

Lord, we pray for those who killed Walter, and for all people who wrongly hold that violence is the only right way for resolving problems. May the power of your Spirit change the hearts of men, and out of Walter's death may there be born a hope which the force of arms will never be able to defeat.

Further, we find the 'whole Christ' of present experience both in the macrocosm of the material world which surrounds us, and in the microcosm of our own personal existence. He is the one in whom 'all things hold together' (Col 1:17); but he is also the one whom we too can 'see with our eyes and look upon and touch with our hands' (1 John 1:1). The Christ present in all the people we meet and in the world we inhabit is the One who reaches us through all our senses. Each of us in our own circumstances can echo St Augustine:

You called to me; you cried aloud to me; you broke my bar-
rier of deafness. You shone upon me; your radiance
enveloped me; you put my blindness to flight. You shed your
fragrance about me; I drew breath and I gasp for your sweet
odour. I tasted you, and now I hunger and thirst for you.
You touched me, and I am inflamed with love of your peace.
(*Confessions*, X, 27).

In his *Summa Theologiae* (1, 54, 5, ad 2) St Thomas Aquinas
includes a lapidary phrase which suggests happily what can
come about through repeatedly meeting Christ within ourselves,
in the world of nature, in worship and through the people
around us. Aquinas observes that 'experience results from
many memories' (*experientia fit ex multis memoriis*). He is
thinking here of the difference between experience understood
as a single, once and for all event, and that experience which
comes about through many particular experiences (or 'memories'): in other words, that stable familiarity with something,
someone or some activity which we recognize in a devoted
couple, a great conductor or an experienced liturgist. The sum
total of innumerable concrete experiences has made them truly
know with whom they relate or how they are to act. What
Aquinas says about such enduring knowledge and lasting familiarity can be properly applied to the sphere of spiritual experience: 'Our experience of Christ results from our many
memories of him'.

The Christ of the future

In seeking the 'whole Christ' we must not stop short of the
future. He is not only the one whom we remember and experience but also the one whom we expect. Our Eucharist means
'proclaiming the death of the Lord until he comes' (1 Cor
11:26). We live with the bridegroom still absent (Mark 2:18ff)
and the master of the household still away (Mark 13:33-37).
His profoundly real presence in the Eucharist reminds us, paradoxically, that he is not yet fully with us.

Of course, the future coming of Christ will be much more
than the return of one who seemed to be absent. It will be the

full realization of his position and power as God's Son. He will then complete the process inaugurated by his resurrection, which was and is the beginning of the end. To be sure, his risen existence has let something of that future already appear in anticipation. Elements of the future are with us now and give life its present meaning. Nevertheless, Christ will be truly and fully Christ for us only at the final stage:

> Then comes the end, when he delivers up the kingdom to God the Father, after abolishing every kind of domination, authority, and power. For he is destined to reign until God has put all enemies under his feet; and the last enemy to be abolished is death ... when all things are thus subject to him, then the Son himself will also be made subordinate to God who made all things subject to him, and thus God will be all in all. (1 Cor 15:24–28).

These words of St Paul vigorously challenge all those approaches to Jesus Christ which remain exclusively oriented to the past and the present but ignore the future. It is not enough to ask, 'Who are you, Jesus?' and 'Who were you, Jesus?' Respect for the 'whole Christ' demands that we also ask: 'Who will you be, Jesus?' We shall never rightly understand and interpret Christ if we leave aside the future end of all things.

About this point the Book of Revelation is strikingly instructive. The work opens with an ecstatic vision experienced one Sunday by 'John, your brother' on the island of Patmos. He sees the radiant, risen Christ who reassures him: 'Fear not, I am the first and the last and the living one: I died, and behold I am alive for evermore' (1:9–18). Revelation begins with this encounter between John and the risen Lord, who recalls his death and resurrection before delivering messages to seven churches of Asia Minor (2:1–3: 22). But then the whole perspective of the book widens so as to include all heaven and earth, a series of cosmic struggles between good and evil, and finally the vision of the new heaven, the new earth and the new Jerusalem. With this promise of a divine future, when all present conflicts will be resolved, Revelation ends by praying, 'Come, Lord Jesus' (22:20). In sum, the Christ of that final end shapes and determines everything.

All in all, Revelation vigorously reminds us that the risen

Jesus who encounters us now does so as the light of the future (21:23; 22:16) and the Lord of the coming world. He is the 'Ad-vent' Christ, who comes to us out of the future. If you like, it is more a matter of experiencing now the presence of the coming Christ rather than acknowledging now the future of the present Christ.

Christ and the Trinity

In conclusion, I would like to relate the 'whole Christ' of Christian life and worship to the Trinity. Any total approach to Jesus Christ which omits the Trinity cannot claim to be fully Christian. And yet, as we know only too well, it is fatally easy for people to dismiss the doctrine of the Trinity as a kind of theological mathematics for specialists. Ultimately, however, it seems to me that the triune God of Christian faith can be seen to be present in all human suffering and activity: that unknown Trinity which men and women everywhere seek and experience.

What I have in mind here is a contemporary version of the *vestigia Trinitatis* or 'hints of the Trinity', which some Fathers of the Church and medieval theologians delightedly recognized in the world. In the created universe they expected to find traces of the triune God who made it. Our more psychological and 'anthropological' age pushes me towards observing the triadic nature of human experience and action. Men and women spend their time avoiding three things and seeking three things. First, they want to escape *death* in all its forms. Death is not merely irreversibly there at the end of their biological existence; it also invades their lives in all the many deaths through which they suffer the loss of people, places, opportunities and personal powers. Everyone wishes to avoid death (understood in that complete sense) and live life to the full (however different individuals interpret what such a full life entails). Second, men and women look for *meaning* in what they do, and constantly flee from absurdity. Where situations appear meaningful, even awful difficulties can be cheerfully faced. But if a sense of hollow meaninglessness dogs people, they can find existence to be intolerable. Finally, as one of my sisters long ago pointed out to me, the human being is like a sponge with an unlimited desire and capacity to be affirmed and loved. We instinctively avoid hatred and indifference, and long to receive appreciation and *love*.

Granted that such a triadic account of human existence matches our experience, we can recognize this radical quest for life, meaning and love to be in fact a quest for the Father, Son and Holy Spirit. In the Father of our Lord Jesus Christ we acknowledge the 'God of the living' (Mark 12:27), the ultimate source of all life. Christ himself comes to us as the wisdom of God, the one who gives point and meaning to our existence. Here we might very well adapt the prologue of John's gospel and make it read: 'In the beginning was the Meaning and the Meaning was with God, and the Meaning was God'. Lastly, the Holy Spirit is the divine love poured into our hearts (Rom 5:5): both to show how God deeply loves and affirms us, and to enable our loving response to take place. In sum, the human search for life, meaning and love can be properly identified as our profound quest for the Father, Son and Spirit.

At the heart of every human being is a deep orientation towards the mystery of Christ. And this orientation towards Christ is nothing more or less than part of a total quest for the only God there is: the Father, the Son and the Holy Spirit.

3

The incarnation under fire

Right from the opening centuries of Christianity there have been those who either refused to accept or else substantially reduced its central doctrine: Jesus of Nazareth as the eternal Son of God who assumed a human existence, to bring salvation through his life, death, resurrection, and gift of the Holy Spirit to all men and women of all times and places. In the first and second centuries the Ebionites, an umbrella term for various groups of Jewish Christians, considered Jesus to be a mere man on whom the Spirit descended at baptism. The Ebionites exemplified an 'Adoptionist' tendency which spread among various Greek Christians and has continued ever since: Jesus was not God the Son but only a man adopted by God at the baptism or the resurrection. For Arius and the Arians of different kinds, Jesus could not be God the Son, as there was no such eternal, divine person to be incarnated. For them the Son of God or Logos did not always exist, and consequently could not be divine by nature but only the first among creatures.

In this low Christology (or better Jesuology) of the Ebionites, Adoptionists and Arians, Jesus differs in degree but not in kind from other human beings. Only One who is God is beyond degrees (and hence differences of degree), because being truly divine means being indivisible. What can be called 'Neo-Arianism' (or 'low' Christology) has flourished from the time of the Enlightenment, especially among nineteenth- and twentieth-century 'liberal' theologians in Germany, Great Britain, the United States and elsewhere. Neo-Arians, in general, diverge from Arius by recognizing Christ's full humanity and by not attributing to the Son any role in creation.[1]

At the moment John Hick is arguably the most prominent English-speaking exponent of a liberal Christology. He presents Jesus as differing from us only in degree and not in kind,[2] and as one who embodies 'the ideal of human life lived in faithful response to God' (ix). In tones that recall the classical liberal theologians of the past, Hick invites his readers to think things through 'in a straightforward and honest way' and so become 'freed from the mass of ecclesiastical dogmas and practices that have developed over the centuries' (14). He acknowledges that 'many Christian theologians today' continue 'to adhere to the Nicene-Chalcedonian teaching on the incarnation' (29). But he dissociates himself from their attempts 'to preserve an endangered dogma' (14), and lines up with 'a large number of highly regarded Christian theologians' of today who question Jesus' divinity and unique role for human salvation (11). In the course of his book Hick mentions some of these 'highly regarded Christian theologians'. One name which is missing in the text and in the extensive (over ten pages) bibliography is that of Don Cupitt. Does Hick now want to avoid any possible 'guilt by association' with a theological iconoclast with whom he was earlier connected? Whatever one makes of those whom he criticizes and those whom he cites in his support, Hick has produced a major challenge to the doctrine of the incarnation. Very many of his arguments against the central Christological doctrine of Christianity are not new, but they are stated in a clear and up-to-date manner. Without pretending to present and react to all the points which Hick raises, this chapter will attend to some of his major anti-incarnational arguments. We begin with the historical Jesus and the post-crucifixion situation.

The historical Jesus and Paul

Like Adolf von Harnack (1851–1930) and other earlier writers, Hick seems to presuppose that the essence of an idea, at its purest and truest best, is to be found in its first form.[3] That means here going back to the initial Christology or Jesuology of the New Testament: the decisive mission and message of Jesus himself. As divine revelation through Jesus is presumed to be completed with his death, no subsequent resurrection or gift of the Holy Spirit should play any valid role in assessing our experience of God through Jesus.

In essence, Hick claims that Jesus understood his work to be that of the final prophet sent to proclaim the divine kingdom which was to be shortly inaugurated upon earth (5). Even though he allows that Jesus 'called disciples and spoke of there being twelve' (18), Hick denies that Jesus ever intended to found a movement (150).[4] Certainly 'the historical Jesus did not make the claim to deity that later Christian thought was to make for him' (27; see 2). When the expectation of his second coming in glory faded, he was 'gradually elevated within the Gentile church to a divine status' (4–5), being transformed by Christian thought into God the Son, the second person of the triune Deity (150). This 'gradual' apotheosis of Jesus, effected by 'later' Christians, began by attributing 'soft' divinity to him and ended with 'hard' metaphysical claims about his being the incarnation of the 'second person of a divine Trinity' (36). Although he at first attributes this gradual elevation to 'the Gentile church', Hick later alleges that the original Christians (first-century monotheistic Jews), along with their Egyptian, Greek and Roman contemporaries, shared in the ancient world's 'elastic' view of divinity (41) that allowed them to 'divinize' outstanding religious and political figures (36, 42).[5]

In putting his account of how the traditional doctrine of the incarnation developed, Hick writes of the New Testament mixing (a) history (in particular, 'memories of memories of Jesus') and (b) theology ('the Church's progressive appropriation and deification' of Jesus). According as 'one focuses on its more historical [= a] or its more doctrinal strands [= b]', one can use this mixture 'to criticize or to support the developed belief in Jesus as God incarnate' (151). Hick himself, however, does much less than full justice to either (a) or (b), the New Testament's 'more historical' or 'more doctrinal strands'. Let us see some examples of biblical evidence being ignored or misused.

The first example concerns the 'Son of man' language. Unlike those who have been pushing the thesis of Jesus as a wandering Cynic-style sage who delivered counter-cultural aphorisms and parables rather than any challenges of a future, eschatological nature,[6] Hick follows E. P. Sanders in holding that an 'apocalyptic expectation of a decisive divine intervention in human history ... must surely go back to Jesus himself' (20). To claim this is to reach some conclusions about the psychology of Jesus – about the way he *saw and understood himself* as God's final prophet (19). It is also to raise the issue of the sayings about the Son of man to come when God intervenes to end human history. It seems to me that those like Hick who present Jesus as expecting 'the imminent end of the age' (21) can hardly deny that the sayings about the future Son of man go back to the earthly Jesus. But Hick himself wants to leave that question open: '*Either* Jesus himself *or* the developing mind of the church believed that when Jesus returned on the great Day', he would be the 'Son of Man appearing in the clouds' (20, italics mine).

Any claim that the 'developing mind of the church' may have produced the sayings about the Son of man to come must reckon, however, with some classic difficulties and challenges.

1. Apart from four marginal cases (Acts 7:56; Rev 1:13; 14:14; Heb 2:6), we never find *others* ever describing or confessing Jesus as the Son of man (in any sense). The Synoptic gospels report people speaking to or about Jesus in a variety of ways, but never as 'Son of man'. If the 'developing mind of the church' created the Son of man sayings, it is puzzling that this designation for Jesus is not found on the lips of others. The puzzle disappears once we agree that we have here a reliable historical recollection: only Jesus used the term, and the evangelists and their sources faithfully recorded that fact. Hick asserts that, 'by the time the Gospels began to be written, the two images of the Son of Man and the Messiah had become more or less fused in the Christian mind' (20). If such a fusion had been taking place, how can one explain the fact that Paul, while calling Jesus 'Christ' or 'Messiah' 270 times, never once uses the term 'Son of man'?

2. The sayings dealing with the coming Son of man turn up in Mark (8:38; 13:26; 14:62) and Q (e.g. Matt 24:27 = Luke 17:24). This multiple attestation or double strand of tradition also supports those who attribute to Jesus himself the sayings about the Son of man to come. Hick simply slips over these and other classic challenges for those like him who doubt or leave as an open question the derivation from Jesus himself of the Synoptic gospels' language about the future Son of man.

Hick remains quite silent about the place in definitive salvation attributed to the coming Son of man (e.g. Luke 12:8–9) and the role this figure will exercise as final judge.[7] Hick quotes 1 Thessalonians about the return of the Lord (21) but tiptoes around the way this first letter by Paul refers to Christ's role as eschatological judge (1 Thess 2:19; 3:13), 'an eminently divine function'.[8] Without speaking expressly of the Son of man, the apostle uses language and images that parallel that found in the Synoptic tradition about the Son of man to come at judgement.

We have focused briefly on the historical Jesus' language about the coming Son of man, language that entails the startling claim to exercise at the end the divine prerogative of judging human beings. This example can serve to illustrate the unsatisfactory nature of Hick's treatment of (a), the 'historical strands' in the Synoptic gospels.[9] What of (b), the 'more doctrinal' strands and the Church's 'progressive deification of Jesus'? What strands do we find, for instance, in the letters of St Paul, whom Hick describes as having moved only 'a third of the way' along the path from seeing Jesus as merely human to divinizing him?

Hick assures his readers that the apostle's central imagery is that of 'father and son' (43). What are the facts here? In seven letters commonly reckoned as authentic (Rom; 1 and 2 Cor; Gal; Phil; 1 Thess; Philem) Paul, while speaking of God as 'Father' 25 times, calls Jesus 'Son' or 'Son of God' only 15 times. Set these statistics over against 'Lord (*Kyrios*)', a divine title which Paul gives Jesus over 200 times, sometimes in passages that apparently or even certainly come out of the pre-Pauline tradition (e.g. Rom 10:9; 1 Cor 12:3; 16:22; Phil 2:11). The apostle's first letter and the oldest Christian docu-

ment, 1 Thessalonians, calls Jesus 'Lord' 24 times, and never
has to argue that Jesus merits this divine title.

The same title turns up when Paul splits the *Shema* or Jewish
confession par excellence of monotheism (Deut 6:4–5), gloss-
ing 'God' with 'Father' and 'Lord' with 'Jesus Christ' to put
Jesus as Lord alongside God as Father: 'For us there is one
God, the Father, from whom are all things and for whom we
exist, and one Lord, Jesus Christ, through whom are all things
and through whom we exist' (1 Cor 8:6). Here the title 'one
Lord' expands the *Shema* to include Jesus Christ. Using the
classic monotheistic text of Judaism, Paul recasts his inherited
perception of God by introducing Jesus as 'Lord' and redefining Jewish monotheism to produce a Christological monotheism.[10] Paul's redefining of Jewish monotheism involves
acknowledging Christ as agent of creation ('through whom are
all things and through whom we exist'). To speak of Christ in
such terms is to attribute to him a divine prerogative, that of
creating human beings and their universe. Besides recasting Old
Testament language about God and applying it to Christ, Paul
(like some later New Testament authors) takes passages in the
Old Testament which call God 'Lord' and refers them to
Christ. Joel's words about deliverance coming to those who
'call upon the name of the Lord' (Joel 2:32) are thus cited and
applied to Christ (Rom 10:13). In brief, Paul's use of the title
'Lord' shows the apostle introducing Christ into the confession
of monotheism, attributing to him the divine work of creation
and setting him on a par with God as presented in the Old
Testament. None of this supports the view that Paul still has
two thirds of the way to go before seeing Jesus in genuinely
divine terms. Although he recommends examining the data in
an 'open and genuinely enquiring way' (29), Hick disregards
relevant material from the Pauline correspondence, some of
which comes from the period when the apostle still expected the
second coming to take place soon (1 Thess and 1 Cor).

When he does take up a classical passage in which Paul
calls Jesus by the divine name of 'Lord' (Phil 2:6–11) and
which he agrees is pre-Pauline, Hick turns a blind eye to several items in the hymn (78–79) – not least that of Jesus enjoying the exalted, divine name of 'Lord' and receiving the
worship of the whole universe (Phil 2:9–11; see the similar

language about God in Isa 45:23–24). Hick's attention is consistently drawn not by the language of 'Lord' but by that of
'Son of God'. Even there he is less than fully accurate. He
detects a 'very early adoptionist strand' in Rom 1:3–4,
according to which 'the human Jesus was raised to an unique
and highly exalted role (though not to deity) shortly after his
death' (28–29; see 43). This comment ignores the fact that in
the very same letter Paul speaks of Jesus as already being
'Son of God' long before his death – namely at his being
'sent' into the world (Rom 8:3; see 8:32). Unless one wants
to charge Paul with indulging highly inconsistent
Christological thought within the same letter, and that his
masterpiece, we may not interpret Rom 1:3–4 as meaning that
Christ became Son of God for the first time after his death.[11]

The resurrection of Jesus

We have looked at some of the evidence from the Synoptic
gospels and Paul that can be cited against those such as Hick
who assert that the historical Jesus lacked any high sense of his
own identity and mission, and who allege that Gentile
Christians gradually elevated Jesus to divine status. A second,
standard move in low Christology's rejection of the doctrine of
incarnation is a revisionist account of Jesus' resurrection. Hick
introduces the resurrection by making the astonishing claim that
among the beliefs which developed around 'the central theme'
of the incarnation were Jesus' atoning death and bodily resurrection (6). Here one should say clearly that, if anything is
widely agreed about Paul and the pre-Pauline traditions quoted
by the apostle, it is that the proclamation of Jesus' death ('for
us and for our sins') and of his resurrection formed the point
of departure around which other beliefs gathered. It is not the
case that beliefs about Jesus' atoning death and resurrection
gathered around a prior, 'central theme' of the incarnation of a
pre-existent, divine Son of God.[12]

At various points which call for a reference to it, Hick quietly ignores Christ's resurrection. Dealing with the doctrine of
the atonement, for instance, he speaks of the possibility of
(wrongly) separating Jesus' death and what preceded it in 'his

self-giving life as a whole' (112). But we also should not sep-
arate this death from what followed it in the resurrection, as
Paul reminds us by citing an early tradition about Christ: 'He
was handed over for our sins and raised again for our justification' (Rom 4:25). By turning a blind eye to the resurrection,
Hick misrepresents Eastern Christianity in general and
Orthodox theology in particular when he tells his readers that
'Orthodox theology' holds that 'Jesus' death was somehow crucial in bringing about human 'deification' (113). In fact,
Eastern theology holds that Jesus' death AND resurrection
bring about this deification.[13] Of course, if someone has no
sense of any divinely effected change occurring in Jesus himself (and through him in others) at his resurrection from the
dead, it will be hard to report faithfully what is held by those
who understand human deification to come through the crucified and risen Christ and his Holy Spirit.

Hick does, however, put the right question about the great
change in the original disciples: 'What ... caused the first
disciples to believe, after Jesus' crucifixion, that he was now
alive as their exalted and glorified Lord?' Hick's reply 'starts
from the earliest account that we have of an "appearance" of
the risen Lord, that to Paul on the Damascus road'. He refers
in passing to 1 Cor 15:8, but ignores both what the first
Christian writer says elsewhere about his Damascus-road
experience (1 Cor 9:1; Gal 1:11–17) and the way the apostle
cites *pre*-Pauline traditions about the resurrection and the
risen Christ's appearances (e.g. Rom 4:25; 10:9; 1 Cor
15:5–7; 1 Thess 1:9–10). Hick builds his 'conjecture' about
the post-crucifixion experience by appealing to the 'blinding
light' which he finds 'later reported' in Acts 9:3–8; 22:6–11;
and 26:12–18. Appealing to Howard Kee, he rightly notes
that Paul had 'equated' his own experience with the paradigm
appearances to Peter and the Twelve (24). Then Hick goes on
to make an extraordinary assertion about 'the story of Paul's
blinding light' coming 'from nearly a generation earlier' than
Mark's gospel – a dating that can only refer to 1 Corinthians
written in the mid-fifties (25). This allows Hick to conjecture
that 'the original resurrection event [sic] consisted in Peter',
and perhaps others, 'having an experience similar to that of
Paul, an experience of a supernatural light around them

within which they were conscious of the glorified presence of Jesus'. Their experiences could have been 'waking versions' of those near-death experiences which Raymond Moody and others have reported – experiences of bright light or of a brightly shining figure who is often identified with Christ by Christians who went through such experiences (24). Elsewhere Hick tries out another parallel of a very different kind: 'during the days and weeks after his death', Jesus may have proved vividly present as is widely reported of recently dead persons who are felt to be 'invisibly present' to comfort, guide or challenge the living (38).

There is much to debate and reject here. First, Hick begs the question by quietly substituting for the epistemological question (what caused the first disciples to believe?) the question of their ontological claim (his conjecture about 'the original resurrection event'). What the first disciples claimed to have happened to Jesus after his crucifixion ('the original resurrection event') should not be silently confused with the question of what led them to believe and claim what they did about Jesus. Second, the 'story of Paul's blinding light' does *not* come from the fifties (1 Corinthians) but from the eighties (when Luke wrote Acts). Paul, while making in 1 Cor 15:8 no distinction between his own encounter with the risen Christ and the earlier encounters enjoyed by Peter, the Twelve and others, does not report any circumstances of those encounters, and certainly not that they involved light phenomena. Hick is reviving a long discredited methodology by privileging later evidence from another author (Luke) over against the earlier testimony from the central protagonist of the Damascus-road experience (Paul).[14] (Hick also misses the way 'the light' mentioned in Acts 26 is even brighter but not blinding as in Acts 9 and 22).

Third, conjecturing that the Easter encounters could have been 'waking versions' of near-death experiences seems like forcibly appropriating to the issue in hand 'data' from a very different context. The whole point of the reports of near-death experiences is that they come from people who were revived after being clinically dead – something which is certainly not the case with Peter, Paul, Mary Magdalene and the other Easter witnesses.[15] Fourth, Hick's other, very diverse parallel, which is drawn from the presence of loved ones who have recently died, seems more plausible. It is obviously worth examining scientific reports of such experiences.[16] But Hick ignores here one massive element which should not be passed over in the story of Jesus and his disciples' grieving process: the crucifixion, a death reckoned to be utterly shameful before God and human beings. In this case the beloved person did not simply die (38), nor was it merely the case of a martyr's death like that of John the Baptist (26). The fact that the Baptist was beheaded and not crucified made a world of difference in the human and religious perception of his martyrdom.[17]

Any low Christology must face the Easter witness which helps to underpin the claims of high Christology. Hick takes one route often followed here by explaining (explaining away?) in 'normal' human and religious terms the post-crucifixion experience of the first disciples. He observes that assertions about what 'occurred in the days and weeks after Jesus' death … can never be fully substantiated from an historical point of view' (25). The qualifier missing here is 'merely'. I would certainly agree that orthodox Christian claims about what occurred can never be substantiated from a merely historical point of view. Nor, as we shall see, can an historical point of view by itself fully substantiate claims about the incarnation. Yet history and historical investigation have a role to play in both issues. Historical accuracy is important and is sometimes missing in Hick's text. For instance, he writes: 'By the time the Gospels were being written … it [the resurrection] was believed to have been a revivifying of Jesus' corpse in a mysteriously transformed state, followed by his bodily ascension up into a cloud' (23). What Hick reports applies not to the gospels (in the plural) but to the scheme adopted by Luke alone. Another example of limited accuracy concerns the assertion that the earlier traditions about the resurrection show 'less and less of the physically miraculous and more of the spiritually transforming'. Such episodes from the later gospels of Luke and John as the stories of the two disciples on the Emmaus road, of Mary Magdalene in the garden and of Thomas' coming to faith are second to none as spiritually transforming narratives; it is odd to write them off as indulging 'prodigious miracles' and 'miraculous physical events' (25).

The incompatible-attributes problem

Fairness to Hick demands leaving behind an area where he is
vulnerable (the Scriptures) to move to an area of his exper-
tise (the philosophy of religion). Like many before him,
including Schleiermacher, he thinks it is not possible to give
a coherent meaning to the traditional doctrine of divine incarnation, developed in its essential lines from the First Council
of Nicea in 325 to the Council of Chalcedon in 451.
Believing Jesus to be simultaneously divine and human leaves
one facing 'the incompatible-attributes problem' (102). What
is being challenged is the Chalcedonian teaching about Christ
as one person in two natures (one divine and the other
human), a doctrine which Hick regards as 'incapable of being
explicated in any satisfactory way' (ix). A satisfactory
account would have (a) to give some 'coherent literal meaning to the idea of divine incarnation' and (b) to do so 'in a
way that satisfies the religious concerns that give point to the
doctrine' (4).

When working out his case, Hick is not always error-free
in what he says about the past and the present. To describe
Christological language before the Council of Nicea as 'generally' having been 'devotional, ecstatic, or liturgical (or all
three), rather than an exercise in precise theological formulation' (101) is to disregard what Tertullian, Origen and other
pre-Nicene writers contributed to the progress of theological
terminology and thought. Apropos of the ecumenical councils
that elaborated the Christological dogmas, Hick changes the
correct language used by others ('divinely guided') when he
states: 'we have no way of determining whether the councils
were in fact divinely inspired [sic] other than by evaluating
their pronouncements. If we can accept these as true we
might accept that the authors were inspired [sic] in making
them' (37). Language is being used loosely here. The
Scriptures were divinely inspired. The solemn pronouncements of ecumenical councils have been divinely guided and
guaranteed but never inspired. Hick seems to understand
'inspired' to be a synonym of 'true'. Second, the idea of evaluating one by one the solemn pronouncements of all ecumenical councils, possibly declaring all the pronouncements to

be true and then being in a position to say that these councils were divinely guided means taking frivolously the question of any special guidance by the Holy Spirit. The real guidance would come from our own personal reason and scholarship that checked the conciliar teaching. Any final declaration, 'Yes, the Holy Spirit must have been guiding the councils after all', would not satisfy religious concerns (see (b) above) and would be downright insulting to God's Spirit. Third, Hick detects a 'circularity' in the position of those like Richard Swinburne who argue for divine guidance: 'one believes the dogma to be true because the ecumenical councils were divinely guided in declaring it, and one believes that they were divinely guided because one believes the dogma to be true' (ibid.). Instead of such false circularity, however, antecedent expectation and subsequent confirmation are at work. On other, prior grounds such as those developed by Swinburne,[18] one can argue and hold that ecumenical councils are divinely guided; the reception and fruitful results of their dogmatic pronouncements then serve to confirm the truth of these pronouncements.

As regards contemporary exponents of incarnational doctrine, not all of those listed as employing the language of Christ's two minds (the divine mind of the Logos/Son and the human mind of Jesus of Nazareth) rather than 'the traditional two-natures language' (48–49) belong on Hick's list. In my *Interpreting Jesus* I pointed out that endorsing two-natures language as I do involves one in grappling with its implications: in particular, the two minds of Christ or his being subject of a double consciousness. I treated these two minds as implications of, but not as a replacement for, the two-natures language of Chalcedon. Further, when criticizing such contemporary Chalcedonians as Thomas Morris and Richard Swinburne (49–60), Hick (unfairly?) presses his two requirements: (a) offering a coherent explication of Chalcedonian doctrine and (b) satisfying religious concerns (see above). Morris and Swinburne, he concludes, have 'forfeited' the 'advantage of mystery' by 'attempting to spell the mystery out in an intelligible way' (60). Hick then debates other contemporary versions of orthodox Christology and maintains: 'a Chalcedonian-type christology cannot be spelled out as a literal theory in any religiously acceptable way. Indeed the more philosophically ingenious christologies have become the less religiously realistic they seem to be' (104). Is the problem created, however, by Hick's own two requirements? Can one simultaneously meet, at least in a fully deployed way, what he requires under (a) and (b)? Space does not allow me to report and evaluate the debate between Hick, on the one hand, and Stephen Davis, Brian Hebblethwaite, Morris, Richard Sturch and Swinburne, on the other. But it should at least be remarked that these philosophers of religion must move on from the first-order, pre-philosophical language of the Bible, the liturgy and personal devotion if they are going to analyse in second-order language basic Christian truths. In doing so, much more than the Council of Chalcedon, they will shift beyond the simple directness of faith language. They must do so if they are going to gain even a little clarity and precision in reflecting on the mystery of Jesus Christ.

Hick touches only briefly on what I understand to be the proper answer to his 'incompatible-attributes problem': what others have called '*qua* clauses' and I prefer to call 'within-a-frame-of-reference clauses'. When Hick asks, 'How can the one undivided divine self be at once unlimited ... and limited ...?' (69), one can reply, 'unlimited *qua* God the Son and limited *qua* Jesus of Nazareth'. Hick remarks that, on 'the evidence of the Synoptic Gospels, we have to say that the historical Jesus lacked at least some of the attributes of God' (61). The observation invites some qualifications: *qua* Son of Mary, Jesus lacked all the attributes of God; *qua* Son of God he still had all the attributes of God. The 'incompatible-attributes problem' should be met by indicating the appropriate frame-of-reference clause. In offering to 'explain' the doctrine of the incarnation, one cannot positively show how a divine person (with an eternal divine nature shared in common with two other divine persons) could assume a complete human nature. But by distinguishing the frames of reference one can at least meet the charge that the doctrine is inherently contradictory in claiming that one subject is simultaneously limited/finite and unlimited/infinite. Christ is limited within the human frame of reference but unlimited within the divine frame of reference.

The incarnation as metaphor

Hick's own proposal is to understand incarnation-talk as metaphorical rather than literal. His examination of some current Chalcedonian Christologies, along with other reasons, has persuaded him that we should no longer try to formulate 'the incarnation dogma as literal assertion' or literal theory (104). It is as such metaphorically rather than literally true. The 'incarnation' depends upon 'its being literally true that Jesus lived in obedient response to the divine presence, and that he lived a life of unselfish love' (105). In itself 'the incarnation of God in the life of Jesus' is 'a metaphorical statement of the significance of a life through which God was acting on earth. In Jesus we see a man living in a startling degree of awareness of God and of response to God's presence' (106).

This reductive re-interpretation of the incarnation could put many hermeneutical nerves on edge by its distinction (separation?) of statements of fact from statements of significance. A 'metaphorical statement of significance' depends upon and hence is at least distinct from statements of (empirical) fact (about the way Jesus lived). But can one make such 'literal' factual statements about Jesus' living in response to God's presence without necessarily implying judgements of significance? What counts as God's presence? What is a startling degree of awareness of God and of obedient response to the divine presence? What counts as a life of unselfish love? To use Hick's terminology, the 'literal' and the 'metaphorical' are inextricably intertwined; the latter does not simply depend upon the former; it is right there in the former. By using an old-fashioned distinction (separation?) between empirical fact and religious interpretation, Hick's positive proposal runs into the classical difficulties which face that distinction.[19]

Right through the book the literal-versus-metaphorical distinction often seems to function as a substantive-versus-verb distinction. Jesus Christ 'embodied' or 'incarnated' the 'divine purpose for human life', rather than being the incarnate God the Son (12). He lived a life of unselfish love that incarnated the ideal human response to the divine reality (152). Verbs – especially, 'lived', 'revealed', 'embodied' and 'incarnated' replace noun-talk (especially, that of two natures) to describe how Jesus behaved historically and how he continues to make God real to those who are inspired by him (132). What we meet here is another functional-versus-ontological Christology, in which Jesus is one 'whose life has revealed to others the reality and love and claim of God' (79) and whose influence has 'powerfully elicited and shaped human transformation' (148). Yet no amount of functional talk can banish the question: Did Jesus' human existence reveal the divine reality, love and claim because he himself was an 'insider' who belonged in person to the divine reality?

Debate with Hick about the divine reality, however, has become problematic as – in a Kantian style – he now distinguishes between the phenomenal world and the divine, noumenal reality which exists quite outside our perception. He ends up with an agnosticism that affirms a transcendent Reality but will hardly take a stand on any particular qualities or activities of God.[20] This raises difficulties for him when he maintains that Christianity is only 'one valid response among others to the infinite transcendent reality we call God' (1). Hick's transcendental agnosticism invites the question: How do we know that any religion at all is a 'valid' response to such an unknown reality?

Hick is well aware that the world religions have their 'rival truth-claims' and present themselves as 'in some important sense absolute and unsurpassable' (134). But he proposes that these 'doctrinal conflicts' simply arise from 'the variations between different sets of human conceptual schemata and spiritual practices' (143). This means that no universalist, 'absolute dogmas' are appropriate about the divine, noumenal Reality (or reality?) (145), except – of course – for Hick's own universalist, absolute ruling that the great religions are 'more or less equally valuable forms of response to the Transcendent' (151). Does he know this in a way denied to others? In any case, how is this assertion reconcilable with his agnosticism about the Transcendent? He courteously grants that 'it is not for us Christians to tell people of other traditions how to do their business' (149). But his opposition to 'absolute dogmas' looks very much like claiming the high ground against *every* tradition and judging all religions from above.

Liberal, low Christologies

As a critique of the incarnation, *The Metaphor of God Incarnate* has the merit of exemplifying, in an updated fashion, many features of older low Christologies. First, they have frequently challenged tradition and aspired to a new, privileged position. Apropos of Jesus' 'voluntary sacrifice' of his 'holy life', Hick himself offers the advice: 'Let us not reduce its [the crucifixion's] meaning to any culture-bound theological theory' (132). But is it possible to leap out of the skin of our own culture? Does Hick in fact manage to do so? Obviously it is impossible to explain what he or anyone else might mean by 'voluntary sacrifice' or a 'holy life' without calling on 'culture-bound' ideas and theories – be they theological or philosophical. Second, there is the role of historical evidence. Hick accurately remarks that 'one cannot justifiably arrive at the belief [in Jesus' deity] simply from the New Testament evidence', yet oddly adds at once the qualifier, 'as this [New Testament evidence] has thus far been analysed and interpreted by the scholarly community' (33). I would deny that historical evidence *simply by itself* could ever generate and support such a momentous belief as that of faith in Jesus as God the Son, no matter how well the scholarly community analyses and interprets the biblical/historical evidence from the New Testament and elsewhere. One thing, however, is clear. Unlike some exponents of low Christology, Hick does not hold that the issue of the incarnation can be decided here and now merely on the basis of historical evidence alone.[21]

Third, low Christologies inevitably bring down the doctrine of the Trinity and produce at best a latter-day version of Sabellianism. (At worst they lapse into Unitarianism). Hick is no exception here: 'God is humanly known – as creator, as transformer, and as inner spirit. We do not need to reify these ways as three distinct persons' (153). This Sabellian doctrine of God, as we saw earlier, includes a challenge to the divine guidance of ecumenical councils. Since there was no Holy Spirit doing that work at the community level, such guidance cannot be asserted at the individual level. A Pelagian-style of life is recommended – one in which 'a great exemplar' (Jesus for Christians) can influence and change us (130). His 'felt impact', rather than any initiatives of his grace through the Holy Spirit, should inspire and challenge each Christian.

Fourth, liberal Christologies, fuelled by free thought and liberated from traditional divine images, have tended to sponsor 'democratic' views of God. Thus Hick, despite his agnosticism about the Transcendent One, somehow knows that a special personal self-communication of God in Christ would be 'incompatible with a universal divine love' (159). *Pace* Matt 20:1-15 and Rom 9-11, God must behave in an equal, democratic way towards all people. Hence Hick decries any talk about 'an important religious advantage to a person's being a Christian' (158), while never reckoning, as far as I can see, with any sense of Christian faith entailing an awesome religious responsibility. Hick seems happy to judge that Christianity has 'definitively ... failed in its project to convert the world' (155). Here, as elsewhere, the more basic issue remains, however, that of Jesus' personal identity. *Pace* John 3:16, Rom 5:6-11, 8:3, and 8:31-32, Hick maintains that the incarnation of God the Son would be 'incompatible' with the divine love.

Lastly, *The Metaphor of God Incarnate* illustrates a persistent characteristic of liberal Christology: it pretends to represent a new, Copernican-style revolution in Christian thought. So much for the old Ebionites, Adoptionists and Arians, none of whom ever rate a mention in this book. Even the classical enlightenment and liberal thinkers hardly enter the discussion: Schleiermacher is mentioned only twice (18, 130), David Friedrich Strauss and Adolf von Harnack only once each (18). Gotthold Ephraim Lessing (who classically endorsed the religion *of* Jesus rather than any religion *about* Jesus, in the spirit of 'the historical Jesus, yes, but the incarnation, no'), Ernest Renan, Albrecht Ritschl are passed over in silence, as is J. J. Rousseau. His *Emile* contains one of the most penetrating criticisms ever made of Christian claims about Christ.

Modern liberal Christologies are philosophically and (in some ways) biblically ahead of their ancient Adoptionist and Arian counterparts. but can Neo-Arianism hope to succeed where Arianism failed?

4

Interpreting Christmas

The birth of Jesus is a profound reality, the kind that defies simple interpretation and demands more than one context. It does not present quite the same face in the settings of study, life and prayer. Scholars, sufferers and worshippers rightly appropriate the Christmas story in a variety of ways.

Immanuel Kant's *Critique of Pure Reason* may seem of little interest to any but the philosophers. Yet that classic work ends with three questions that retain a permanent validity everywhere: 'What can I know? What ought I to do? What may I hope for?'

Those questions readily suggest three major lines of inquiry about the Christmas story: What can I know about the historical formation and theological meaning of the infancy narratives in the first two chapters of the Gospels according to Matthew and Luke? What ought I to do or leave undone when the story of Jesus' birth parallels the movement of my life? What may I hope for when that story becomes my prayer?

The first question invites us to station ourselves in a place of biblical and theological thought – let us say, the University of Notre Dame, Yale Divinity School or Union Theological Seminary in New York City. The second question takes us off to the world of action and suffering, like the suburbs of São Paulo. The final question could turn us toward the Church of the Nativity in Bethlehem.

Let us first join the scholars and students in their academic setting. Here we enter a community whose tradition – at least in the Western world – stretches back through the Enlightenment and the achievements of medieval Europe to the glories of ancient Greece. Plato's conversational approach has shaped this tradition for all time. We raise questions, concede points and draw conclusions as the dialogue runs along. Error is the villain and carefully trained reason the solution in this rigorous pursuit of the truth.

The intellectual approach to Christmas scrutinizes the intentions of Matthew and Luke, searches out the sources they used and tries to tell at this distance the precise historical events that first gave rise to the stories about Jesus' birth and babyhood. In the best sense of the word 'theory', biblical scholars have their theories about the meaning, formation and origins of the infancy narratives. They focus on the past in seeking to verify their answers to such questions as: Where did the story of the Magi come from and what did Matthew mean by it? Did the Romans take that census (Luke 2:1–5) and was Jesus really born in Bethlehem? What are Luke's major concerns in his opening chapters?

Theories are judged by one's competent use of the available evidence. Truth has the primacy when exegetes practise their academic discipline. Theirs is the work of an intellectual elite. They have enjoyed a privileged education as the heirs to the great tradition formed by the old universities of Bologna, Cambridge, Heidelberg, Oxford and Paris.

A second view of Jesus' birth comes from the *favelas* where people suffer terrible deprivation and struggle to survive. Here it is a matter of consulting the poor, not the scholars, about the meaning and message of Christmas. In this setting it is not so much intellectual error but injustice, poverty and sin that stand in the way of appropriating the story of Jesus' birth.

Stripped to its simplest terms, Christmas here means something to be lived and done. The mystery of God born among us calls for a transformation of our world. It invites those who suffer and those who cause their suffering to seek and find a new kind of human existence.

This second way of understanding the Christmas story challenges us to 'repent and believe in the good news of Jesus' birth' rather than to 'interpret the infancy narratives more scientifically'. We justify and verify the story of Bethlehem more by practising it than by studying it.

This second approach is focused on the here and now – on the present history of suffering, sin and evil. Its vision of Christmas takes shape around the question: What good ought I to do for all those for whom Jesus was born into this world?

The wise men from the East symbolize the third approach to the 'silent and holy night' of Christmas. They followed their star to come and worship the new-born Saviour of the world (Matt 2:1–12). They represent all those whose hearts continue to catch fire at the Child in the manger, that exquisitely beautiful expression of the divine love for us all. On our knees with the Magi we glimpse the grandeur of God, who comes among us to 'save his people from their sins' (Matt 1:21).

Contemplating the new-born Child, we know that 'the hopes and fears of all the years' find their answer in him. We need fear no more but can hope that we are on our way home to a God who cherishes us with everlasting love.

Such then are three different but complementary approaches to the Christmas story: through the head, the hands and the heart. The scholar studies and analyses the story for its historical and theological truth. Those who suffer and struggle in the marketplace can let the story enter and enrich their lives like Luke's poor shepherds who 'watched their flocks by night' (Luke 2:8). Finally, the faithful take in the story when they come rejoicing to worship our newborn King. He appeared among us as Mary's tiny Baby but will come again as Lord to take us to himself.

Christmas is the story of the Child who holds out to us the full and final answers in our triple quest for what we can know, what we ought to do and what we may hope for. We can encounter that Child in the university setting, along the roads of life and in our places of prayer. In him we find the plenitude of truth, the ultimate good and the utterly satisfying beauty of God. It will take all our study, life and worship to know him.

5

Emmanuel

Some years ago a friend of mine was complaining about what he took to be the decline and fall of Roman Catholicism in France. His voice faltered, and he summed things up: 'The French went in for Catholic Action. Then they pushed the line of *témoignage*, or witness. Now they are satisfied with mere presence.'

At the time I wondered whether my friend was right in being disenchanted with the move from action to witness and from witness to presence. I put it to myself this way: 'When I come to die, no one will be able to do anything for me, and I won't want anyone preaching to me. But I will certainly be reassured by the presence of a close relative or some other person I love dearly.'

Nowadays I wonder whether, inadvertently, my friend had stumbled on a good way of expressing the move from creation, through the history of Israel and down to the birth of Jesus himself. God acted in creation. Moses and the prophets were called to give witness to the people. But Jesus Christ was God's personal presence among us.

In his infancy narrative, Matthew calls Jesus 'Emmanuel, which means "God with us"' (Matt 1:25). The prologue of John's gospel climaxes with the announcement: 'The Word became flesh and dwelt among us' (John 1:14). This presence came about through the free love of God: 'In this way the love of God was made manifest among us, that God sent his only Son into the world that we might live through him' (1 John 4:9).

Thinking of the Christmas message in terms of a new divine presence carries several advantages. First, we are moving in the area of something we look for every day of our lives – the personal presence of those whom we care for and who care about us. We cannot endure to leave friendship and love at a distance. Photographs, memories, letters and even phone calls are not enough. We want to enjoy the personal presence of those who fill our minds and let us live in their hearts. We live in God's heart, and Christmas visibly brought among us the Son of God who cares infinitely for each of us. God did not want to live that love at a distance. God gave us and gives us God's personal presence, that most precious gift of those who care for us.

Second, the theme of divine presence has at least a small advantage over some of the other language we use and hear in our worship at Christmas. The reading for the Mass at dawn, for example, recalls the birth of Jesus as the time 'when the goodness and loving kindness of God our Saviour appeared' (Titus 3:4). Beyond doubt, this language of 'appearance' indicates the divine good will toward human beings. All the same, there is a direct sense of personal relationship communicated by the name 'Emmanuel'. God is no longer merely 'for us' but now 'with us'. The Word has come to dwell 'among us'. This presence had initiated a new relationship between the human race and our God. As never before, God is with us and personally related to us.

Third, a personal presence, whether human or divine, always has something mysterious about it. We appreciate the qualitative difference between the mere physical nearness of other people on a crowded bus and the supportive presence of a friend at a time of crisis. We are dealing here with something that is utterly real and yet quite difficult to understand and interpret. 'Presence' and various kinds of presence can seem a straightforward matter, but on analysis they remain mysteriously elusive. This may partly account for the fact that over the centuries Western philosophy has failed to reflect very much on this notion. Apart from Gabriel Marcel (1889–1973) and a few others, philosophers have largely left alone the idea and reality of presence and personal presence.

To speak of the Son of God coming 'among us' to live 'with us' sounds like simple talk. But we have little help here from the philosophers, and in any case this belief points to a unique mystery, the qualitatively new, personal presence of God in our world.

Fourth, as Vatican II's Constitution on the Sacred Liturgy noted, Christ's personal presence takes different forms (no. 7). This 1963 document naturally addressed itself to the variety of ways Christ becomes present in worship and left it at that. But the link between liturgy and life suggests looking also to the many other forms of Christ's presence around us. In a special way, the poor and oppressed bring us his presence. The Child in the manger shows us his face in a thousand needy victims of our world. The Christmas message means not only Jesus himself in the arms of Mary but also his presence in the arms of those who carry our suffering brothers and sisters.

I do not know whether my friend feels happier now about the state of French Catholicism. But I remain grateful for the language he offered me. In our human history, we find God in action. We hear the prophetic witness given us through the inspired Scriptures and inspired speakers. But at Christmas we can rejoice in a uniquely rich and mysterious gift, the new personal presence of 'God with us'.

Christmas shows us that we contact God not only through what we see and hear, but also through what we touch. We can see God acting in history. We can open our ears to hear the divine message to us. But we can also reach out and touch the Son of God, now mysteriously but truly present among us in a rich range of new ways.

6

Jesus between poetry and philosophy

In 1976 I heard a lecture by Hans Georg Gadamer (a retired professor of philosophy from Heidelberg University) on the history of relations between philosophers and poets. Gadamer mused on the ups and downs, the loves and hates, the convergences and divergences of that relationship. It runs all the way from Plato to the later Heidegger. Plato called the poets' stories of the gods 'theologies'. His ideal republic – he believed – would be better off if it severely controlled this kind of theology and even banished the poets. Plato refused to accept that his own master in philosophy, Socrates, had corrupted the youth of Athens, but he clearly believed that poets could be corrupting influences. Other philosophers have been much kinder to poets. In our own century Heidegger turned from his earlier work to draw from poetry the material for his later philosophical reflections.

All in all, it was a brilliant lecture by Gadamer. It set a number of questions buzzing in my head. Would a period that was high on poetic imagination prove likely to be low on philosophical thought? Do poetry and philosophy represent completely different ways of approaching reality, which neither match one another nor even have much to do with one another? And then came the question that gave rise to this chapter. *Would reflection on some of the ways poets and philosophers work throw light on the mind behind the preaching of Jesus?*

Let us explore that last question and see what comes up. First of all, the philosophers and their revolutions. Some philosophers like Wittgenstein have stood back from their culture, surveyed centuries of intellectual history, and quite consciously tried to take philosophy and human thought in new directions. In their own way such philosophers could appropriate the sentiment of Jesus, 'Of old such and such was said to you. But I say to you.' Beyond question, some poets have attempted a similar form of revolution. Wordsworth and T. S. Eliot creatively re-examined poetic language, rejected standard traditions and initiated new styles of poetry. But, on balance, more philosophers than poets have attempted such revolutionary changes.

When they made such radical breaks with the past, philosophers employed general formulae. The generalizations offered by Aristotle, Descartes and Kant separate them from Jesus. He expressed himself in concrete language, not general formulae. He often delivered his message in the form of parables. His instructions and invitations could often take very specific forms: 'Go, sell what you have and give to the poor. Then come, follow me.' Nevertheless, not all philosophers have indulged in lofty generalizations. Wittgenstein could introduce particular cases with a strong imaginative impact. Even Plato himself gave myths a key place in several of his major dialogues. But, after allowing for some exceptions, we can risk a generalization. The vernacular vigour and earthy directness of Jesus' language sets him apart from most philosophers and their talk.

Of course, Jesus resembles the philosophers in their passion for truth. At the same time, he differs from the philosophers on two further scores. He is not interested in clear thinking, exciting speculation or accurate speaking for their own sake. His preaching aims at presenting the truth which will set his hearers free to live as genuine sons and daughters of God. Secondly, Jesus does not spend time clarifying concepts or hunting down ultimate truth through Socratic dialogues with lakeside listeners – let alone arguing matters out with close attention to logic. He already knows how things are and bluntly confronts his audience with his vision of reality.

Like a poet Jesus presents a vision – a vision of the Father who 'makes his sun rise on the evil and on the good, and sends his rain on the just and on the unjust' (Matt 5:45). He presents that vision as poets might, and does not argue for it as philosophers do. When philosophers try to turn human thought in new directions and declare: 'Of old such and such was said to you. But I say to you' – they do not merely communicate their vision. They add their arguments: 'But I say to you X and Y – for the following reasons.' Jesus, however, confronts us with his insights. He does not lead us through his set of arguments.

All things considered, any comparison between the preaching of Jesus and the work of philosophers fails to yield very much. Normally philosophers have dealt with concepts, made speculation their medium and reached for generalizing principles. At times Jesus shares their concern for logic. Is healing on the sabbath always to be avoided as a forbidden work? Jesus handles that issue by appealing to a calculus of values. 'I ask you, is it lawful on the sabbath to do good or to do harm, to save life or to destroy it' (Luke 6:9). Doing good by restoring the sick and maimed to full human health logically takes precedence over observing the prohibition against work on the sabbath. For the most part, however, Jesus appeals to logic far less frequently and clearly than the philosophers. His style of preaching makes him no latter-day Socrates, nor some first-century anticipation of a Kant or a Wittgenstein.

What of the poets? Can we sort out and relate some ways in which Jesus and the poets match each other? His commitment to language suggests a significant point of likeness. He shows a striking respect for words and does not tolerate their misuse. 'On the day of judgement men will render account for every careless word they utter; for by your words you will be justified, and by your words you will be condemned' (Matt 12:36f). Jesus uses language with care, creates concise, unforgettable parables, and like most poets speaks of what we see, hear, taste, touch and smell. 'Dogs came and licked' the sores of Lazarus (Luke 16:21). The crowds who heard John the Baptist did not go out in the desert to see 'a reed shaken by the wind' (Matt 11:7). The disciples of the Baptist are told to go and tell him what they heard and saw (Matt 11:4).

Furthermore, Jesus resembles most poets by talking as a man committed. Here poetry differs from philosophy. What philosophy accomplishes in the world of thought need not directly project what philosophers are as men and women. But poems, like deeds, tend to manifest the standards and personality of their makers. Not always, of course. Not every poet speaks with his or her own voice. Only feeble sentiments and a faint experience may back up what he or she says. Yet frequently poems express keen feeling and intense experience. We do not expect such strong emotion from the philosophers, but only rational clarity.

Under the headings of language and experience we can then spot some likeness between the preaching of Jesus and the practice of poets. But we would let ourselves off too easily, if we slipped over the differences. Poets as poets depend on language not only far more than philosophers but even more than Jesus himself. His ministry extends beyond his preaching to include his miracles and his symbolic actions. He eats and drinks with sinners. He thus offers them divine pardon, and conveys the promise that they will share in the great party which God will throw at the end of time. If Jesus depends on his chosen language more than philosophers, he depends on it less than poets. Language in its sound, meaning, music and overtones is all the poets have.

Poets use expressive language to order and interpret their experience. Strong experience and deep commitment may back up what they say. Nevertheless, once they publish their poetry, they leave it to speak for itself. Their texts take over from them. But we never hear of any impulse from Jesus to write and publish. He betrays no interest in getting his message down on papyrus. Nor does he seem attracted by the challenge of wrestling with words as such. Language for its own sake fails to preoccupy him.

A few words of summary may now be in order. The question triggered off by Gadamer's lecture on poetry and philosophy seems to have led me into a blind alley. We can sort out and list some resemblances between the preaching of Jesus and the work of poets and philosophers. But we run the risk of making strained and artificial comparisons. Jesus was neither a poet nor a philosopher, but a wandering rabbi martyred like John the Baptist and other prophets before him. Yet that is not quite that. By discussing the language of philosophers and poets, Gadamer ultimately left this question like a burr in my mind: Does the language of Jesus give us a clue to his imagination and sensibility? I would like to spend the rest of this chapter tackling that question. Does the language used by Jesus suggest anything about the way his imagination worked?

Before exploring the imagery of Jesus, let me interject three disclaimers. First, I am not dealing with – let alone calling into question – his divine identity. Of course, any appeal to his status as Word of God become flesh will tell us nothing significant about the actual way in which his human imagination functioned. We may get some clue about that from the material in the gospels. Second, the historical method – as developed in form criticism, redaction criticism and other techniques – has indicated that the gospels do not give us exact transcriptions of what Jesus said during his ministry. We simply cannot take the preaching, even as found in the Synoptic gospels, as an unmodified version straight from the lips of Jesus. However, in appealing to Matthew, Mark and Luke, I will select and use *only those sayings* which – *at least in their substance*, if not necessarily in the precise wording – seem to go back to the preaching of Jesus.

My third disclaimer is perhaps the most important. Obviously Jesus used much expressive language which others had provided. He inherited the Old Testament and extra-canonical traditions – a rich and diverse storehouse which he could adopt and creatively employ. This imagery drawn from the past appeared both to liberate – not block – his originality and to serve his strongly individual style of preaching. Nevertheless, in this chapter I am not trying to assess his degree of originality. The question is *not*: How uniquely inventive did Jesus show himself in his language? Rather my question is: Does the imagery and language that Jesus used suggest anything about his imagination and sensibility?

Let me single out three features of Jesus' preaching. The first thing we may note is this. He shows himself aware of and responsive to many forms of human activity, suffering and happiness. He observes what happens when farmers sow crops, see how they may need to build extra barns to house the proceeds of a bumper harvest, and recalls their methods for forecasting the weather: 'When you see a cloud rising in the west, you say at once: "A shower is coming"; and so it happens. And when you see the south wind blowing, you say: "There will be scorching heat"; and so it happens' (Luke 12:54f). He has watched how people put patches on torn cloaks and use fresh wineskins for new wine. Jesus speaks of financial loans, taxation, the role of stewards in large households, the practices of fishermen, the work of shepherds in guarding their flocks, the soft clothing of the wealthy, dogs waiting for scraps to fall from the table, travellers turning up late at night and looking for food, the administration of the law, the current price of sparrows, and much else besides. Jesus' eye sweeps across a very wide range of human activity. If we put together all his images, we would have a fairly extensive picture of daily life in ancient Galilee.

Jesus does not flinch from facing human suffering. One of his most memorable stories features a traveller who is robbed, beaten up and left half-dead on a country roadside. He points to the greed of rich men which allows them to over-indulge, although sick men may lie starving in the streets outside. He recalls the calculations made by princes before they lead their armies into war. Human happiness does not pass Jesus by: the joy of a father whose renegade son returns, the celebrations at weddings, a housewife delighted to have recovered some missing money.

For the most part, Jesus reveals an imagination that has grown to be sensitively aware of what is going on in his world. Nevertheless, there are some gaps in the picture. And this is my second point about his preaching. He delights in children, but he has next to nothing to say about the mother–child relationship. At times he glances at the father–child relationship. 'What father among you, if his son asks him for a fish, will instead of a fish give him a serpent; or if he asks for an egg, will give him a scorpion?' (Luke 11:11f). But Jesus somehow finds his way round the mother–child relationship almost without pausing to notice it. When his eye runs forward to the troubles to come, he sympathises over the sufferings that will afflict pregnant women and nursing mothers: 'Alas for women with child in those days, and for those who have children at the breast' (Mark 13:17). Except for one or two such tangential remarks, Jesus bypasses the mother–child relationship. Did he have such an utterly untroubled relationship to his own mother that this intimate area of life produced nothing for his language? Or was there such a deep and pervasive tradition against a rabbi using such imagery, that in

this regard Jesus had no ready storehouse of language to draw
on? Whatever the reason, his preaching does not derive imagery
from the mother–child relationship.

Almost as remarkable is his silence about the husband–wife
relationship. He defends married life by rejecting divorce, and
insisting that even in their minds men should not go lusting after
other men's wives. But nothing survives from his preaching
about the loving and caring life together of married people. To
illustrate the nature of prayer Jesus tells a story about troubling
one's neighbour at midnight to borrow some food:

> Which of you who has a friend will go to him at midnight
> and say to him: 'Friend, lend me three loaves; for a friend
> of mine has arrived on a journey, and I have nothing to set
> before him'; and he will answer from within: 'Do not bother
> me; the door is now shut, and my children are with me in
> bed; I cannot get up and give you anything'? I tell you,
> though he will not get up and give him anything because he
> is his friend, yet because of his importunity he will rise and
> give him whatever he needs. (Luke 11:5–8)

We might have expected the story to run: 'Do not bother me.
The door is now shut, and my wife is with me in bed'. But
Jesus has the man say: 'My children are with me in bed.'

Besides the mother–child and husband–wife relationships,
there are other facets of human life which fail to get reflected
in the language and imagery of Jesus. Despite his reference to
the ravens and the lilies, he shows no delight in nature and natural beauty. Nor does he indulge in any pathos at the transience
of things. He is so busy urging his audience to live like genuine children of God, that he has no time to indulge in wistful
sadness at the world – still less disillusionment with it. He
could never make Virgil's sentiment his own: 'There are tears
for human affairs and mortal things touch the mind (*sunt
lacrimae rerum et mentem mortalia tangunt*).' Admittedly Jesus
does weep over Jerusalem and shakes his head sadly: 'O
Jerusalem, Jerusalem, killing the prophets and stoning those
who are sent to you! How often would I have gathered your
children together as a hen gathers her brood under her wings,
and you would not' (Luke 13:34). But, by and large, Jesus says
very little about his own failures and perplexities.

Finally, images drawn from non-religious literature, history and current world affairs hardly surface in the preaching of Jesus. There is a hereness and nowness about his language, a preoccupation with the scene right in front of him. He recalls, of course, a few episodes from biblical history or myth like the story of the flood and the destruction of Sodom. But Jesus betrays little interest in the past. The Maccabean revolt, the Hasmonean period, the capture of Jerusalem by Pompey, the switch of Jewish allegiance to Julius Caesar, the reign of Herod the Great (37–4 BC) and all the other crowded events of recent history never even get a passing nod in Jesus' preaching. That larger world of politics fails to come into sight. Apart from a brief remark about paying taxes to Caesar and a comment on some victims of Pilate's brutality, Jesus hardly even suggests that he is living under Roman rule. Once he draws a lesson from a military build-up – the king with 10,000 troops deciding not to risk war against a king with 20,000 troops. But Jesus names no specific king nor any particular cold-war situation in the Mediterranean world of the first century. Another time he speaks vaguely of 'a nobleman' who 'went into a far country to receive kingly power and then return' (Luke 19:12). But he mentions no historical figure as the peg on to which he hangs the parable of the pounds that follows. Jesus' mind reaches out to the immediate situation here and now. He neither scans history, not even the most recent history, nor lets his eye run around the Roman Empire for images and examples that he could press into service.

So much for my second observation that the language of Jesus did not represent the whole of the world in which he lived. One could, of course, argue that his preaching did actually introduce historical references, include imagery drawn from the mother–child relationship and so forth: but the early Church and/or the evangelists censored out nearly all this language. One can only respond, however, that there are no plausible reasons for believing that such censorship took place. In general, we do best to work with what we have rather than speculate about missing material.

Third, we throw away any right to comment on the way Jesus perceives reality, if we ignore the earthy particularity of his language. Characteristically, he answers general questions like 'Who is my neighbour?' by telling a story (Luke 10:29–37). Of course, other rabbis have done that – both before and after Jesus. But the fact that they can also display this habit does not make it any less his. He thinks from below, not by way of deduction from above. He offers cases from which his audience can draw general principles, if they want to. Even his generalizing remarks stay close to the earth: 'No one after drinking old wine desires new' (Luke 5:39). There is a common touch in the proverbial sayings he cites: 'Doubtless you will quote to me this proverb: "Physician, heal yourself"' (Luke 4:23). He invites his hearers to perceive the particular things around them. His imagery is attuned to the earthy wisdom of ordinary people. All of this makes him the supreme preacher with the common touch. He speaks with us and to us, not merely at us.

To sum up. The imagery and language that Jesus uses suggests at least three conclusions about his sensibility.

(1) A very wide range of things in his immediate environment catch his eye. If he is intensely aware of God, he also seems intensely aware of what he experiences on the human scene.

(2) There are some surprising gaps in what he appears to notice.

(3) His mind works from below – from the concrete case. In his own unique way he betrays the earthy wisdom of ordinary people.

That then is the yield from the question triggered off by Hans Georg Gadamer's lecture. I might have persevered with the job of comparing and contrasting Jesus with the poets and philosophers. Plenty of further points spring to mind.

(a) Jesus could weep over Jerusalem. On occasions poets too can shed tears. But has there ever been a weeping philosopher?

(b) By and large poets and philosophers have not been men and women of action. Admittedly Plato tried to put into practice his theory of philosopher-kings. Dante was deeply involved in the affairs of Florence and other city-states. But most poets and philosophers have dealt in words. Was

Jesus a man of action? And in what sense? Clearly he showed himself concerned with what people did or left undone.

(c)   At the end Jesus went into action and died for his cause. How many poets have done that? One Greek philosopher died for the sake of truth. But no one has ever even claimed that the virtuous acts of Socrates remain with us in the sense that the virtuous acts of Jesus are believed to remain with us. Belief in Jesus and beliefs about Jesus constitute Christology. But there is no Socratology.

Nevertheless, as we admitted earlier, comparisons with the sincerest poets and the noblest philosophers fail to take us very far in understanding Jesus. All the same, poets and philosophers may lead us to reflect on language. The imagery that Jesus employed gives a clue to the way his imagination and perception of the world worked. To move through his language to some insights into his sensibility can only be a real gain.

7

Jesus the communicator

In 1983 I took part in an interdisciplinary seminar made up of twelve specialists in communications, eight theologians and two philosophers coming from twelve nations. It was organized by Robert White, SJ, of the Centre for the Study of Communication and Culture in London, Peter Henrici, SJ, director of the Interdisciplinary Centre of Social Communication at the Gregorian University in Rome, and their associates. We met for a week in the autumn, south of Rome in an eighteenth-century villa that stands among olive groves on the slopes of the Alban Hills.

Down the road from the villa is Frascati, famous for its white wine but also remembered for being badly bombed during the Second World War. Across the folds of the hills are the ruins of the Roman town of Tusculum, where Cicero came to write some of his philosophical works. War always expresses some dreadful failure in international communication. Philosophy is concerned to lay bare and communicate questions about the ultimate nature and meaning of things.

In the shadow of Frascati and Tusculum the seminar grappled with the challenge of transmitting the gospel in the new world of mass media and electronic communication. Obviously suitable strategies must be found by all who wish to communicate effectively the Christian message toward the end of the twentieth century. Theology itself also needs to perceive and define its task in fresh ways.

In the past Christology has enriched itself by confronting the New Testament story with contributions coming from various disciplines such as philosophy and history. What help could it find today by applying some concepts, findings and theories taken from studies on interpersonal, cultural and mass communication? Of course, none of this communication material can be applied without change to Christology, and some of it may work only by contrast.

One could begin by noting the essential difference between the Old Testament prophets and Jesus Christ as communicators of God's revelation. In the Old Testament the mediators were only partly identified with their messages. With Jesus the Mediator was the Message. The divine Communicator was the divine Communication. In Christ, God was not only communicating with us but also personally present.

All the same, this kind of general talk about Jesus the Communicator may fail to grip us by the soul. Nowadays it is certainly not enough to drop an older language about the 'Christ-event', talk of him as *the* communication-event and leave it at that. What did this communication-event look like in its political, social and, above all, religious context?

To begin with, there was the strange nature of the event in question. The good news Jesus proclaimed and acted out was a far cry from what normally counts as a media event today. Much of the news reported and interpreted by press, radio and television concerns the acquisition and use of money. One way or another wealth fills the screen and the front pages, from government decisions about defence expenditure, through changes in taxation rates, to the purchase of top athletes. Jesus, however, spoke of a fundamental option: We cannot serve God and mammon. He gave special attention to poor, sick and marginalized persons. Our mass media prefer the rich, the powerful and the beautiful. It takes no great effort to spot these and other dramatic differences between what counted as good news for Jesus and what counts as exciting news nowadays.

No matter what one's faith, Jesus' power of language entitles him to be ranked as one of history's most extraordinary communicators. He spoke with authority and at times in a remarkably innovative way. Nevertheless, he never employed linguistic skills to dominate or manipulate his audiences. The parables called on people to respond freely to the divine presence that was powerfully at work to heal and transform their lives. Jesus never used his powers of communication to demand submission, but rather invited others to identify with him in sharing a vision of the Father who offers an unconditional love to all persons. Jesus had at his disposal far more words and images than his peers. Yet he never made language an instrument of social or religious domination. Children knew that and came to be blessed by him.

Both the Synoptic gospels (Matthew, Mark and Luke) and John report and portray Jesus as thoroughly 'receiver-centred' in his mode of communication. He did not treat his audience as passive hearers to whom special information about God could simply be transmitted. Rather he took seriously their circumstances and reactions. He shared freely, and his listeners could freely respond or refuse to respond. The parable of the sower (Mark 4:3-9) classically expressed this aspect of Jesus' communicative activity.

Our media world lives off symbolic objects, events and persons – whether they are yachts that sail faster than the wind, papal visits, summit conferences between world leaders or nuclear weapons which could devastate our earth. An appreciation of its symbolic terms can help us to elucidate more successfully the story of Jesus. His miracles of healing, for instance, meant much more than mere acts of kindness toward sick and crippled persons. They were part of an open invitation to his public to let his presence and activity make new sense of their human and religious situation. Some groups like the people of Chorazin and Bethsaida missed the point of these symbolic events and failed to integrate his miraculous actions into the way they read off the world and responded to God (Matt 11:20-24; Luke 10:13-15).

One could speak of a symbol-clash with the authorities in Jerusalem. They did not understand the way Jesus used his central symbol of God's kingdom and were scandalized by the meaning expressed through such symbolic acts as dining with public sinners and healing on the sabbath. His claim that 'something greater than the temple is here' (Matt 12:6) threatened the central religious symbol of the Sadducean ruling class, the magnificent temple in Jerusalem.

As the Rev Michael Traber (World Association for Christian Communications, London) pointed out during the seminar, there is a startling paradox in naming Jesus 'the perfect Communicator'. From the normal perspective of communication studies, Jesus proved himself almost a total failure. After an initial success, he was misunderstood and abandoned by the large crowds he first attracted. The core group of disciples could not fathom his warnings about his coming fate and almost all fled in fear at his arrest. Some few individuals did better at receiving and interpreting his meaning: an army officer (Matt 8:5–10), certain women whom he had healed (Luke 8:2–3) and perhaps some children (Matt 21:15). According to Mark, it was only after the crucifixion that someone finally grasped the secret of Jesus' real identity 'Truly this man was the Son of God' (Mark 15:39). With his resurrection and the sending of the Holy Spirit, Jesus' power to communicate dramatically changed. But during his earthly ministry he failed or at least appeared to have failed as a communicator.

Nothing expresses this more poignantly than the 'mercy-seat' paintings and carvings of the crucifixion. The Father receives the cross that bears the dead body of the Son, or else simply holds the corpse in his arms. Above or below the Holy Spirit appears under the form of a dove. The Christian artists who produced these works knew that through the brutality and seeming silence of Calvary the presence and power of Father, Son and Holy Spirit were communicated. Even Calvary had not broken the circle of communion within the triune God, who invites human beings to accept true life from that death and build a new human community in the image of the Trinity, the ultimate communicative reality.

In general, communication is essential to Christianity. More specifically, at the heart of Christian life and theology is Jesus Christ who lived, died and rose to communicate new life to us. A global revolution in communications and developments in the field of communication studies can help to interpret, appreciate and share more effectively the lived experience of him who came to redeem us through suffering and apparent failure. If this communication does not take place, not even the noblest philosophy promises to save our world from something far worse than what happened to the town of Frascati in the Second World War.

8

The founder of Christianity

Scholars have frequently raised the question: Did the historical Jesus intend to found the Christian Church?[1] But it has not been very common to call Jesus 'the Founder of Christianity'. C. H. Dodd used the title for a first-rate study of the gospels.[2] But he did not develop to any great extent what he believed that title to entail. Dodd wrote of Jesus standing behind the events out of which the Church arose and as Founder remaining a permanent feature 'of contemporary society's continuing existence'.[3] Especially at the Eucharist the Church remembers the moment of its foundation when its Founder 'suffered under Pontius Pilate'.[4] The New Testament, above all the gospels, record in writing the living tradition about Jesus 'at various stages of its transmission during the first century of the church's existence'.[5] Those are the main details which Dodd explicitly and directly applied to the picture of Jesus precisely as 'Founder of Christianity'. The book contained a fine account of what we can retrieve about the life, death and resurrection of Jesus. But the title as such seemed relatively incidental to Dodd's project.

In this chapter I want to explore the usefulness of calling Jesus 'the Founder of Christianity'. Some data from the New Testament can support the possible role of this title in Christology. After examining several implications in fundamental theology and ecclesiology, I will end by reflecting on

Jesus and the founders of other religious movements. Hence the word 'founder' will be used first in a positive, historical context, and then more in a theological context. The argument moves from historical questions about Jesus as 'the Founder of Christianity' to Christological issues.

I

Apropos of the earthly Jesus' intentions recent scholarship (represented by exegetes like Raymond Brown and theologians like Walter Kasper) has moved to a middle ground between maximalizing and minimalizing positions.

Maximalists held that from the outset Jesus clearly aimed at founding the Church with all its structural components. Usually such a maximal approach rested on two presuppositions. First, the historical Jesus was credited with more or less unlimited knowledge. From the moment of his conception he was alleged to have enjoyed (in his human consciousness) the beatific vision. That meant, among other things, precise and detailed information about everything that was to happen, including the emergence of Christianity in the aftermath of his death and resurrection. Second, behind the maximal view there often seemed to have lurked the fear that unless the earthly Jesus explicitly intended to found the Church with *all* its institutional elements, its origin would not be divinely authorized. Hence he was held to have planned and prepared (at least from the start of his public ministry) the establishment of the Christian religion in all its details.

Minimalists stressed the difficulty of recovering very much reliable information about Jesus' words and deeds. They often argued that we really have no access whatsoever to Jesus' interior states of mind, let alone to any possible intentions to set a new religious movement going. Claims about his motivation and aims were dismissed as illegitimate psychological constructions. To echo Alfred Loisy, all that we know is that Jesus preached the Kingdom of God and what emerged was the Church.

Various arguments built up against the maximalizing interpretation. It is after all orthodox faith to believe that Jesus of Nazareth was (and is) true God and true man. Being limited in knowledge and foreknowledge is precisely part of being human, and not some unfortunate imperfection from which he had to be miraculously freed. Among other things, some limitation in knowledge makes it possible for human beings to act freely in this world. Genuinely free acts entail entrusting oneself to situations and a future which are to one degree or another unknown. Hence in the name of Jesus' true humanity and genuine liberty (not to mention other reasons), theologians and church teachers have accepted real limitations in his knowledge and foreknowledge about matters like the foundation of Christianity.

It has been frequently pointed out against the minimalizers (represented classically by Rudolf Bultmann) that they had abandoned one unacceptable position for another equally unacceptable extreme. Granted that those elaborate reconstructions of intentionality indulged in by many nineteenth- and twentieth-century 'lives' of Jesus were almost totally subjective projections of modern authors, that does not justify heading to the other extreme and rejecting any claims whatsoever about the interior intentions of Jesus. The absence of adequate data about his psychological states is not the same as the absence of all data about his intentions. At least here and there the Synoptic gospels, as we will see in a moment, do allow us to draw some conclusions about what Jesus aimed at doing.

Furthermore, the minimalizers finish up with a strange account of what God effected through the whole Christ-event. Jesus, the primary protagonist on the visible scene, preached the Kingdom without the slightest idea or intention about what was to come with the rise of the Church. We are expected to believe that Christianity got under way without any proper 'input' from the conscious aims of Jesus. He founded this new religious movement, and yet in no way wanted or intended to do so! Certainly we should not simply identify the rule of God with the Christian Church. But it is equally unacceptable to separate completely Jesus' proclamation of the Kingdom from the emergence of the universal Church. Some data from the Synoptic gospels tell against any such rigid separation between the ministry and the post-resurrection situation.

We should, of course, admit that Jesus directed his primary appeal to his own nation. According to Matthew's account, he told the Canaanite woman, 'I was sent only to the lost sheep of the house of Israel' (15:24). Likewise he instructed the twelve when he sent them on their trial mission: 'Go nowhere among the Gentiles, and enter no town of the Samaritans, but go rather to the lost sheep of the house of Israel' (Matt 10:5-6).[6] The very call and sending of *twelve* disciples expressed some intention to gather again the twelve tribes (Matt 19:28; Luke 22:30).[7] We glimpse Jesus' sense of his own mission when we (rightly) translate his remark: 'I was sent only to the lost sheep *who are* the house of Israel.' (We can be sure that this saying came from the earthly Jesus himself. It stands in such manifest discontinuity with the early Church's sense of her universal mission (Acts 11:19ff.; 13:1-3 etc.) that, so far from being invented in the post-Easter situation, the saying was fortunate not to be suppressed.) Whatever the precise meaning of his statement about the rebuilding of the Jerusalem temple (Mark 14:58; 15:29 and parallels), it also indicated Jesus' intention to reform and restore the Jewish nation at its religious and political centre.[8]

Nevertheless, granted that Jesus saw his own people as the primary beneficiary of some final revelation and salvation, his vision was universal. Although he directed his preaching to the chosen people, he called humanity as such to decision. He addressed his Jewish audience as human beings, not as Jews and still less as a holy remnant, some special group of the saved within Judaism. He spoke to them in parables, the language of ordinary life and a language which has proved itself capable of communicating to the whole human race. He demanded a realistic love towards other human beings in need, a love which was willing to cross racial boundaries (Luke 10:25-37). He called for a new brotherhood and sisterhood which denied any absolutely sacrosanct value to family or tribal bonds within Israel: 'Whoever does the will of God is my brother, and sister, and mother' (Mark 3:35 parr.). There was the same kind of universal ring to the parable of the tax-collector and the Pharisee (Luke 18:9-14). There Jesus asserted that the extent of God's generosity had been hitherto ignored: the divine pardon was offered to all.

Hence Jesus' vision of Israel's future entailed 'many coming from east and west to sit at table with Abraham, Isaac and Jacob in the kingdom of heaven' (Matt 8:11 par.). The restoration of Israel to come through Jesus' ministry would bring salvation to the nations. The reformation of the twelve tribes would benefit the human race.

Thus evidence from the public life of Jesus supports two conclusions which tell against any rigid separation between his personal mission for God's Kingdom and the subsequent rise of the Christian Church. The call of the Twelve and what that implied represented some minimal organization. Second, in various ways Jesus showed that he was aware of the universal import of his mission. Not only in terms of the historical sequence of events but also in his conscious intentions, some line led from his proclamation of the divine rule to the establishment of Christianity as a new religious movement.[9]

This second conclusion can be confirmed by the evidence about Jesus' intentions in the face of death. Material from the Synoptic gospels supports the view that Jesus anticipated his coming death and accepted it as an obedient service which would atone for the sins of others and in some way bring a new relationship with God for the wider human family.[10] His death was not unrelated to Jesus' proclamation of the divine rule. The message of the Kingdom led more or less straight to the mystery of the passion. That message included and culminated in the suffering ordeal to come: a time of crisis and distress which was to move towards the day of the Son of man (Mark 13 parr.), the restoration of Israel (Matt 19:29 par.), the banquet of the saved and the salvation of the nations (Matt 8:11 par.). Thus his arrest, condemnation and crucifixion dramatized the very thing which deeply engaged Jesus' intentions, that rule of God which through a time of ordeal was to come for both Jews and Gentiles.

Much of the difficulty in relating Jesus' aims in life and death with the rise of the Christian Church has been concerned with his eschatological vision of the future.

(a) Did he (mistakenly) expect the *parousia* or end of history to occur imminently (the 'consistent' eschatology of Albert Schweitzer)?

(b) Did he announce that the 'end' had already happened (the 'realized' eschatology of some reactions to Schweitzer)?

(c) Or did he proclaim a future end but without expecting it all to happen either during his ministry or immediately after his death and resurrection (the 'mediating' eschatologies of many scholars)?

If hypothesis (c) is correct and Jesus believed or knew that after his suffering, death and resurrection some interval was to elapse before the *parousia*,

(i)   did he expect the end to come during the lifetime of his audience, or
(ii) was a delayed end to be preceded by various signs (the persecution of his followers, disasters for the Jewish people, their capital city and temple, etc.)?

Those who accept interpretations (a) and (b) and some of those who hold (c, i) cannot really credit Jesus with any intentions to found an enduring religious movement. In those cases he happened to be the Founder of Christianity, but did not aim at bringing about that result. He never even envisaged some possibility in time which would allow such an effect to follow. It was only if the earthly Jesus expected some kind of delayed end to history that he could have intended to launch a lasting religious movement, and thus have been in some sense the conscious Founder of Christianity.

Rather than attempt to argue matters out in detail, I can only make several general points. First, whether (in Mark 13 parr.) he was speaking of the impending destruction of Jerusalem (which did actually happen) or of the *parousia* (which has not yet happened) or both, Jesus spoke of the future in heavily symbolic, prophetic language. It is wrong to interpret such prophetic discourse as precise predictions which could have been expected to enjoy a precise fulfilment. Prophetic knowledge was limited knowledge which offered, not an exact forecast of events, but a symbolic vision of the near future which gave meaning to the present and made exceptional demands on people whom the prophet saw to be confronted with an emergency situation. Anthony Harvey expresses very well the timescale of a single generation adopted by those who, in the light of some future end, prophetically discovered and proclaimed to the people new possibilities in the present.

> The end could not be prophesied as if it were upon them in the next few days: a suspension of all routine activity was not what the prophet aimed at; at the other extreme, it could not be proclaimed as something which might take place only

in a subsequent and distant generation, for it would then cease to have any influence on the motives [and actions] of those alive at the time.[11]

That meant that if Jesus wanted to address the people in such a prophetic, apocalyptic way, in general he had no choice but to speak of a dramatic intervention of God to come within the lifetime of his hearers. When he said, 'there are some standing here who will not taste death before they see the kingdom of God has come with power' (Mark 9:1), he was observing the time-scale of that kind of prophetic discourse. This was part of what Harvey calls 'the constraints of history', those limits and conditions imposed by the human environment in which Jesus lived and worked.

Second, we should also take Jesus at his word when he stated that he did not know just when the *parousia* was to occur: 'Of that day or that hour no one knows, not even the angels in heaven, not the Son, but only the Father' (Mark 13:32). We seem to have here an authentic saying. This is the only place in Mark's Gospel where Jesus is reported as referring to himself absolutely as 'the Son', and yet the logion goes against the early Christian tendency to glorify Jesus by frankly admitting his ignorance about the timing of the *parousia*. It is difficult to imagine this saying being created by the Christian tradition and attributed to the earthly Jesus. The saying was fortunate not to have been suppressed.

Third, there are no solid reasons for supposing that Jesus foresaw and planned in detail the various future developments of the Church. Moreover, not only his ministry but also other causes (like the coming of the Holy Spirit) collaborated to initiate the rise of Christianity. Nevertheless, since Jesus called the Twelve and saw his mission with them as bringing salvation to the nations, he was in some truly conscious way the Founder of Christianity. No particular problems about the interpretation of his language of apocalyptic eschatology can tamper with that conclusion. In fact Harvey's appreciation of the 'constraints' of that kind of prophetic language effectively alters the whole debate between the protagonists of 'consistent', 'realized' and 'mediating' eschatologies.

Before leaving the gospels and the New Testament, I want to add some observations about the post-Easter situation, when the foundation of Christianity visibly got under way with the apostolic mission to Jews and Gentiles. Jesus was then called *archēgos* not only in his risen and exalted state (Acts 5:31), but also with reference to his suffering and death (Acts 3:15; Heb 2:10; 12:2). The title meant 'ruler', 'leader', 'originator' and 'founder'. In secular Greek the term was applied to the hero of a city who founded it, often gave it his name and became its guardian. It should be noted, however, that the passages from Acts and Hebrews never call Jesus precisely the Founder of the Church or of Christianity. Rather he is named 'author of life' (Acts 3:15) and the one who leads the way to salvation (Acts 5:31; Heb 2:10) and faith (Heb 12:2).[12]

Elsewhere, however, images of the Church as a building, house and temple encouraged language about Christ as the corner-stone or foundation-stone (Eph 2:20) of that new community.[13] Paul understood the preaching of the gospel to be 'laying a foundation' like a master builder, and the foundation which had already been laid was Jesus Christ himself (1 Cor 3:10–11; see Rom 15:20). This imagery may have originated with Jesus' challenge to his Jerusalem opponents. It can be argued that he was the first to use Psalm 118:22–23 to illuminate and interpret the deadly conflict his ministry provoked: 'Have you not read this scripture: "The very stone which the builders rejected has become the head of the corner: this was the Lord's doing, and it is marvellous in our eyes"?' (Mark 12:10–11 parr.). The symbol of Christ as the rejected stone which became the cornerstone turned up in Acts 4:11. Part of the image was also taken up by Paul who drew on Isaiah 28:16 to present Christ as a 'stone to trip over' and 'a rock to stumble against' for those who sought righteousness not through faith but through the works of the law (Rom 9:30–33).

1 Peter gives this imagery a further twist by presenting Christ not only as the rejected stone of scandal which became the corner-stone of God's new temple, but also as 'the living Stone' into which believers are built like 'living stones':

Come to him, to that living stone, rejected by men but in God's sight chosen and precious; and like living stones be yourselves built into a spiritual house, to be a holy priesthood ... For it stands in scripture: 'Behold, I am laying in Zion a stone, a cornerstone chosen and precious, and he who believes in him will not be put to shame.' To you therefore who believe, he is precious, but for those who do not believe, 'The very stone which the builders rejected has become the head of the corner', and 'A stone that will make men stumble, a rock that will make them fall'; for they stumble because they disobey the word (1 Pet 2:4–8).

In the following section I will return to this New Testament theme about the rejected stone which became the corner-stone. The imagery links Christ as *the* Foundation-stone with the apostles as secondary foundation-stones of Christianity. For the moment I simply wish to note the strong New Testament support for calling Christ *the* Foundation-stone of the Christian movement (the Synoptic gospels, Acts, Paul, a Deutero-Pauline letter (Ephesians) and 1 Peter). In that sense there is more direct scriptural warrant for naming him 'the Foundation of Christianity' than 'the Founder of Christianity'.

II

It pushes language to the limits to speak of a 'living Stone'. Yet this is a vivid reminder that Jesus is no Founder or Foundation-stone who once existed 'back there' and 'back then' and who simply gave the Christian movement its initial support and impetus. His resurrection makes him more dynamically alive and present than ever before. If we are to adopt and use the title 'Founder of Christianity', we must understand this 'Founder' to be still uniquely with us. In other words, this title will prove properly viable if associated with a Christology of living presence.

Here it is as well to recall some other Christologies which have been in the field since New Testament times. John 1:14 ('the Word became flesh') stood behind the classical Christology of incarnation. The Letter to Titus provided the basic texts for a Christology of appearance (2:11, 13; 3:4). Philippians 2:7 ('he emptied himself') encouraged an almost opposite, 'kenotic' approach which stressed the humble hiddenness of God's Son that culminated in the silent 'disgrace' of Calvary. An 'image' Christology has drawn on 2 Corinthians 4:4 and Colossians 1:15 to reflect on the Son as not simply a likeness but the very image of God the Father. Presumably Karl Rahner's proposals about Christ as the 'real symbol' of God are to be related to this 'image' Christology.[14]

Without then claiming any special monopoly for this approach, what do I see a Christology of *presence* bringing to the title of Christ as 'Founder of Christianity'? Even more than the notion of founder, 'presence' is a personal rather than a metaphysical category. At its best 'presence' speaks of a 'being-with' which is entered into through the freedom of love and exercises a transforming influence on those who enjoy that personal presence. This is the special presence of God with the chosen people to which Deuteronomy witnesses: 'What great nation is there that has a god so near to it as the Lord our God is to us, whenever we call upon him?' (4:7; see 7:6, etc.). It is this kind of rich personal presence which the Second Vatican Council's Constitution on the Sacred Liturgy (*Sacrosanctum Concilium*) acknowledged in the liturgical celebrations:

> Christ is always present in his Church, especially in her liturgical celebrations. He is present in the Sacrifice of the Mass not only in the person of his minister ... but especially in the eucharistic species. By his power he is present in the sacraments so that when anybody baptizes it is really Christ himself who baptizes. He is present in his word since it is he himself who speaks when the holy scriptures are read in the Church. Lastly, he is present when the Church prays and sings (no. 7).

A Christology of presence will prove unsatisfactory unless it develops this line of *Sacrosanctum Concilium* to suggest the different kinds and qualities of presence. If that is done, it can help greatly to fill out ways in which the Founder of Christianity continues to live among us.

In *Redemptor Hominis* Pope John Paul II highlights that mystery of Jesus Christ, 'in which each one of the four thousand million human beings living on our planet has become a sharer from the moment he is conceived beneath the heart of his mother' (no. 13). The Founder comes to us behind four thousand million faces; they are signs and sacraments of his presence. What does the mystery of his union with them say to us now as we seek to clarify his person and saving work? In particular, we should expect those who suffer to be privileged carriers of his presence. Left to ourselves, we would hardly turn to sectors of human suffering for help in understanding and interpreting the continuing presence of Christianity's Founder. But the truth comes through clearly from the gospels, St Paul's letters and other books of the New Testament. Jesus points to the hungry, imprisoned, sick and displaced persons as identified with him in a special way (Matt 25:31–46). Then he dies in seeming failure and atrocious pain, crucified between two criminals. That is precisely the moment when the Roman centurion breaks through to the deepest truth of Jesus' identity and declares: 'Indeed this man was the Son of God' (Mark 15:39). This event of powerless suffering remains paradigmatic. Paul discerns and interprets the passion of his own missionary experiences as *the* means through which Christ the Founder remains peculiarly present and active in the apostle's life (2 Cor 4:8ff; 6:4ff; 11:23ff; 12:7ff).

Events of contemporary history also manifest something of Christ's present Lordship and the working out of the salvation which he has brought.[15] St Paul sees all humanity and creation 'groaning' together in a history of suffering as they move towards the fullness of liberating redemption (Rom 8:18ff). Through Christ the story of the world unfolds as a story of cosmic and human reconciliation (Rom 5:10–11; 2 Cor 5:18ff; Col 1:20ff). By means of its vivid scenarios and apocalyptic language, the Book of Revelation invites its readers to contemplate the triumph of Christ in human history. Now it would be very odd to agree in theory that his reconciling power is presently shaping the world's history towards the day of full and final salvation, and at the same time refuse to acknowledge any visible signs of his presence around us. In 'the signs of the times' Christians recognize and seek to read off current indications of their Founder's personal presence and influence.

An increasing dialogue with other religions and various ideologies – partly interpreted through a return to the thought of

Justin, Clement of Alexandria, Irenaeus and other fathers of the Church – picks up another area of contemporary experience which can enrich our reflections on the ongoing presence of Christianity's Founder. The Second Vatican Council initiated a theme which was taken up by Paul VI, by the closing statement from the bishops' synod of 1977 (no. 15) and by John Paul II in *Redemptor Hominis* (no. 11): the 'semina Verbi' (seeds of the Word) which disclose a kind of 'inchoate' presence of Christ beyond Christianity. In *Evangelii Nuntiandi* Paul VI described non-Christian religions as 'all impregnated with innumerable "seeds of the Word"' (no. 53).

This attitude encourages us to acknowledge and reverence Christ actively present in other religions even before any contact has been made with the gospel. These other faiths and their cultures have proved a matrix in which the revelation and salvation brought by the Founder of Christianity have in some way been effectively present.

I do not wish to make the mistake of developing too far subordinate themes. But I hope enough has been said about liturgy, suffering, history and other religions to illustrate the varied ways in which the Founder of Christianity continues to be dynamically present to the Church and the world.

Measured against the usual founders of political, social and religious movements, Jesus proves startlingly different in at least two ways. Often founders (like the founders of a new nation) did their work in a much more conscious way by drafting constitutions, foreseeing future developments and providing elaborate structures for maintaining the community they launched into existence. The earthly Jesus did none of that. At the same time, his sense of a universal mission and the call of the Twelve made him in some real sense the conscious Founder of Christianity. 'Quantitatively' he did little when compared with many other founders. Yet 'qualitatively' it was enough to justify calling him the *archēgos* who gave the Christian Church its originating impulse. Second, the resurrection has made Jesus dramatically present in a way which is simply not true of other founders. They can remain present through their writings and the community's memory of them. The personal presence of the risen Jesus, however, expresses itself in a rich span of ways, some of which I indicated above.

It is this personal presence which makes it vitally necessary to acknowledge *the actual reality* of the saving revelation Jesus brought through his life, death, and resurrection. On the one hand, God's self-communication reached a full, absolute and unrepeatable climax with the whole Christ-event. The first Christians, and above all the apostles, testified to that foundational history of revelation and salvation, because they had known the once-and-for-all experience of living intimately with Jesus, encountering him in his risen glory and through the power of the Holy Spirit becoming the basic witnesses to the resurrection. (In the special case of Paul, of course, this apostolic experience did not include an association with Jesus during his ministry.) On the other hand, however, the revealing and saving presence of Christ did not cease with the apostolic age. He remains 'the living Stone' (1 Pet 2:4), 'the living One' who is 'alive for evermore' (Rev 1:18) and who says here and now to every community and individual: 'Behold, I stand at the door and knock; if anyone hears my voice and opens the door, I will come in to him and eat with him, and he with me' (Rev 3:20). The Founder of Christianity is far more than an historical figure who each year slips further and further back into the past. He is a living presence, 'the same yesterday, today and forever' (Heb 13:8).

Here I have been considering an issue which concerns fundamental theology – namely, the challenge of relating the fullness of revelation at the outset of Christianity with the actual reality of revelation here and now. In my *Fundamental Theology* I proposed the distinction between 'foundational' and 'dependent' revelation.[16] In equivalent terms we could also speak of the Founder who never went away but who transcends space and time to be with us all more intimately than ever before (Matt 28:20). I turn next to some ecclesiological and apologetic implications of the title 'Founder of Christianity'.

III

If we go back for a moment to Ephesians, we find 'the apostles and prophets' called the *themelios* or foundation for the Church of which Jesus Christ himself is the foundation-stone:

You are fellow citizens with the saints and members of the
household of God, built upon the foundation of the apostles
and prophets, Christ Jesus himself being the corner-stone, in
whom the whole structure is joined together and grows into
a holy temple in the Lord; in whom you also are built into
it for a dwelling place of God in the Spirit (Eph 2:19–22).[17]

Here the apostles are associated with Christ like foundation-
stones with *the* Foundation-stone. Matthew's gospel names
Simon Peter 'the rock' on which Christ builds his Church
(16:18). The city wall of the new Jerusalem in the Book of
Revelation will have 'twelve foundation-stones' and on these
stones the name of 'the twelve apostles of the Lamb' (21:14)
will be written. Although it employs the imagery of 'thrones',
Matthew 19:27–28 promises that Peter and his companions will
serve as foundations for the new Israel. All of this can rightly
encourage us to speak of the Founder (in upper case) and the
founders (in lower case) of Christianity.

In the narrower sense the Twelve, Paul and other apostles[18]
were the founders of the Church. In a wider sense all Christians
of the first century can be considered to have been in a variety
of ways the founding fathers and founding mothers of the
Church. Let me concentrate on the apostles themselves whom
Matthew, Ephesians and Revelation describe as the foundation-
stones. St Paul offers a useful way in.

Paul knew his meeting with the risen Christ to be a stun-
ningly unexpected, utterly 'abnormal' birth into new life, *the*
experience which drastically reorganized all his values and
shaped his subsequent story. 'Last of all, as to one untimely
born,' he recalled, Christ 'appeared also to me' (1 Cor 15:8;
see 9:1; Gal 1:11ff). That once-and-for-all experience not only
turned Paul's life around (Phil 3:7ff), but also brought him into
the ranks of the apostolic founding fathers of the Church. That
'last of all' encounter closed the series of appearances by the
risen Christ which gave Paul and a limited number of others the
unique, unrepeatable and non-transferable task of officially witnessing the resurrection (Acts 10:40–41) and of founding the
Church. No later Christians would ever again have precisely
the same experience or exactly the same role as Easter witnesses and Church founders.

As a consequence it is preferable to call bishops successors *to* the apostles. 'Successors *of* the apostles' too easily implies that bishops are called to play completely the same role as the apostles. 'Successors to' reminds us that bishops do not follow on the apostles in the way, for example, that President Ronald Reagan took over from Jimmy Carter and assumed an *identical* set of powers and responsibilities. We cannot say that of the bishops *vis-à-vis* the apostles. To be sure, all that could be handed on from the apostles to the bishops was handed on. But as resurrection witnesses and Church founders the apostles had a once-and-for-all function, which associated them intimately with the once-and-for-all character of the total Christ-event and which could not as such be passed on. The Easter encounters brought the official resurrection witnesses a special experience and a special function (which died with them).

Finally, I wish to move beyond the Church (in which the bishops can be properly called successors *to* the apostolic founders) and reflect on what might be said of Christ over against the founders of various other religions.

Here the advantage of the title 'Founder of Christianity' shows up. Unlike 'high' Christological titles like 'Lord' and 'Son of God' or 'low' titles like 'Messiah' or 'Prophet', 'Founder' comes across as more factual, historical and even relatively value-free. This title allows Hans Küng to develop an updated apologetic for Jesus and Christianity. He not only notes how 'superficial' it is to place all 'founders of religion' in a kind of interchangeable series, but insists on the dramatic differences between Jesus and other founders. Obvious human factors which help to explain, at least in part, their power and lasting influence were absent in his case.

> Jesus was not brought up at court as Moses apparently was, nor a king's son like Buddha. but neither was he a scholar and politician like Confucius nor a rich politician like Muhammed. The very fact that his origins were so insignificant makes his enduring significance all the more amazing.

Add too the deep divergences between Jesus' message and those of Moses, Buddha, Muhammed and Confucius. All of this leaves us with the questions: 'What really impelled' Jesus? What was his 'centre'? Who was he? How do we account for him?[19]

Küng goes on to develop this argument for Christianity and its Founder in terms of an 'historical enigma': it was 'only after Jesus' death that the movement invoking his name really started'. In the case of Buddha, Confucius and Muhammed we can point to various visible causes which helped to account for the spread of their religious movements. Historically speaking, the origin of Christianity remains puzzling.

> How different this was from the gradual, peaceful propagation of the teachings of the successful sages, Buddha and Confucius; how different also from the largely violent propagation of the teachings of the victorious Muhammed. And all of this was within the lifetime of the founders. How different, after a complete failure and a shameful death, were the spontaneous emergence and almost explosive propagation of this message and community in the very name of the defeated leader. After the disastrous outcome of this life, what gave the initial impetus to that unique world-historical development: a truly world-transforming religion emerging from the gallows where a man was hanged in shame?[20]

Here too Küng successfully contrasts Jesus with the founders of other religious movements. Those other founders and their movements can hardly be called historical enigmas. With Christianity, however, it is difficult to account for its rise and success after Jesus' disgraceful crucifixion, unless we admit his resurrection from the dead.

In conclusion, it should be added that other religious movements do not identify divine truth and spiritual growth with the historical person of their founders as Christianity does. Muhammed received and proclaimed the truth for his followers, whereas Christians acknowledge Jesus to be the *truth*. Unlike Buddha and other Eastern sages, Christ does not merely show the way. He is the *way*.

The founders of other religious families and movements preached and taught doctrines which were 'external' to their own person. They normally were not proposed as the object of their disciples' faith. In the case of Christianity, however, we face a founder who through his life, death and resurrection was accepted as being in his own person the absolute fullness of divine revelation and the supreme sign of God's desire to share friendship here and hereafter with the whole human race.

In *Jesus the Man and the Myth* James Mackey has some interesting pages on what he calls 'the final myth' of religious founders.[21] There are a number of points in Mackey's Christology over which I would part company with him.[22] But I wish to support thoroughly his contrast between Jesus and the founders of non-Christian religions. He writes:

> The Christian faith is more closely bound to the person of its founder than any other faith living or dead, or, to put the matter the other way round ... the actual person of Jesus of Nazareth, its historical founder, is more central to the Christian confession of faith than is the founder of any other religion to its formulated confessions.

Mackey then adds some examples to clarify the difference:

> The Buddhist need not confess Gautama Siddartha his Lord, much less his God, and the Parsee proffers no such claims about Zoroaster. Muhammed was the prophet of Allah; he was the one who uttered to the human race the truths of Allah, but he did not think himself, nor was he thought to be, their subject.

It is precisely in terms of its Founder that Mackey interprets the historical nature of Christianity.

> Whatever else the statement that Christianity is an historical religion may mean, it must certainly mean that the actual person of its founder is infinitely more at the centre of, infinitely more of the essence of the Christian religion than is the case with the actual historical founder of any other of the world's great religions.[23]

Küng and Mackey do not talk of 'Founder of Christianity' as a title, but they do in fact illustrate its usefulness in the area of comparative religion. As we have also seen, the title has a valuable role to play in Christology, ecclesiology and fundamental theology.

9

Our peace and reconciliation

It has frequently been remarked that the passion narratives of our gospels are most sparing in their description of Jesus' physical sufferings. There is, in fact, only one reference to Christ's shedding of his blood – if we leave aside Luke's allusion to the sweat which was 'like' drops of blood in the garden of Gethsemane (Luke 22:44): this is to Jesus hanging on the cross, his side pierced by the soldier's lance in order to make certain that he was already dead; 'and immediately there flowed out blood and water' (John 19:34). So runs the litany, from which the title of this chapter is taken:

> Heart of Jesus, pierced with a lance;
> ... source of all consolation;
> ... our life and resurrection;
> ... our peace and reconciliation;

Thus the invocations associate the world's 'peace and reconciliation' with a particular reality and symbol; the Sacred Heart of our Lord. St Paul's letter to the Colossians is the clear biblical foundation for the litany here – stating what it is that Christ has done as Saviour: 'Through him ... God chose to *reconcile* the whole universe to himself, making peace through the shedding of his blood on the cross: to *reconcile* all things, whether on earth or in heaven through him alone' (Col 1:20). God reconciled the entire universe (Paul repeats the assertion in Ephesians: 'Now in Christ Jesus you who were once far off have been brought near through the blood of Christ ... our peace ... through his cross' [2:13–17]) through an historical execution which took the *specific* form of crucifixion: a death which, unlike many other forms of dying, involves a massive loss of blood. Universal redemption was achieved when a man from Nazareth suffered a bloody execution on a particular day outside Jerusalem, 'the city of peace' (cf Luke 19:41ff). I stress this link between the universal and particular because of a noticeable unwillingness, both in recent translations of the New Testament and some theological writings, to mention the blood of Jesus. *Good News for Modern Man*, the New Testament in *Today's English version*, repeatedly refuses to translate exactly references to Jesus' blood and often introduces a vaguer term, death. The version renders Colossians 1:20 as follows: 'Through the Son, then, God decided to bring the whole universe back to himself. God made peace through his Son's death on the cross, and so brought back to himself all both on earth and in heaven.' A key Pauline passage about the nature of redemption speaks of Jesus expiating sins through his blood (Rom 3:25). The *New English Bible* modifies Paul's concreteness and calls Jesus 'the means of expiating sin by his sacrificial death'.

When contemporary theological works deal with the suffering and death of Jesus, they regularly fail to discuss how he made peace 'through the shedding of his blood upon the cross'. An easy way of verifying this apparently sweeping judgement is to review the chapter (or sections) devoted to Jesus's death in the Christologies of Kasper, Küng, Moltmann, Pannenberg, Schillebeeckx, Schoonenberg and others. Let me cite two recent examples: James Mackey and Jon Sobrino. The former has one passing reference to the spilling of Jesus' blood.[1] Jon Sobrino also seems reluctant to do more than merely touch the theme.[2]

I wonder whether Bible translators and theologians are losing something of great religious importance when they downplay or even ignore the blood of Jesus shed for us on Good Friday. We have here a theme which runs through the New

Testament. At the Last Supper Jesus takes the cup and says, 'This is my blood of the new covenant, which is poured out for many' (Mark 14:24 and parallels). St Paul teaches that we are 'justified' by the blood of Christ who 'died for us' (Rom 5:8ff). The first letter of Peter assures its readers that they have been 'ransomed' by 'the precious blood of Christ' (1:18ff). The letter to the Hebrews expounds the priestly service of Christ whose blood purifies us 'to serve the living God' (9:12, 14; 13:12). Revelation pushes language to its limits when it 'explains' that the heavenly multitude in white garments 'have washed their robes and made them white in the blood of the Lamb' (7:14).

No one who saw them has remained unmoved at the sight of the pictures of Archbishop Oscar Romero assassinated at the altar, his priestly vestments stained with his life's blood. Again, in St Peter's Square, on 13 May 1981, the white of the Pope's cassock contrasted with the red blood issuing from the bullet wounds. It needed ten pints of blood to save his life. People wanted to know these details about the operation. Like water, milk and other fluids, blood is a natural symbol expressing a wide range of social and religious meanings. The press, radio and television appreciate that blood and what it symbolizes have a stronger hold on the popular imagination than some theologians and Bible translators would apparently like to think.

The current scholarly and theological 'distaste' for the blood of Christ is understandable: one is reminded, for example, of the annual 'performance' over the liquefaction of the blood of St Januarius in Naples. The Dominican, M.-D. Chenu, was one of the distinguished theological architects of the Second Vatican Council. Yet his article '*Sang du Christ*' indicates what might be called a morbid not to say unscientific approach to 'theological haematology' up to the recent past.[3] Chenu describes how the generality of theologians agree that Christ's blood was personally united to the Word of God. He then lists the questions which remain open: Was the precious blood separated from the Word during the passion? If so, did it merit adoration? If Christ's blood has in fact been preserved as a relic, should we adore such a relic? Devotion to the blood of Christ had somehow become separated from the reality of his humanity and his historical life and death. We had devotion to the 'five wounds', the Sacred Head as well as the Sacred Heart, as though those were separate objects of a quaint and primitive piety rather than integral to the entire mystery of Christ's redemption.

Yet in spite of these exaggerations, and the reactions to which they have given rise in recent years (for example, the feast of the Precious Blood, raised to a double of the first class in 1934, was suppressed altogether as a separate feast in 1969), it is important for us to appreciate what it originally meant, and still must mean today when it is proclaimed that Jesus effected 'our peace and reconciliation' with God through 'shedding his blood on the cross'. Certainly there is ample biblical and theological justification for addressing the Sacred Heart of Jesus as 'our peace and reconciliation'. What I wish to do is to show the special foundation for the reconciliation by taking our cue from the Pauline statement (Col 1:20) and restricting our reflections to this shedding of his life's blood during the passion.

Our Jewish heritage

It is hardly possible, however, to comprehend the symbolism of blood in the Old Testament and early Christian thought without some recognizable typology. Otherwise the information is so complex and culturally conditioned that it threatens to frustrate any attempt at clear understanding and interpretation. So much diverse material is at hand to provide answers to the basic question: How did the Israelites think about blood in their relationship with God? It is true that pure or ideal types do not exist in our world: they belong, as the philosophers say, to an exaggerated realism. None the less, typology can be useful, inasmuch as it helps both to classify the data on the religious symbolism of blood and to elaborate some kind of ordered understanding. For example, it is simple enough to discern a threefold typology of blood-symbolism employed by the Israelites in a religious setting.

First, there is the sign which brought deliverance from death. Before leaving Egypt the Israelites smeared their doorposts with the blood of a lamb (Exod 12:7, 13, 22ff). This sign delivered them from the destruction which afflicted the homes of the Egyptians. The blood of the paschal lamb saved the Israelites from losing their first-born. There were other ways, too, in which blood was closely associated with *life*. The Israelites understood life to be 'in the blood' (Lev 17: 11ff; cf Deut 12:23). Since life was sacred, they regarded blood also as sacred. Yahweh was the God of life. Hence blood, the seat of life, belonged to God alone. In the ancient Near and Middle East, the Israelites appear to have differed from all their neighbours *in linking blood with life, and hence with what was sacred and divine*: at least in the symbolism dealing with sacrifice.[4] In its own way, modern science has more than vindicated the Old Testament conviction that life, the divine and sacred gift *par excellence*, is 'in the blood'. Oxygen, nutrients, hormones and other items essential for life are carried by our blood. Its complex structure enables us to endure wide variations of temperature and changes of diet. Every day around the world massive transfusions of blood save lives that are slipping away. Medical discoveries and practice have dramatically associated the miracle of life with the miracle of blood.

Second, besides expressing deliverance and life, blood was believed to cleanse the stains of human sin. On the Day of Atonement the high priest sprinkled blood as part of a ritual recalling God's willingness to purify the Israelites from their sins. Yahweh wished to remove human guilt, destroy sin and effect reconciliation with his people. The ceremony of sprinkling blood on the 'mercy seat' symbolized the divine desire to wipe away the contamination of sin (Lev 16). Today, of course, we may not appreciate the practice of slaughtering bulls and goats to release and use their blood. But we should still be able to recognize the religious logic of the Israelites. In so far as it was the element in which life resided, blood enjoyed a peculiarly divine and sacred character. Hence it appropriately served and stood for the purification of sin and the restoration of loving relations between Yahweh and his people.

Third, blood sealed the covenant at Sinai (Exod 24:3-8). Even today some cultures and sub-cultures maintain this symbolism. Rituals involving blood bind together formerly hostile groups and bring new relationships of peace, friendship, and love. In the desert, the Israelites solemnly accepted Yahweh's offer of a special relationship with them and used blood to represent this loving union with their God. The sacrificial blood was shared by the people and their God (represented by the altar).

Here then are three perspectives on blood recorded in the Old Testament: as a sign of deliverance and life, as a ritual means of expiating human guilt, and as a way of sealing and expressing a new relationship of friendship. Even in the advanced industrial culture of the late twentieth century this triple typology persists at least dimly. When a society lacks life, we call it anaemic. Parents show alarm when their children suffer cuts. There is a danger that blood will be lost and dangerous infection will set in. The blood-stained seat of a car can speak very powerfully of a precious life being terminated by terrorists. Blood donors literally give new life to others. The point does not need to be laboured. Both positive and negative associations of ideas link blood with deliverance from death to life. Admittedly we have become sadly used to the fact that noble people – the J. F. Kennedys, the Romeros, the Sadats – may dedicate themselves in heroic service only to be murdered and soon forgotten. So much bloodshed seems irrelevant for the purifying and healing of a contaminated world. Yet there always remains the hope that the love inherent in the true sacrifice of a Martin Luther King or an Oscar Romero will somehow make its impact: that in some way the deaths of these victims work to cleanse and atone for the sins of our society. Though it remains true that the call to give one's life for others has been introduced in a thousand evil causes, no abuse can rob Jesus' words of their truth: 'Greater love has no man than this, that a man lay down his life for his friends' (John 15:13). Whether in fiction or in real life, there can be no more powerful way of symbolizing and enacting a relationship of love than by shedding one's blood for others. True love always makes people vulnerable. Sometimes it literally turns them into targets for killers.

The blood of Jesus

It takes no great imaginative leap to see how this triple typology is supremely realized in the case of Jesus' bloody crucifixion. As our paschal lamb (1 Cor 5:7), he freely accepted death

to deliver us from the power of sin and bring us life and freedom. To eat the flesh of the Son of man and drink his blood is
to receive eternal life (John 6: 53–56). Secondly, the first Letter
of John witnesses to 'the blood of Jesus' which 'cleanses us
from all sin' (1:7). Finally, the shedding of his blood effected
a new covenant of love between God and the whole human race
(Mark 14:24 and parallels). This death expresses the divine
love towards us (Rom 8:31–39), and aims at bringing a loving
reconciliation between God and all people (Rom 5:10ff).

The Litany of the Sacred Heart rightly calls Jesus '*our* peace
and reconciliation'. His crucifixion was not a death which
changed God, but an act of loving self-sacrifice directed at changing us and reconciling us with God. The shedding of Jesus' blood
in no way means that he is punished in our place, placating, so
to speak, the divine anger at human sin. On the contrary, this
death offers us life and invites us to dwell with our God in peace.
As Sebastian Moore puts it: 'God uses the crucifixion of Jesus to
convince us that, even at our worst, as crucifiers of the good, we
are accepted by him.'[5] The victim gave his life for the crucifiers,
and his blood called down upon them infinite love, not
vengeance. It is, however, a sorrowful fact that even now many
Christians continue to think that through his suffering and death
Jesus propitiated an angry God, turned away the divine wrath,
and in that sense won us peace and reconciliation through shedding his blood. It is a heresy that dies a slow death, that the
Father treated the Son as a sinner, judging and punishing him in
our place as a substitute for guilty humanity. In the past we find
such a view reiterated and endorsed by Bishop Bossuet
(1627–1704) in one of his sermons on the passion:

> The man, Jesus Christ, has been thrown under the multiple
> and redoubled blows of divine vengeance ... As it vented
> itself, so his [God's] anger diminished; he struck his inno-
> cent Son as he wrestled with the wrath of God ... When an
> avenging God waged war upon his son, the mystery of our
> peace was accomplished.

Such language of anger, punishment and propitiation has flourished down to our own day. Theologians, preachers and hymn-
writers continue to represent the suffering Christ as being
punished in substitution for sinful men and women. We find it,

for example, in the writings of Jürgen Moltmann, who interprets Jesus' cry of abandonment (Mark 15:34) as revealing his 'rejection' by the Father, becoming 'the accursed of God', divided from his Father by 'the utmost degree of enmity', and suffering 'the torment of hell'.[6] Similarly, Hans Urs von Balthasar: 'Hell is ... a reality that Christ knew fully in his dereliction'; and Easter meant raising 'the already stinking body of *the sinner* from the grave'.[7]

It would certainly appear to be stepping beyond the bounds of poetic licence to represent Jesus as a criminal condemned in our place to appease the divine anger and thus to reconcile the world with God. There is nothing in the great servant-songs of Isaiah, for example, to justify the portrayal of the Father acting with such extreme cruelty towards his Son, treating him as a sinner, and demanding his life's blood from one utterly innocent. Any image of God as an angry punisher requiring such propitiation has nothing in common with the parable of the Prodigal Son. In that story the Father does not need to change from anger to gracious love. He is not waiting to be appeased; he is simply waiting for the return of his son. When that happens, he runs to fling his arms around the boy and kiss him.

The New Testament does not allow us to construe the passion and crucifixion as punishment from God. When hostility is shown him from Pharisees, Herodians or priests, Jesus never interprets this as indicating divine displeasure, let alone a desire to punish him as a substitute for sinners. On the contrary, he associates himself with the fate of persecuted prophets (Luke 13:33ff). In their case and in his, suffering and death in no way implied condemnation by God. Such persecution was due to the hardness of heart of those to whom they were sent.

Supporters of this penal substitution view are quick to point out a detail of the agony in the garden: the 'cup' which Jesus prayed to be taken from him (Mark 14:36 and parallels). Undoubtedly, in the Old Testament a 'cup' can not only be 'the cup of salvation', but also can symbolize the divine anger: that wounded love of God which tries to win human beings back from their sins. In Revelation the guilty must drink the cup of God's anger (14:10; 16:19; 18:6). However, the 'cup' in Gethsemane stands for the suffering and representative death which Jesus *freely accepted* (Mark 14:23 and parallels). His followers would also be invited freely to accept similar suffering and even martyrdom. That would be to share in the cup which Jesus himself drank (Mark 10:38ff). In the description of the arrest given in the Fourth Gospel, Jesus' rebuke to Peter coheres with what Mark reports: 'Shall I not drink the cup which the Father has given me?' (18:11). Jesus does not ask, 'Shall I not drink the cup which the Father has *imposed* on me and with which the father is *punishing* me?' Rather, here, as in Mark, he freely accepts the violent and bloody death he is to undergo.

To understand and interpret the redemption Jesus brought, we can do no better than to turn to a classic passage where St Paul proclaims that 'through his blood' Jesus became 'the means of expiating sin for all who believe' (Rom 3:25). The three perspectives mentioned above stand behind the apostle's words. This blood delivered us from death and bondage, like the blood smeared on the doorways of the Israelites at the time of their liberation from Egypt. Jesus died on a new Day of Atonement, which was not simply valid for a year (Lev 16) or even for half a century (Lev 25); his act of expiation concerned all men and women for all time. Finally, his blood sealed a relationship which went beyond the covenant made with the Israelites at Sinai: a new covenant of love was established with all men and women for all time.

The symbol of blood

Undoubtedly there are ample biblical reasons for acknowledging that Jesus gave his heart's blood to bring reconciliation and peace to the world. But we are dealing here with a symbolic reality. Something further needs to be added about the power and meaning of this symbol. Symbols enter our imagination, affect our feelings and influence our behaviour by making things present. Symbols are felt to be powerful and important even before we consciously perceive their possible meanings. Further, over and above those meanings which society generally associates with given symbols, different people will recognize and appreciate different meanings for themselves. Cultural and historical conditioning brings it about that the perception of symbols vary from period to period and from place to place. In all cases, rational explanations will always fall short of the potential range of meanings expressed by given symbols. Particularly when we take up religious symbols, like the precious blood of Christ, which point to ultimate, transcendent realities, we can expect these symbols to prove inexhaustible.

Small but precious details in the passion story suggest the richness of the symbol we are examining. For instance, Jesus shed his heart's blood before *and after* death. In a brutal act of aggression, a Roman soldier ran a spear through the side of the corpse on the cross. At once water and blood flowed from this final wound (John 19:34). The memory of this symbolic episode evokes the sense that in life, at death, and even beyond death, Jesus gave himself *totally*, even as his crucifixion and resurrection aimed to reconcile the entire universe with the Father. Further, the opened side of Jesus released grace into the world under the signs of blood and water. The dead victim offered life, cleansing and love to his crucifiers, and to the sinful humanity they represented. Earlier I sketched the Jewish understanding which, as we have said, links blood with all three. Here we might catch the nuances better by associating life and love with the blood, and cleansing with the water, which flowed from the wounded side of Jesus. In re-reading the Litany of the Sacred Heart before writing these words, I was intrigued to find that the litany makes no explicit reference to the blood of Jesus, even though it contains such invocations as 'Heart of Jesus, pierced with a lance'. Does it need the addition, 'Heart of Jesus, giver of your life's blood for us'? The blood which issued from Christ's wounded side and flowed down the body on the cross was blood which had passed through the heart of the Crucified.

From the outset I have argued that, as a symbolic reality, blood maintains its hold on the popular mind and feelings. We can still hear the message of Colossians: by shedding his blood on the cross Jesus brought peace and reconciliation to the whole world. At the same time, however, the symbol has its distasteful, cruel aspect. But consummately, as a symbol touching the divine-human relationship it exemplifies wonderfully well the 'frightening and fascinating mystery' (*mysterium tremendum et fascinans*) that we encounter in God. To reflect on Jesus' blood is to think of something which concerns and evokes both desire and dread.

Not far from where I live in Rome there are two crucifixes which belonged to an alumnus of the Gregorian University, St Vincent Pallotti (1795–1850). He was dissatisfied with the way he found them and dabbed on them some red paint to represent the blood which issued from Jesus' wounds. St Vincent was moved to emphasize this specific detail for his personal meditation on Christ crucified. To the cultured and cultivated his action might seem a 'stumbling block' and 'folly' (1 Cor 1:23). Yet so too in its own way was the faith expressed by the letter to the Colossians; that Jesus ushered in the time of cosmic peace and reconciliation 'through shedding his blood upon the cross'.[8]

10

Did Joseph of Arimathea exist?

For a critical assessment of the New Testament tradition(s) about Jesus' empty tomb much depends on one's evaluation of the burial story (Mark 15:42–47 in its first intracanonical form). A reference to Jesus' burial turned up in the early kerygma quoted by Paul (1 Cor 15:4a; see Rom 6:4). But it was ten or fifteen years later before Mark ended his passion narrative with the episode about Joseph of Arimathea following the prescriptions of Deut 21:22–23 and burying Jesus' body before sunset on the day of the crucifixion. Obviously if we deny any historical reliability in this burial story and dismiss it as a legend created either by the evangelist (or one of his sources), we would have to make the same negative judgement about the subsequent empty tomb narrative (Mark 16:1–8 in its first intracanonical form).

Among the pioneers of form criticism, Rudolf Bultmann accepted the essential credibility of the burial narrative. He described the basic story (Mark 15:44–45, 47) as 'an historical account which creates no impression of being a legend'.[1] More recently Joseph Fitzmyer wrote: 'Joseph of Arimathea is otherwise unknown, but in all four gospels he is linked to the burial of Jesus, clearly a historical reminiscence being used. Who would invent him?'.[2] In his *Anchor Bible Dictionary* article on 'Joseph of Arimathea', Stanley E. Porter[3] obviously followed

Bultmann, Fitzmyer and many other biblical scholars who acknowledge an historically reliable core in the story of Joseph of Arimathea burying Jesus' body after the crucifixion.[4]

Nevertheless, every now and then the burial story is dismissed as completely non-historical, a story created by the evangelist Mark. In three recent books[5] John Dominic Crossan has argued *inter alia* that the tradition about Joseph of Arimathea originated with Mark and was then derived from him. Essentially four arguments come into play to support Crossan's position: three are general propositions (about the original source for the gospel passion narratives in an earlier version which, though no longer extant, is embedded in the Gospel of Peter; the tendency to historicize Old Testament prophecies; and Mark's extraordinary creativity), and one deals with a specific point (Joseph of Arimathea as an 'in-between' figure). Let us look at them in turn.

From the first of his trilogy, *Four Other Gospels*, Crossan has argued that much of the apocryphal Gospel of Peter antedated Mark, Matthew, Luke and John, and provided the narrative from which all their passion (and resurrection) stories derive. In particular, the passion narratives in the four canonical gospels can 'all be adequately and plausibly explained as layers of redactional expansion on that single primary source' (p. 145). In *Four Other Gospels* Crossan calls the source or major part of the Gospel of Peter 'the original Passion-Resurrection Source' (pp. 145, 160–161, 164). In *The Cross that Spoke* it becomes the 'Cross Gospel, a document presently embedded in the Gospel of Peter, just as Q is in Matthew and Luke' (p. XIII). According to 'the original Passion-Resurrection Source' (soon to be called 'the Cross Gospel'), 'Jesus' burial was completely under the motivation and control of his enemies'. Crossan refers his readers to the Gospel of Peter 2:15; 5:15 and 6:21 – verses which belong, he claims, to the original Passion-Resurrection Source or Cross Gospel.[6] Denying incidentally the presence of the female disciples at Jesus' death and burial, Crossan draws an important conclusion from his position that Jesus' enemies were totally in charge not only of his execution but also of his burial: 'Those closest to Jesus had fled his Crucifixion and had no idea how or where he was buried'.[7] In *The Historical Jesus* he makes the same claim more rhetorically: 'With regard to the body of Jesus, by Easter Sunday morning, those who cared did not know where it was, and those who knew did not care' (p. 394).

In his 1986 presidential address to the Society of New Testament Studies, Raymond Brown exposed the weakness in Crossan's first general claim: the dependence of the canonical gospels on the apocryphal Gospel of Peter (or rather the first half of it, 1:1—6:22, but without 2:3–5a) for their passion narratives.[8] Brown denied all such literary dependence: there are noticeable inconsistencies in the narrative of the Gospel of Peter which cannot be explained by Crossan's thesis of an earlier self-coherent passion story (=Crossan's 'Passion-Resurrection Source') and a later redaction under the influence of the canonical gospels. Brown then points to examples of a massive transferral or switching of details affecting the dramatis personae when incidents in the Gospel of Peter are compared to similar incidents in the canonical gospels. This all tells against Crossan's thesis. Brown concludes that the Gospel of Peter 'does not constitute or give the earliest Christian account or thoughts about the passion' (p. 339).

One might have expected Crossan to have explicitly answered this very public challenge to his thesis that the sole source for the passion narrative in all four canonical gospels was embedded in the Gospel of Peter. Instead he made no reference to Brown's 1986 address when developing at length his same thesis in his 1988 *The Cross That Spoke* and using it in his 1991 *The Historical Jesus*. As much as anything, this silence about Brown's sustained critique gave substance to Meier's remark in *America* magazine for 7 March 1992 about 'Crossan's refusal to debate other scholars who hold alternate views' (p. 199).

Apart from one or two sympathetic reactions,[9] scholars generally have remained quite unconvinced by Crossan's 1988 lengthy and tortuous attempt to rehabilitate the Gospel of Peter and claim that its core (his 'Cross Gospel') served as the sole source for Mark's story of the passion (and resurrection). The reviews of *The Cross That Spoke* by Black, Fuller, Green, Matera, Meier, Wink and others were little less than devastating in demolishing Crossan's case for an early date for the core of the Gospel of Peter and a literary dependency from it on the part of Mark and other canonical gospels. As regards the passion narrative, our earliest source remains Mark's gospel. The existence still has to be proved of any written passion narrative antedating the canonical gospels – let alone such a mid-first-century document embedded in the second-century apocryphal Gospel of Peter.[10] In his (later published) 1993 presidential address to the Society of New Testament Studies, Martin Hengel spoke for many scholars when he stated that the attempt to 'fix earlier dates' for apocryphal gospels, including the Gospel of Peter, 'have not convinced me at all'.

A second presupposition that underlies Crossan's rejection of the historicity of the Marcan burial narrative is his conviction that historical prophecy rather than historical recall 'ruled the creation of the passion narrative', particularly the earliest such narrative (= that, according to him, embedded in the Gospel of Peter).[11] Such historicizing of Old Testament 'prophecies', *Four Other Gospels* assures its readers, was a 'pervasive process' (p. 138); right from the original passion narrative, biblical prophecy dictated 'the very details' in the formation of the story (p. 147). Historical memory could hardly play any role, as the followers of Jesus knew 'absolutely little' about the events of his passion, crucifixion and burial (p. 148). (So much, once again, for any information coming, for example, from faithful women disciples of Jesus!) Hence the burial tradition found in the Passion-Resurrection Source to be identified in the Gospel of Peter was simply derived from Old Testament texts, especially from Deut 21:22–23 and its legal injunction about burying the executed on the same day. 'It is because of respect for this law', Crossan maintains, 'that the [earliest Christian] tradition presumed the Jewish authorities would have buried Jesus themselves. Since they were in total charge of the crucifixion, they were in total control of the burial as well' (p. 164; see pp. 153–154). Right through to the last work of his trilogy, *The Historical Jesus*, Crossan has maintained the Old Testament origins for the Cross-Resurrection Source or Cross Gospel. His hypothetical Cross Gospel created from different prophetic allusions 'a narrative passion' in 'a coherent and sequential story' (p. 389).

In short, Crossan presumes the highly creative contribution of Old Testament texts to a passion tradition that practically lacked all historical memory. In their reviews of *The Cross*

That Spoke, C. Clifton Black, Reginald Fuller and Joel Green challenged this presupposition. Green writes:

> Crossan here walks along what has become a well-trodden path opened earlier in this century by Martin Dibelius (though Dibelius was much less sceptical about the possibility of historical information for the passion than Crossan). In opting for this route, Crossan failed to consider substantial works of the last decade on the hermeneutics of late Judaism, especially on the question whether the creation of current history from OT texts was an accepted and widely-practised phenomenon. In fact, while more work needs to be done, study of *pesharim* texts from Qumran, postbiblical historiography, and selected apocalyptic writing is already suggesting that the direction of influence was *from event to biblical text* (*Journal of Biblical Literature* 109 (1990), pp. 357–58).

What Green names as influence from event to text, Fitzmyer calls 'literary embellishment'. The Old Testament references and resonances help to tell the story, not to create it (p.1501). Hence Fitzmyer insists that the gospel passion stories contain historical narrative: 'If there were ever a part of the gospel tradition which must be so characterized, this is it' (p.1368). Specifically apropos of the story of Jesus' burial, Hooker finds 'nothing to commend' the suggestion that 'the incident was created' to 'fulfil' Old Testament texts (p. 380).

Crossan's third presupposition concerns Mark's creativity, allegedly of quite an extraordinary kind. In *The Historical Jesus* Crossan speaks of the evangelist's 'consummate theological fictions' and informs his readers: 'It is impossible, in my mind, to overestimate the creativity of Mark' (p. 390).

Two obvious problems emerge at once from this third presupposition. First, if Mark's creativity is impossible to overestimate, why did he bother at all to use any written passion narrative? Such an exceptionally creative author would not have needed to adjust and add to Crossan's hypothetical Cross Gospel in composing his own story of Jesus' death. Second, if one credits Mark with extraordinary, impossible-to-overestimate creativity, how can we know that the evangelist made the three (major) 'profound changes' in the passion narrative of the Cross Gospel which Crossan alleges (pp. 389–391)? The formation of any text from an author of such unique theological and literary creativity would be very difficult indeed to track. In other words, the more Crossan emphasizes Mark's creativity, the more precarious become any hypotheses about the genesis and composition of the second gospel.

Lastly, there is the specific claim that the story of Jesus' burial by Joseph of Arimathea originated with Mark, who 'began the process of taking Jesus' burial away from his enemies and giving it to his friends'. He did so by inventing and using the in-between character, Joseph of Arimathea, 'who mediates' between enemies and friends.[12] This 'limbo' character is described in Mark 15:43 with two carefully balanced qualities.

> First, he is 'a respectable member of the council' but, second, he is 'one who was also looking for the kingdom of God'. This locates him somewhere in between the 'Jewish' side and the 'Christian' side. Still one recognizes a problem in that description. If he was a member of the Sanhedrin, where was his voice when Jesus needed him earlier during the trial? The rest of the intracanonical tradition would solve, each in its own way, the problem created by Joseph's ambiguous position and Mark's difficult description.[13]

Three questions can show up the weakness of explaining away the burial story as simply originating with Mark. First, was Mark ready to create an entire episode, invent its central protagonist, give him a name and assign him an origin from a relatively obscure city? Crossan obviously sets no limits to what the evangelist might do 'creatively'. The standard, recent commentators on Mark (Ernst, Gnilka, Haenchen, Harrington, Hooker, Pesch, Schweizer, etc.), however, while recognizing the redactional contribution of the evangelist, do not invest him with the kind of 'creativity' needed to invent the burial story as asserted by Crossan.

Second, do the redactional changes introduced by Matthew and Luke show that these two evangelists found some special problem in the story of Joseph of Arimathea? Matthew's antipathy to the Sanhedrin, interest in discipleship and (apologetical?) desire to explain why Joseph easily secured the body from Pilate may account, respectively, for his no longer being named as 'a respectable member of the council', but being called 'a

disciple of Jesus' and 'a rich man' (Matt 27:57–58).[14] Luke
23:50–56 makes various redactional omissions and additions in
the Marcan burial narrative. For instance, he names Joseph as
'a good and upright man' who is not a party to the Sanhedrin's
decision against Jesus – thus stressing his 'moral character'
(Fitzmyer, p. 1525) and perhaps also, indirectly, the innocence
of Jesus and his followers. The redactional changes Matthew
and Luke introduce in the burial story reflect their normal theological interests rather than show them grappling with some difficult problem created for them by Mark.[15]

'The rest of the intracanonical tradition' which had to solve
the problem (that Crossan believes was left by Mark's creation
of Joseph of Arimathea) includes John's gospel, which – he
claims – depends on the Synoptics at least for the passion.[16]
However, as Meier points out, 'most of the major commentators on John in recent decades' hold that John represents 'a tradition independent of the Synoptics'.[17]

Third, is there anything historically so suspicious about
Mark's burial story centering on an 'in-between figure', someone 'within the Jewish leadership elite' and 'still connected with
Jesus'?[18] By the end of Jesus' public ministry we would expect
the presence of some 'in-between' figures, devout and leading
Jews who were attracted by Jesus' message of the kingdom but
had not (yet) become his disciples. Crossan's suspicions here
fly in the face of antecedent historical probability.

Unquestionably, the essential historicity of the burial story
in Mark cannot be demonstrated absolutely, but at least we
can conclude that Crossan has done nothing to undermine its
historical credibility, which remains accepted by very many
biblical scholars from Bultmann to Fitzmyer and beyond.

11

The resurrection of Jesus: some current questions

In 1983 a non-scholarly but thoroughly well-read person in Holland started writing me long letters about biblical and theological matters. This Dutch correspondent has filled pages with questions about Jesus' resurrection. I do not begrudge the time it takes to read and answer these letters. They continue to remind me of something that is utterly important: the mysterious and endless richness to be found in the resurrection of the crucified Jesus.

In this chapter I make no attempt to raise, let alone answer, all the significant questions that have emerged in recent discussions of the resurrection. I will limit myself to the following issues: What does the New Testament primarily claim about Jesus' resurrection? What is to be said about the two ways in which the disciples came to know about the resurrection (the appearances of the risen Jesus and the discovery of his empty tomb)? Were those Easter appearances special and even unique, or did they simply initiate the kind of experience that any subsequent Christian could have? Is the empty tomb a reliable part of the Easter tradition? What major gaps can we detect in present scholarly reflection on Jesus' resurrection?

In modern times certain writers have maintained that 'resurrection' was an event that affected the disciples, not Jesus himself. The 'something' that happened after his death and burial was only a change in their minds and hearts, not a new, transformed life for Jesus. In concluding his *On the Trial of Jesus*[1] Paul Winter movingly expressed this view: 'Crucified, dead and buried, He yet rose in the hearts of His disciples who had loved Him and felt He was near. Tried by the world, condemned by authority, buried by the churches that profess His name, He is rising, today and tomorrow, in the hearts of the men who love Him and feel: He is near.' In these terms, 'resurrection' was not a fact about Jesus himself, but simply a fact about his disciples, past and present. After the crucifixion, a new beginning was to be found only with those disciples, not with Jesus.

Whereas Winter emphasizes the affection and devotion of the disciples, others speak of their new consciousness. The ministry and death of Jesus eventually helped his followers to grasp the real point and purpose of human existence. The 'something' that happened after the crucifixion was merely a discovery of meaning, a transforming change in the disciples themselves. The new event lay totally on their side and in no way directly affected the dead Jesus.

The basic problem with any such 'change of heart' or 'new insight' version is that it must deny that the early Christians and the New Testament authors mean what they repeatedly say. There are kerygmatic and credal fragments that survive from the first decades of Christianity and pre-date even the writing of Paul's letters: for example, 'He was raised' (1 Cor 15:4), 'God raised up Jesus' (Acts 2:23ff, 32) and 'the Lord has risen indeed' (Luke 24:34). Then there are many affirmations by Paul himself about Christ's resurrection (for example, Rom 14:9; 1 Cor 15:12ff). The four gospels and other New Testament writings again and again proclaim Jesus' resurrection. The 'new insight' theory, however, supposes that in these and many other instances the early Christians, although appearing to claim some new fact *about Jesus* (his personal resurrection from death to new life) were really using a deceptive form of discourse and talking only about some new, seminal idea that now possessed their hearts and minds.

This explanation entails the conclusion that the basic Easter message of the first Christians has been fundamentally misunderstood for many centuries. Their assertive propositions about Jesus' personal resurrection from the dead – so it is claimed –

expressed a hidden meaning that one can now see differed drastically from the conventional sense of the words they used. They were speaking only of themselves, never of a new event affecting Jesus himself.

This position is quite implausible. When Paul quotes an early Christian formulation about 'Jesus Christ and God the Father, who raised him from the dead' (Gal 1:1), the ordinary conventions covering the use of language indicate that this confession primarily concerned Jesus and offered some factual information about what happened to Jesus himself after his death. A new event, distinct from and subsequent to the crucifixion, brought Jesus from the condition of death to that of a new and lasting life.

To allege that the true, primary referent in the proposition 'the Father raised Jesus from the dead' was not Jesus, but his disciples, is to open up an extraordinary gap between what Paul and other New Testament witnesses wrote and what they meant. They introduced Jesus as the object ('God raised Jesus') or subject ('Jesus was raised' or 'Jesus rose from the dead') in their fundamental claims about the resurrection. Did they put down the name 'Jesus' but secretly mean some other object or subject ('the disciples') in these sentences? Are we to imagine that the New Testament authors were deliberately deceptive in their use of language? Or were they remarkably incompetent? These are the only plausible alternatives open to us if we wish to maintain that their assertions about Jesus' resurrection were 'merely' assertions about themselves.

In the end, the problem comes to this: The exponents of the 'new insight' thesis fail to distinguish between people holding something to be true and the effects of this claim on those who make it. In speaking of his resurrection, Jesus' followers claimed a new fact about Jesus himself. Holding his resurrection to be true, then, had deep and transforming effects on them. These effects, however, depended on the fact that they held something to be true: namely, that Jesus had passed from the state of death to a new and final life.

Thus far, I have discussed the bottom line in the early Christian claim about Jesus' resurrection. But how did the disciples come to know about this event? The New Testament never alleges that anyone witnessed the actual resurrection itself. Rather, it names the appearances of the risen Christ and the discovery of his empty tomb as the two dramatic causes that triggered the knowledge of his resurrection.

The early Christian kerygma or proclamation (for example, 1 Cor 15:5, 7; Luke 24:34), Paul's letters (1 Cor 9:1; 15:8; Gal 1:12, 16), the four Gospels (Matt 28; Luke 24; John 20 and 21; and, by implication, Mark 16:7), Acts (1:3; 10:40; 13:31) and the appendix to Mark (16:9–20) attest that the risen Jesus appeared both to various individuals and to groups of witnesses, above all 'the twelve' or 'the eleven' as Luke 24:33 more accurately calls them after Judas' defection. The appearances of the living Jesus were the primary way the disciples came to know that he was risen from the dead.

There is a curious 'ordinariness' about the Easter appearances as reported by the Gospels and Paul. Unlike other communications from God, they do not take place during ecstasy (Acts 10:9ff; 2 Cor 12:2–4; Rev 1:10ff), nor in a dream (Matt 1:20; 2:12, 19–22), nor by night (Acts 16:9; 18:9; 23:11; 27:23). The appearances occur under 'normal' circumstances and without the traits of apocalyptic glory that we find elsewhere (Mark 9:2–8; Matt 28:3ff). The one exception comes in the way Acts describes Paul's experience on the Damascus Road when he sees 'a light from heaven, brighter than the sun' (Acts 26:13; see also 9:3; 22:6, 9). But there is no mention of this phenomenon when Paul himself writes of his encounter with the risen Christ (1 Cor 9:1; 15:8; Gal 1:12, 16).

Largely on the basis of the Nag Hammadi papyrus codices (third to fifth century), James M. Robinson has proposed that the original Christian tradition told of the risen Christ's disembodied appearances in light on a mountain. But the evidence for such luminous appearances comes almost entirely from later, Gnostic sources that do not provide us with any independent and trustworthy data about the origins of Christianity.

Since the appearance of *Jesus* in English,[2] Edward Schillebeeckx, OP, has modified his view of the Easter experiences of Peter and the other disciples. According to that book, through the real but invisible influence of the risen Lord, the disciples experienced a deep forgiveness and conversion that they expressed in the model of 'appearances'. But their talk of 'appearances' was only a means for articulating what the invisible Jesus had done for them after his death and resurrection, and did not refer to genuinely historical events. In his *Interim Report*, Father Schillebeeckx concedes that when the first Christians speak of 'appearances', this 'need not be a pure model; it can also imply a historical event'.[3] Nevertheless, he continues to play down the role of such appearances – and, for that matter, of the discovery of the empty tomb – in generating Easter faith.

Furthermore, Father Schillebeeckx relativizes the special character of the appearances by interpreting them as the first instance of something available to all later Christians – a 'renewal of life and the experience of Jesus' spiritual presence'. This 'experience of the new (spiritual) presence of the risen Jesus in the gathered community' can be shared by any of his followers anywhere and at any time. Peter, Mary Magdalene, Paul and the other Easter witnesses were only chronologically the first to experience 'Jesus' new saving presence in the midst of His people on earth'. All later Christians can gather together to know the same forgiveness and conversion through the same, new presence of the risen Lord. There is no very significant difference between the first disciples' Easter experience and subsequent experiences of the risen Lord (Jesus).

Father Schillebeeckx names only one special aspect of the first apostles' Easter experience: the fact that they had known Jesus before his death. The disciples who were with Jesus during his ministry recognized the risen Christ as being identical with the master whom they had known and followed: 'It is the Lord' (John 21:7). No later group or individual believer, not even Paul, could duplicate this aspect of those first post-resurrection meetings with Jesus. Peter, Mary Magdalene and other disciples served as bridge persons who linked the period of Jesus' ministry with the post-Easter situation. In that way their experience of the risen Lord was unique and unrepeatable. But much more should be added about their 'once only' experience and its aftermath.

Peter, Paul and other apostolic witnesses who meet the risen Christ have the mission to testify to that experience and found the Church. These witnesses have seen for themselves and believed. In proclaiming the good news and gathering together those who have not seen and yet are ready to believe, these original witnesses do not need to rely on the experience and testimony of others. Their function for Christianity differs from that of any subsequent believers, inasmuch as they alone have the once-and-for-all task of inaugurating the mission and founding the Church. Others will bear the responsibility to continue that mission and keep the Church in existence. But the coming into being of the mission and of the Church cannot be duplicated. The way in which that unique function rests upon some difference in their respective experience is expressed by John's classic distinction between those who have seen and believed and those who are 'blessed' because they 'have not seen and yet believe' (John 20:29).

Paul also draws attention to certain real differences between the fundamental post-Resurrection encounters and all later experiences of the risen Lord. 'Last of all', he recalls, Christ 'appeared also to me' (1 Cor 15:8). The episode constituted Paul's apostolic calling and the basis for his mission (1 Cor 9:1; Gal 1:11ff). Other Christians share with him the gift of the Holy Spirit and life 'in Christ', but they did not and do not experience that fundamental meeting with the risen Lord that made Paul a founding father of the Church. He never remarks to his readers: 'Christ has appeared to you', or 'Christ will appear to you'.

This is not to say that Christians other than the resurrection witnesses were thought to have no access whatsoever to the risen Jesus. He remained present through word and sacrament (Luke 24:30ff), in the community (Matt 18:20), in his body (1 Cor 12:27), through persons who suffer (Matt 25:31–46) and through his Spirit (2 Cor 3:17). Nevertheless, the risen Lord did not appear to all those other Christians and make them normative witnesses to his resurrection and authoritative founders of the Church.

Father Schillebeeckx's position on the Easter appearances undercuts this normative function of the apostolic founders of Christianity. Here he stands apart from those such as Walter Kasper, Hans Küng, Karl Rahner, sj, and Jon Sobrino, sj, who, despite their differences, all recognize more clearly the unique, unrepeatable nature of the Easter appearances.

The discovery of the empty tomb was the secondary confirmatory cause when the first disciples came to know that Jesus was risen from the dead. There is very good evidence that the Church of the Holy Sepulchre in Jerusalem does in fact contain Jesus' grave. Moreover, the story of women finding Jesus' tomb open and empty (Mark 16:1–8 and parallels) seems unique to Christianity. But is the story reliable?

Here it does no harm to recall that, for all the reports about a Christian bishop and other scholars doubting or even denying the empty-tomb story, very many critical exegetes and historians defend it. There is a reasonable case to be made for their conclusion.

As regards the fate of Jesus' body, both the tradition behind the Synoptic gospels (Matthew, Mark and Luke) and that which entered John's gospel testified to one (Mary Magdalene) or more women finding Jesus' grave open and empty. Early polemic against the message of his resurrection supposed that the tomb was known to be empty. Naturally the opponents of the Christian movement explained away the missing body as a plain case of theft (Matt 28:11–15). But we have no early evidence that anyone, either Christian or non-Christian, ever alleged that Jesus' tomb still contained his remains. Furthermore, the place of women in the story of the empty tomb speaks for its historical reliability. If this story were a legend created by early Christians, they would have attributed the discovery of the empty tomb to male disciples rather than women, who in that culture did not count as valid witnesses. Legend-makers do not usually invent positively unhelpful and counterproductive material.

If we are satisfied about the historical case for the empty tomb, the further challenge is to explore and appreciate what this discovery could and does mean. How would it improve our Easter faith and theology if we were to understand something of the empty tomb's significance?

First of all, the emptiness of Jesus' grave reflects the holiness of what it once held, the corpse of the incarnate Son of God, who lived for others and died to bring a new covenant of love for all people. This 'Holy One' could not 'see corruption' (Acts 2:27). Second, the very emptiness of the tomb can suggest and symbolize the fullness of the new and everlasting life into which Jesus has gone.

Third, the empty tomb expresses something vital about the

nature of redemption: namely, that redemption is much more than a mere escape from our scene of suffering and death. Rather, it means the transforming of this material, bodily world with its whole history of sin and suffering. The first Easter began the work of finally bringing our universe home to its ultimate destiny. God did not discard Jesus' earthly corpse, but mysteriously raised and transfigured it so as to reveal what lies ahead for human beings and their world. In short, that empty tomb in Jerusalem is God's radical sign that redemption is not an escape to a better world, but an extraordinary transformation of this world.

I have lingered over three things: the essential New Testament claim about Jesus' resurrection, his appearances and the discovery of the empty tomb. Let me complete this chapter by noting three tasks not yet carried out in contemporary discussion of the resurrection.

In our day, liberation theologies have little to say about Jesus' resurrection. It is not that Hugo Assmann, Leonardo Boff, OFM, Jon Sobrino, SJ, and others fail to mention the Easter mystery, but they inevitably underplay the full significance of the resurrection because they are often bent on developing Christologies in the light of Jesus' ministry and death. These liberation theologies are deeply concerned with issues of justice and injustice. They would be greatly enriched if they reflected more on a major aspect of Jesus' resurrection: the full and final justice it promises to the poor and oppressed. Of course, that theme is not totally missing in the work of Father Sobrino and other liberation theologians. Nevertheless, they cannot develop it adequately, since in general they fail to focus very much on the resurrection.

In the whole interreligious dialogue, Christians have dwelt incessantly on questions about creation, incarnation and ministry, while largely ignoring the resurrection of the crucified Jesus. Paul Knitter inadvertently testifies to this phenomenon.[4] His report on the present state of the interreligious dialogue rarely mentions Jesus' resurrection. Yet it is this event that reveals the fact that the particular, human story of Jesus has absolute and decisive value for all men and women of all times, places and cultures. To pass over the Easter mystery is to omit something utterly essential for the dialogue with other religions.

Another task for current discussion of the resurrection comes from a question that in various forms has repeatedly surfaced in recent British theology. How should we understand and interpret 'special' divine interventions in the 'ordinary' course of history? The issue extends beyond the resurrection to such matters as the role of God in Israel's history, the event of the incarnation, the writing of inspired Scriptures and episodes of special grace in the lives of believers. All the same, the event of the resurrection is the climactic case of such divine interventions. What sense, then, can we give claims about the divine activity involved in raising Jesus from the dead and thus inaugurating the end of all history? Sooner or later this task must be tackled by anyone who thinks deeply and systematically about the pasch al mystery.

In this chapter I have made no attempt to explore other vital questions about Christ's resurrection. For example: How can we legitimate belief in it? Second, what is its transformative value for us? The long letters from my Dutch friend continue to remind me that in the matter of Christ's resurrection our questioning and exploring will never end.

12

The uniqueness of the Easter appearances

Does the New Testament indicate that the appearances of the risen Lord were limited to certain individuals and groups and that, even at the beginning of Christianity, others beyond those individuals and groups did not and indeed could not share in that experience? Or would the New Testament data be consistent with the thesis that those 'appearances' were simply the first examples (chronologically) of ecstatic, pneumatic, and/or revelatory encounters with the risen Jesus that early believers widely experienced and that later believers could also experience? Any well-argued answer will have to deal with evidence from Paul, Luke, John, and elsewhere. As such this is an exegetical issue, but it obviously carries serious theological implications for the normative role of the apostolic experience and witness at the origins of Christianity.[1]

Inevitably our sources will oblige us to say something about the nature of the Easter appearances and their consequences.[2] But the primary scope of this chapter is simply to ask the question: do the New Testament witnesses claim that the post-resurrection appearances were experienced only by certain individuals (e.g., Peter, Paul, and Mary Magdalene) and groups (e.g., the Twelve)? Or does the New Testament fail to indicate that these experiences were in principle unique to that limited set of early Christians?

To answer these questions we have divided this chapter into four parts with a conclusion. The first part will summarize what the New Testament indicates about the nature of the Easter appearances; the second part will take up the evidence from Paul and 1 Peter about the closure of these post-resurrection appearances; the third part will examine the Lucan scheme of the appearances as found in the third gospel and Acts; and the fourth part will conclude with the Johannine testimony about 'those who have not seen but have believed' (John 20:29).

The nature of the Easter appearances

In a statement that expresses a wide scholarly consensus R. H. Fuller describes the post-resurrection appearances as follows:

> They were not in their innermost essence open to neutral observation or verification, but revelatory events in which the eschatological and christological significance of Jesus was disclosed, and in which the recipient was called to a particular function in salvation history.[3]

The evidence from Paul, the Gospels, and elsewhere in the New Testament amply supports the five major points in Fuller's summary account of the appearances. These self-disclosures of the risen Jesus, while (1) not open to neutral observers, were (2) events of revelation that revealed (3) the eschatological and (4) christological status of Jesus and (5) called the recipients to a special mission.

Once we move beyond this spare description, we face various questions in an attempt to specify more closely the nature of the encounters with the risen Jesus. Were they luminous, mystical experiences? Were they primarily events of conversion and forgiveness? Did they merely entail a verbal revelation without any visual perception being involved? Were they ecstatic experiences? Or experiences of the Holy Spirit?[4]

Answers to these more specific issues about the post-resurrection appearances will probably decide one's position on the central question raised in this article. Ecstatic and 'spiritual' experiences, for example, are obviously not limited in principle to a small set of witnesses at the origins of Christianity.

Interpreting the Easter encounters as no more than events of interior verbal revelation could readily lead to the conclusion that, both in the early Church and later, innumerable believers have experienced such an 'appearance' of the risen Christ. Hence it seems advisable to examine briefly at least some versions of the Easter appearances which, right from the start, would undercut claims about their being reserved to a small group of witnesses at the beginning of Christianity. In particular it is worth looking at views that interpret post-resurrection encounters as merely episodes of verbal revelation or else ecstatic and 'spiritual' experiences.

Wilhelm Michaelis remains the most significant exponent of the view that the Easter appearances do not emphasize either sense or mental perception but rather revelation and encounter with the risen Lord.[5]

1. In dealing with the LXX's use of *horaō* ('I see') and its passive form *ōphthē* ('he appeared' or 'was seen by'), he notes the clear preponderance of hearing over seeing in the prophets, especially the great writing prophets: 'Mostly revelation by word is also to the fore; revelation by picture is more and more a framework for revelation by word.'[6] Revelation in 'vision' is in fact revelation by word. The use of *ophthēnai* ('to appear') 'simply denotes the presence of revelation as such with no necessary reference to its perceptibility.'[7]

2. As regards the LXX use of *ōphthē*, which the New Testament (and the kerygmatic traditions behind it) will apply to the risen Jesus' appearances (1 Cor 15:5, 6, 7, 8; Luke 24:34; Acts 13:31), Michaelis observes that it 'is for the most part the characteristic term to denote the (non-visual) presence of the self-revealing God.'[8] He draws attention to the LXX formula *ōphthē kyrios tō̦ ... kai eipen autō̦* found in Gen 12:7; 17:1; 26:2, 24; 35:9, and comments that when God 'appears', we 'are simply told what God had to say'. Even when, as in Gen 26:24 'the *ophthēnai* takes place by night or in a dream', we 'are not on this account to think in terms of dreams'. God is not seen but 'is simply heard, and the *ōphthē* marks the beginning of the revelation by word, i.e., it indicates the presence of the God

who reveals himself in His Word'.[9]

3.   Turning to the New Testament, Michaelis notes that the Gospel accounts of the appearances of the risen Lord are always associated with revelation by word.[10] Further, the witness of Gal 1:16 encourages Michaelis to interpret the apostle's Damascus road experience (see also 1 Cor 9:1; 15:8) as an event of revelation, without any special indication about a visible reality being perceived. Paul, who bases his apostleship on that experience, holds it to be similar in kind to the other appearances listed by him in 1 Cor 15:5-7.[11] Thus Michaelis argues for his thesis that interprets the Easter appearances in general as events of (verbal) revelation and plays down any suggestion of their visual or eyewitness quality.

4.   Finally, Michaelis's argument might easily have led him to allow for Easter appearances in the case of later Christians – that is to say, to accept that they could encounter the (non-visual) presence of the self-revealing Christ. However, he guardedly recognizes that the Easter appearances are limited to a certain period. He interprets Paul's 'last of all he [Christ] appeared to me' as meaning that the apostle has not heard of any further appearances after the Damascus encounter. Not even opponents are laying claim to similar experiences. While refusing to state unequivocally that the 'last of all' implies that 'there *can* be [italics ours] no similar or equivalent event,' Michaelis concludes: 'The material connection between the appearances and the resurrection certainly sets a temporal limit to the appearances, which, while extended by the special time of the Damascus experience, is not removed.'[12] He explains why the Easter appearances came to an end. Their role is to steer believers away from expecting an imminent *parousia* and to prepare them for 'the age of the Church and the work of the Holy Spirit'.[13]

The weight of evidence, however, tells against the Michaelis line of interpretation. Certainly hearing and revelation by word predominate in the case of the great prophets. Nevertheless it is never said of a prophet *ōphthē kyrios autō*. That theophany language of the LXX is used of the saving presence of God in the *patriarchal* period.[14] Hence the secondary role of seeing in the prophetic literature should not guide an interpretation of *ōphthē* in 1 Cor 15:5–8, Luke 24:34 and Acts 13:31. Furthermore, in the LXX usage, like the Hebr. *rā⁼â* behind it, *ōphthē* implies some kind of seeing, an element that may not be sacrificed to claims about a mere reception of revelation by word.[15]

As regards Paul's reference to the Easter appearances, like others R. J. Sider points out that 1 Cor 9:1 clearly denotes visual perception. Since 1 Corinthians 15 argues for bodily resurrection, it seems that the apostles understood that Jesus was visible to the eyes of those to whom he appeared.[16] In commenting on 1 Cor 15:5–8, Hans Conzelmann also disagrees with Michaelis, maintaining a true perception ('a real visible manifestation') of the risen Christ and locating the element of 'word' in the 'fact that the manifestation at once makes the person concerned a witness and presses towards proclamation.'[17] Hans Kessler takes the *ōphthē* of 1 Cor 15:5–8 to entail an experience of the risen Christ making himself visible and being seen, even if this was 'not necessarily' a seeing with one's 'external, bodily eyes'. About revelation by word nothing is said here explicitly.[18] One can press this point by noting that, unlike the passages in Genesis to which Michaelis refers, 1 Cor 15:5–8 says that 'Christ appeared to Cephas' and the rest but does not add, 'and said to him/them'. The second half of the LXX formula is simply not found either here in 1 Cor 15:5–8 or, for that matter, in Luke 24:34 and Acts 13:31.[19]

Finally, like others, Karl Dahn rightly points out that an element common to the Easter narrative in the gospels is that the risen Christ is seen and visibly recognized. Certainly the appearances are events of revelation, also involving hearing the word and being commissioned to witness. Nevertheless, the genuine seeing of the risen Christ may not be played down in favour of hearing.[20]

To sum up: according to the theophanies found in the patriarchal narratives and elsewhere (e.g., Exod 3:2–10; Judg 6:11–21; 1 Sam 3:1–14) the communicating presence of God is experienced. In the Easter Christophanies the presence of the risen Christ is revealed and somehow visibly perceived. This sixth element of visible perception should be added to the five points listed above in Reginald Fuller's account of the post-res-urrection appearances. Such a visible perception of the risen Jesus, together with the call to a foundational mission, belongs to an experience that, as we shall see, remains limited to Peter, Paul, and the other Easter witnesses and is not shared by other later Christians.

Michaelis's view of the Easter appearances as revelation by word means that he neither understands Paul's Damascus road experience as 'ecstatic rapture' nor classifies it with the ecstatic visions and revelations mentioned in 1 Cor 12:1.[21] Like some others, however, Hans Dieter Betz interprets the Damascus road encounter in ecstatic terms. Commenting on Gal 1:16 ('[God] was pleased to reveal his Son in me'), Betz explains:

> The 'in me' corresponds to Gal 2:20 ('Christ ... lives in me') and 4:6 ('God has sent the Spirit of his Son into our hearts'). Paul does not explain how the three passages are related to each other, but we may assume that they comple-ment each other. This would mean that Paul's experience was ecstatic in nature, and that in the course of this ecstasy he had a vision (whether external or internal or both – 'I do not know, God knows' [cf 2 Cor 12:2, 3]). This interpreta-tion is supported by the debate about Paul's vision in the ps.-Clem. *Hom.* 17.13–19.[22]

Thus for Betz, Paul's 'seeing' Christ points to a visionary expe-rience and verbal revelation, an experience which can be more closely described as an internal/external ecstatic vision. In reaching this position Betz appeals to 2 Cor 12:2–3, a passage which, as we shall note later, does not refer to Paul's Damascus road experience, and to a late and dubious authority, the *Pseudo-Clementine Homilies*. His assumption that Gal 1:16, 2:20, and 4:6 'complement' each other in clarifying Paul's experience does not hold. Betz slips over the *once-and-for-all* nature of Paul's personal call in Gal 1:16: '[God] was pleased [aorist] to reveal his Son to me, in order that I might preach him among the Gentiles.' In Gal 4:6 and elsewhere (e.g., Rom 5:5; 8:11) Paul indicates the *common* Christian experience of the *ongoing* indwelling of the Holy Spirit. Very occasionally, Paul speaks of Christ living [present tense] 'in me' (Gal 2:20) or 'in us' and 'in you' (Rom 8:10). Normally he expresses the new communion of life all Christians enjoy as our being 'in Christ' (e.g., Rom 8:1; 16:7; 1 Cor 15:22; Phil 3:8–9). Either way, Paul reports the common, ongoing Christological ('we/I in Christ' or 'Christ in us/me') and pneumatic ('the Spirit in us/me') experiences of all believers. But these experiences (in the present tense) are not the same as the special, once-and-for-all experience (in the aorist tense) that made Paul the apostle to the Gentiles (Gal 1:16).

Before examining more fully the data offered by Paul and 1 Peter about the closure of the post-resurrection appearances, we should say something about the alleged 'pneumatic' character of those appearances. To interpret them primarily as experiences of the Holy Spirit would obviously suggest that they were not limited to a small group of witnesses at the start of Christianity.

Alone among the Easter texts, John 20:22 links a Christophany and the receiving of the Spirit. This scene encouraged Joachim Jeremias to attribute a pneumatic character to the post-resurrection Christophanies and to support the hypothesis that 1 Cor 15:6 (the appearance to more than 500) and the coming of the Spirit to the 120 followers of Jesus at Pentecost (Acts 2:1–13) are simply two different traditions about one and the same event.[23] Jeremias also claimed that Christ's appearance to Paul, 'which consisted in a vision of shining light (2 Cor 4:6, Acts 9:3; 22:6; 26:13), clearly attests to the pneumatic character of the Christophanies (cf. 1 Cor. 15:44; *sōma pneumatikon*); it may be regarded as typical of all of them.[24]

Both claims about Paul seem, however, quite doubtful. The language of light in 2 Cor 4:6 refers to the general Christian experience of conversion, not to Paul's particular experience on the road to Damascus.[25] Even if the three texts in Acts come from a historically reliable tradition, the language of light from heaven could simply have been a conventional way of saying that Paul encountered a heavenly reality, the risen Jesus through whom the glory of God was revealed.[26] Furthermore, even if Paul literally had a vision of shining light, there is no good reason for holding that this evidence was 'typical of all' the appearances.[27]

What of the alleged 'pneumatic character of the Christophanies'? The first four texts invoked by Jeremias (2

Cor 4:6; Acts 9:3; 22:6; 26:13) have nothing to say about
any pneumatic character of the appearances. What of 1 Cor
15:44 on the 'spiritual body'? Here Paul is speaking of the
resurrection of the dead in general (1 Cor 15:42) and not
attending to the particular case of Christ. Moreover, it is a
question of what has been 'sown a physical body' being
'raised a spiritual body', *not* of its appearing to impart the
Holy Spirit to those still living a perishable, weak, and physical existence like the first Adam (1 Cor 15:42–49).

Paul writes at length about the experience of the indwelling
Spirit (Gal 4:6) and various gifts of the Holy Spirit (1 Cor
12:1–13; 14:1–40). But he never identifies that common experience of the Spirit and the spiritual gifts with the once-and-for-
all encounter with the risen Christ that gave him his own special
mission (1 Cor 9:1; 15:8; Gal 1:12, 16). Neither Jeremias nor
others have established the case for interpreting the post-resurrection appearances as equivalent to experiences of the Spirit.[28]

Having faced the challenge coming from some views about
the nature of the Easter appearances, we can turn to the central
theme of this chapter. How long did these Christophanies continue? Were they experienced by only a few hundred men and
women at the beginning of the Christian movement?

Data from Paul and 1 Peter

Many commentators understand the list in 1 Cor 15:5–8 (of
individuals and groups to whom the risen Christ appeared) to
follow a chronological sequence.[29] Within the context of this
article, two points are important: the tense of the verb *ōphthē*,
and Paul's phrase 'last of all'.

The aorist tense of 'appeared' which Paul uses in 1 Cor
15:5–8 suggests events over and done with in the past and not
repeated.[30] As regards 1 Cor 15:8 and the appearance to Paul,
C. F. Evans wonders whether Paul meant 'last of all' to be a
factual statement. Or is it an expression of Pauline egoism?[31]
Evans does not answer his own questions but implies that the
apostle holds that the appearance to him was in principle the
last: 'Paul envisages the whole series as coming to a close only
with the appearance of the Lord to himself.'[32]

Hans Conzelmann argues that the long list of witnesses, starting with 1 Cor 15:5 and ending at 1 Cor 15:8, is there to maintain the resurrection's 'temporal distance from the present and thereby to rule out the [present] possibility of a direct appropriation of it.[33] Here Conzelmann seems to be saying that the witnesses, from Peter to Paul, directly appropriated the resurrection (directly encountered the risen Lord) in a way that was simply not possible for believers when Paul wrote 1 Corinthians.

Fuller is quite clear in holding that the appearance to Paul (1 Cor 15:8) is in principle the last appearance of the risen Lord. He argues for two types of appearances (founding the eschatological community and inaugurating the Christian mission). He asserts that Paul not only knew of no other appearances during the past twenty years after his own, but also ruled out in principle any such appearances.[34] Fuller sums up his points by saying: 'The appearances occurred over a period of some three years or so, the last and definitive one being that to Paul' (p.49).[35]

In commenting on 1 Cor 15:8 Jacob Kremer argues that the 'of all' refers to all the Easter witnesses listed in 1 Cor 15:5-8, and not simply to 'all the apostles' just mentioned in v. 7. He further argues that even if 'last of all' might in theory mean 'least of all the apostles' (a sense of value), it reflects the 'then' of vv. 5-7 and clearly carries a temporal meaning.[36]

Charles K. Barrett faces the same question and decides more emphatically for the temporal sense of 'last of all'.[37] Similar opinions are expressed by Grosheide ('Paul was the last to see the glorified Lord with his own eyes, in order that he might be a true apostle'),[38] Morris ([Paul] 'thinks of himself as the last in the line of those who have seen the Lord'),[39] Wand (the 'historical accuracy [of Paul's preaching] was guaranteed by a number of witnesses of whom Paul himself was the last'),[40] and Rengstorf.[41] Finally, Gordon Fee states that the appearance to Paul 'was a unique and gracious gift that occurred after the time when such appearances were understood to have ceased.'[42]

The conclusion seems well supported: Paul understood the risen Lord's appearance to him to be, both in fact and in principle, the last of a series. With his special case such experiences ended.

Another passage that is relevant to our theme is 1 Pet 1:8: 'Without having seen[43] him, you love him; though you do not now see him, you believe in him.' By the time this letter is written (probably in the 60s) Christianity has spread far beyond the original disciples who had known Jesus during his lifetime and/or seen him after his resurrection. A second generation of Christians has entered the Church. These subsequent followers of Jesus in Pontus, Galatia, Cappadocia, Asia, Bithynia (1 Pet 1:1), and elsewhere love and believe in him, without having seen him in the past and without seeing him in the present.[44] In the midst of suffering, these new Christians relate to Jesus through a faith and love that is based neither on a direct acquaintance with him (during his ministry) nor on an encounter with him when risen from the dead, but on the good news or the 'word' which has been preached to them (1 Pet 1:12, 25; 2:8; 4:17).

The verse implies two further points. First, in the final future the present Christian experience will give way to a direct vision of Christ.[45] Second, the writer of the letter, unlike the readers, has seen Christ and enjoys apostolic authority. Beare dismisses this implication as 'far-fetched'. But his comment seems a little curious, as he has just recalled John 20:29 where one of the Twelve (Thomas), *unlike* those blessed for a faith that does not come from their having seen, sees the risen Jesus and so comes to believe.[46] In milder tones than Beare, E. Best suggests that there is 'no need' to find 'in the contrast' in 1 Pet 1:8 between seeing and believing/loving 'a claim on the part of the writer to have been a personal disciple of Jesus'.[47] This is to slip over the presentation of the writer of the letter as 'Peter an apostle of Jesus Christ' (1 Pet 1:1)[48] and the implications of 1 Pet 5:1, 12–13 for the status and (possible) experience claimed by the letter's author.[49] Other commentators correctly detect in 1 Pet 1:8 a contrast between the writer who claims to have been an authoritative eyewitness of Jesus (during his ministry and then as risen from the dead) and his addressees who love and believe in the Lord without ever having seen him.[50] As Kelly observes, to recognize the presence of such a contrast in our text does not depend on establishing the direct Petrine authorship of the letter. The contrast is there, even if it 'might be [only] a lifelike touch inserted by someone claiming to write in the Apostle's name'.[51]

Thus 1 Pet 1:8 joins not only 1 Cor 15:8 but also other voices in the New Testament. 'Seeing' Jesus was an experience restricted to the first generation of disciples, above all to the apostolic eyewitnesses of that generation. Other and later Christians relate personally to Jesus (through faith and love), but they do not see him. Their 'seeing' will come at the end, in the final 'revelation of Jesus Christ' (1 Pet 1:7). In the meantime, accepting the testimony of those who have seen him, they believe in him (Rom 10:14; Gal 2:16; 1 John 5:10). They 'walk by faith, not by sight' (2 Cor 5:7), by a faith that makes them certain about realities they do not see (Heb 11:1). Above all, through their love they relate personally to Jesus (1 Cor 16:22; Eph 6:24; 2 Tim 4:8; John 8:42; 14:15, 21, 24; 21:15-16). Thus they wait in hope for what they do not yet see (Rom 8:24-25).

The evidence from Luke and Acts

In the Lucan scheme, the closing of the Easter appearances is closely connected with the risen Jesus' ascension (Luke 24:50-51; Acts 1:9-11),[52] the role of the (twelve) apostles as eyewitnesses to him (Luke 1:2; 6:12-16; Acts 1:3, 9-11, 21-22)[53] and the transition from the period of Jesus (which begins with the Holy Spirit descending upon him when he is baptized by John (Luke 3:21-22; 4:1, 14, 18) to the time of the Church (which begins when Jesus is taken away into heaven out of sight of the apostles and they are baptized with the Holy Spirit Acts 1:5, 9).[54] Let us see these points in a little more detail.

In Luke's two-part account of the origins of Christianity, the work of Jesus begins with his baptism (Luke 3:21-22; Acts 1:22; 10:37-38). It ends with his ascension when a new stage in salvation history opens the period of the Church that will bring the witnesses of Christ right to the ends of the earth (Luke 24:47-48; Acts 1:8) and will close when he comes again at the *parousia* (Acts 1:11).[55] We argued above that the aorist tense of *ōphthē* in 1 Cor 15:5, 6, 7, 8 suggested that the Easter appearances were over and done with – a point made quite explicit by Paul's 'last of all' in 1 Cor 15:8. This notion (that the appearances of the risen Jesus had come to a close) probably helped in the making of Acts 1:1-11.[56] The period when the risen Jesus had let himself be seen (Acts 1:3) ended with the ascension (Acts 1:9-11), an episode which stresses the role of the apostles as eyewitnesses right to the finish:

> And when he had said this, as they were *looking on*, he was lifted up and a cloud took him out of *their sight*. And while they were *gazing* into heaven as he went, behold, two men stood by them in white robes and said, 'Men of Galilee, why do you stand *looking* into heaven? This Jesus, who was taken up from you into heaven, will come in the same way as you *saw* him go into heaven.'[57]

Thus Jesus' activity was followed by eyewitnesses from the beginning of his ministry (Luke 1:2; 3:23), through the crucifixion (Luke 23:49), and on to the time of post-resurrection appearances (Luke 24; Acts 1:1-11) that terminated with the ascension. These disciples not only report on the ministry and death of Jesus but also witness to the resurrection and testify that the Risen One was and is personally identical with the earthly Jesus (see also Acts 10:39-42; 13:31). From among these disciples the witnesses *par excellence* are 'the Twelve' whom Luke practically identifies with 'the apostles'. The account of the choice of Judas' successor (Acts 1:15-26) summarizes the Lucan view on the conditions and function of the apostolic office. Peter says: 'One of the men who accompanied us during all the time that the Lord Jesus went in and out among us, beginning from the baptism of John until the day when he was taken up from us – one of these men must become with us a witness to his resurrection' (Acts 1:21-22). After prayer Matthias was chosen by lot to become one of the Twelve and through the Spirit (Luke 24:49; Acts 1:8) to be empowered (with the others) in his function as apostolic witness.[58]

Thus with the ascension and the coming of the Holy Spirit the period of the Church begins, a period that opens with Peter and the college of twelve apostles bearing witness to Jesus and their particular experience of him – an experience that ends when he is taken up into heaven. For the twelve apostles the post-Easter appearances have definitively come to a close. That being their situation, *a fortiori* is it so for others. Henceforth, instead of seeing him, the new 'disciples' (Acts 6:1, 7; 9:1, 10, etc.) or 'Christians' (Acts 11:26) 'turn to' Jesus (Acts 9:35; 11:21), receive the forgiveness of sin through his name (Acts 2:38; 3:26; 4:31; 10:43), 'believe in' him (Acts 9:42; 10:43;

11:17; 14:23; 16:31), have 'faith' in him (Acts 26:18), are 'baptized in his name' (Acts 2:38; 8:16; 10:48; 19:5) and are 'saved' through his name (Acts 4:12) or through his grace (Acts 15:11). In these and other ways Acts presents the (old and new) disciples' experience of and relationship to Jesus in the post-ascension situation. He does not, however, 'appear' to them nor do they 'see' him. Let us look at the exception of Paul.

Along with Barnabas, Paul is twice called an 'apostle' (Acts 14:4, 14) – accidental exceptions to Luke's otherwise consistent limitation of the title 'apostle' to the Twelve. Like Stephen (Acts 22:20) Paul is called a 'witness' (Acts 22, 15; 26:16). Like the twelve apostles, Paul is to witness to what he has 'seen' and 'heard' during his Damascus road experience (Acts 22:14–15; see Acts 9:27) and later during a trance in the Jerusalem temple (Acts 22:17–21). Nevertheless, in the Lucan scheme the real witnesses to Jesus and his resurrection are the twelve apostles (Acts 4:33) and their leader, Peter (Acts 2:32; 3:15; 5:32; 10:39–41). Hence in one of his major addresses (in Pisidian Antioch) Paul speaks not of himself but of those others (who are, above all, the Twelve) as *the* witnesses to the risen Jesus: 'For many days he [Jesus] appeared to those who came up with him from Galilee to Jerusalem, who are now his witnesses to the people' (Acts 13:31). Thus even if Luke twice calls Paul an apostle and witness, it is only by way of analogy to the qualifications and function of the twelve apostles.

Where then does that leave the Damascus road encounter which Luke emphasizes by including it three times (Acts 9:1–19; 22:5–16; 26:12–18)? In the encounter 'a light from heaven flashes' around Paul (Acts 9:3; see 22:6 and 26:13) who falls to the ground and hears a voice which identifies itself as that of Jesus (Acts 9:4–5; 22:7–8; 26:34–35). It is not in the actual narration of the encounter but only afterwards that the text says that 'Jesus appeared to' Paul (Acts 9:17) or that Paul 'had seen the Lord' (Acts 9:27; see Acts 22:14–15). In the third version of the encounter it is Jesus himself who adds that language of appearing and seeing: 'Rise and stand upon your feet; for I have *appeared* to you for this purpose, to appoint you to serve and bear witness to the things in which you have *seen* me and to those in which

I will *appear* to you' (Acts 26:16).

The promise about those things 'in which I will appear to you' refers to other (subordinate) encounters with the heavenly Jesus, three of which are narrated by Acts. First, after returning to Jerusalem, Paul goes to pray in the temple, a place of central importance in the Lucan picture of salvation history, and later reports: 'I fell into a trance and saw him [Jesus] saying to me, "Make haste and get quickly out of Jerusalem"' (Acts 22:17–21). What Paul hears is much more significant than what he sees, as the heavenly Jesus sends him as apostle to the Gentiles. Hearing likewise takes precedence over seeing in a second episode which, though chronologically later, turns up earlier in the text of Acts. In Corinth Paul is encouraged to teach bravely and prolong his stay after the Lord Jesus *spoke* to him 'one night in a vision' (Acts 18:9–10).

The same emphasis on what Paul hears holds true on the third occasion: 'The following night the Lord [Jesus] stood by him and said, "Take courage, for as you have testified about me at Jerusalem, so you must bear witness also at Rome"' (Acts 23:11). Thus the three episodes that fulfil the promise 'I will appear to you,' even if they use the language of 'seeing' and 'vision,' concentrate rather on what Paul hears Jesus 'saying' and 'speaking' to him about the apostle's mission to the Gentiles and about the difficulties to be overcome on that mission. These messages from the heavenly Jesus, given during prayer in the Jerusalem temple or at night, are somewhat akin to what Paul himself reports in 2 Cor 12:7–9. On some occasion (after an 'abundance of revelations') Paul suffered from 'a thorn in the flesh,' prayed three times, and received from the Lord a message of comfort – the only word from the risen and heavenly Jesus cited by Paul in his letters.[59]

To sum up: in the Lucan scheme the risen Jesus' only clear appearance to Paul is the Damascus road encounter. Even there, when narrating the encounter, Luke does not state straightforwardly that Jesus appeared to Paul (as in 1 Cor 15:8) or that Paul saw Jesus (as in 1 Cor 9:1). This detail is added subsequently by Ananias (Acts 9:17; 22:14–15), Paul (Acts 9:27), or Jesus himself (Acts 25:16).[60]

We have seen the Pauline, Petrine, and Lucan testimony about the post-resurrection appearances being limited to certain individuals and groups. Let us turn now to the Johannine data.

'Those who have not seen but have believed'

What is the difference between those who have seen the risen Lord and believed, and those who believe without having seen him? This question is taken up by Raymond Brown in his commentary on John 20:29.[61] Brown emphasizes that the contrast here is between seeing and not seeing rather than between seeing and believing. Brown is reacting to Bultmann who thinks the appearances did not really occur but are merely symbolic pictures for the fellowship which the Risen Lord has with his own; the appearances are mentioned only to show their unimportance.[62] Brown, in maintaining his position, is in good company. C. K. Barrett points out that John 20:29 contrasts seeing with believing apart from sight – Thomas who saw contrasted with the later Christians believers who did not see. Barrett adds: 'but for the fact that Thomas and the other apostles saw the incarnate Christ there would have been no Christian faith at all.'[63] Barrett stresses the unique importance of those who saw the risen Lord: 'The disciples of the first generation had the unique distinction of standing as a link between Jesus and the church; John indicates this in saying that their successors equally may believe, and that their faith places them on the same level of blessedness with the eye-witnesses, or even above it' (p. 574). Barrett then concludes his comments as follows: 'It is not true that the first apostles have no particular and unique importance; for later generations believe through their word (17.20), that is, it is in their word that later generations encounter the Risen Christ and become believers' (pp. 574–75). While the era of visible signs and appearances has ended, it remains indispensably important for all subsequent believers.[64]

Some distinction between those witnesses ('we') who saw (and heard and touched Christ), and later believers ('you') who did not, focuses the opening three verses of 1 John

'That which was from the beginning, which we have seen with our eyes, which we have looked upon and touched with our hands, concerning the word of life – the life was made manifest, and we saw it, and testify to it, and proclaim to you the eternal life which was with the Father and was made manifest to us – that which we have seen and heard we proclaim also to you, so that you may have fellowship with us ...' (RSV) .

'What' (1 John 1:1) the tradition-bearers witness to is the whole career of Jesus, i.e., his 'person, words, and deeds "from the beginning" of his self-revelation to his disciples after being pointed out by John the Baptist until his victory over death.'[65] Brown sums up the dependence of later (Johannine) Christians on the tradition-bearers and behind them the original eyewitnesses. He does so in language that recalls Bultmann's distinction between historical and eschatological contemporaries: 'The whole community does share an eschatological existential encounter with the Word become flesh. But this is possible only because there was a group who encountered Jesus historically.'[66]

Exegetes diverge over the 'we' of ' John 1:1. Some insist on the eyewitness quality of the testimony to Christ's life, death, and resurrection (Brooke,[67] Marshall,[68] and Westcott[69]). Others, while recognizing that this testimony is rooted in personal contact with the earthly and risen Jesus, understand the 'we' to be the authoritative bearers of the tradition (Brown,[70] Bultmann,[71] and Perkins[72]). Even in this latter interpretation, however, the later believers ('you') depend indirectly on the testimony of the 'contemporaries of the historical Jesus' (Bultmann), 'original disciples' or 'first witnesses' (Perkins) or 'the Beloved Disciple' and the 'group who encountered Jesus historically' (Brown). Those later believers (the 'you' of 1 John 1:2–3) cannot simply repeat for themselves the experience of those who historically heard, saw, and touched Jesus.

Conclusion

Does the New Testament data support the view that the appearances of the risen Jesus were limited to certain individuals and groups at the start of the Christian movement? Attempts have been made to explain these Christophanies as episodes of merely verbal revelation, ecstatic events, and/or the reception of the Holy Spirit – experiences that could be shared by later

Christians. But these views are not convincing. The exegesis of
1 Cor 5:8 and related passages shows that Paul understood his
encounter with the risen Lord to be, both in fact and in principle, the last of the post-resurrection Christophanies. 1 Pet 1:8
suggests that 'seeing' Jesus was an experience limited to the
apostolic eyewitnesses among the first generation of disciples.
Through faith and love, other (later) Christians personally
relate to him but they do not see him.

In the Lucan scheme the Easter appearances close with the
risen Christ's ascension. Neither the vision of Stephen and
Ananias nor the experience of Paul's companions on the
Damascus road modify this pattern of no Christophanies after
the ascension. The only (partial) exception is the appearance to
Paul himself. Even here what Paul hears is more important than
what he sees.

Finally, there is the clear distinction between eyewitnesses
and non-eyewitnesses in John 20:29-31. The former group
came to faith through the visible signs of Christ that ended with
his post-resurrection appearances. Their testimony to what they
had experienced of the earthly and risen Lord remains essential
for later Christians who believe without seeing. The text of 1
John 1:1-3 does not clearly draw quite such a sharp distinction
between eyewitnesses and non-eyewitnesses. Nevertheless, the
testimony of the authoritative bearers of the tradition ('we') is
at least rooted in the once-and-for-all experience of the original
disciples who encountered Jesus historically.

In this way the Pauline, Petrine, Lucan, and Johannine data
converge to indicate the unique role of those who witnessed to
their experience of Jesus that ended with the post-resurrection
Christophanies. Later disciples cannot simply repeat that experience but are called to believe in dependence on the testimony
of the original disciples. The New Testament does not support
those such as Schillebeeckx who underplay the special nature of
the Easter appearances and so reduce the role of the apostolic
witness as authoritative founders of the Church. Instead, the
New Testament upholds a significant difference between the
post-Easter encounters with the risen Lord and subsequent
Christian experience, a difference which helps to validate the
normative witness of those to whom the risen Lord appeared.

13

St Ignatius Loyola on Christ's resurrection

For twentieth-century Christians the *Spiritual Exercises* of Ignatius Loyola continue to assert their power and persuasion. Those open to the possibility of deep personal reform have repeatedly experienced the graces mediated by this iron-hard school for conversion. To help celebrate the more than five centuries which have elapsed since the birth of Ignatius, I present these reflections on the resurrection, reflections emerging from the fourth, or Easter week, of the *Exercises*.

I

After guiding us through the life and death of Jesus, Ignatius asks us to 'consider how the divinity, which in the Passion seemed to hide itself, now appears in the most holy Resurrection and now most miraculously shows itself by its true and most holy effects.' Here Ignatius folds into a few words the shared experience of first-century Christians.

Right from their earliest writings Christians have associated the resurrection with a) the final vindication and revelation of Christ's divine identity and b) the full deployment of his saving power. Paul, for example, found in the Damascus road encounter the revelation of the Son of God (Gal 1:16). Echoing an earlier formula, the apostle expresses the resurrection as Jesus' being 'declared Son of God in power' (Rom 1:3), a lapidary phrase parallelled by the language of Ignatius about the divinity 'appearing in the most holy Resurrection' and 'showing itself by its true and most holy effects'.

Ignatius has here summarized two strictly interrelated truths that also come through the Easter stories of our gospels. The female disciples, and then the core group of male disciples, worship the risen Jesus (Matt 28:9, 17), recognizing in him a divine authority that extends over the whole universe (Matt 28:18). The people of all nations are now called to become a worldwide community of disciples who share new life through baptism and Christ's teaching. This 'holy effect' will be made possible through the enduring presence of the risen Jesus: 'I am with you always, to the close of the age' (Matt 28:20).

Right from the outset, John's gospel professes the divinity of Jesus. But it does so even more intensely in its final two chapters. Mary Magdalene, the beloved disciple, Peter and others acknowledge the risen Jesus as divine Lord (John 20:18, 25; 20:7, 12, 15–17). The confession of his divinity reaches its explicit climax with Thomas's profession 'My Lord and my God' (John 20:28). From the beginning of his ministry, Jesus has been manifesting his divine glory (John 2:11). But this self-disclosure develops to its full in the context of the resurrection.

The 'most holy effects' of the risen Lord are summed up in his gift of the Spirit on the first Easter Sunday. In an act of new creation, Jesus breathes on the disciples and says, 'Receive the Holy Spirit' (John 20:22).

The final chapter of John depicts the revelation of the risen Christ and His 'holy effects' – the *light* of the world who is the *life* of the world – in more picturesque and familiar terms. After a night of unsuccessful fishing, the disciples see Jesus standing on the beach just as dawn is breaking and light is coming into the sky (John 21:4). Through the beloved disciple they recognize him as the Lord and are invited to breakfast on the food Jesus has already provided and the catch of fish he directs them to make. The 'holy' promise of life in abundance (John 10:10) is being fulfilled, a fact symbolically expressed by the catch which, though huge, leaves the net unbroken (John 21:4–14).

St Paul, and even more the gospels, illuminate memorably Ignatius's conviction that the resurrection manifests Christ's divinity and the redemptive power he now exercises in the world. For Ignatius, as for the New Testament, revelation and salvation go hand in hand. There is no final disclosure of Christ's divine person without his salvific power coming fully into play.

II

Love is the second leitmotif in Ignatius's handling of the resurrection. Those following the *Spiritual Exercises* are asked to 'regard the office of comforter, which Christ our Lord exercises, comparing it with the manner in which friends are wont to console one another'. Such Easter prayer dwells on the immense consolation the appearances of the risen Jesus communicated to their recipients. This love practised by Christ toward his first-century disciples is to be reciprocated now by those coming to the end of the *Exercises*. They are 'to be intensely glad and to rejoice in such great glory and joy of Christ our Lord'. Ignatius takes for granted the mutual quality of love. The risen Jesus actively worked for the welfare and happiness of those to whom he appeared. In a reverse direction Ignatius' retreatants should go out of their way to 'rejoice in the exceedingly great joy and gladness of Christ our Lord'.

The active, bilateral nature of love sharply characterizes the 'contemplation for obtaining love' attached to the Easter week of the *Exercises*. The choice of Easter as the right place for that contemplation testifies to the way Ignatius grasps the paschal mystery – that is, in terms of love. Easter first happened through the freedom of God's love and will never cease to invite the free, lifelong commitment of our love.

III

Ignatius's appreciation of the resurrection as a mystery of love comes across as something immediately attractive and thoroughly acceptable. Much more problematic is the very first meditation he proposes for the Easter week of the *Exercises*: an appearance of Jesus to Mary, his Mother. In an unusually firm, even polemical way, Ignatius insists that this appearance, even though not mentioned by the New Testament, took place.

It can seem thoroughly strange that the New Testament, while reporting a number of post-resurrection appearances, remains silent about any such appearance to the Virgin Mary. In John's gospel she is there at the foot of the cross with her sister (the wife of Clopas), the beloved disciple and Mary Magdalene (John 19:25-27). In the Easter narratives of John, the beloved disciple and Mary Magdalene bulk large. Mary Magdalene discovers the tomb to be empty and is the first to see the risen Lord (John 20:1-2, 11-18); the beloved disciple is the first to believe and the first to identify the risen Christ on the shore at daybreak (John 20:8; 21:7). But curiously, the Easter chapters of John's gospel say nothing about the Blessed Virgin Mary and her sister. In their case, unlike that of the beloved disciple and Mary Magdalene, there is no follow-up to their presence at the crucifixion.

Where the New Testament was silent about the Blessed Virgin Mary's role at the first Easter, imaginative writers soon supplied the missing data. Several of the apocryphal gospels added Mary to the holy women who visited Christ's tomb on Easter morning. Some of these apocryphal gospels went further by describing an appearance of the risen Christ to his Mother, the earliest example coming from the so-called *Gospel of the Twelve Apostles* (which probably dates from the second century). In the same century, Tatian found the appearance to Mary in one of our canonical gospels, when he turned the Mary Magdalene of John 20:11-18 into Christ's own Mother.

In Eastern Christianity two decisive influences were Romanos the singer, a great sixth-century poet who introduced *kontakia*, or a new type of canticle, into the Byzantine liturgy, and the ninth-century metropolitan, George of Nicomedia. In his hymn 'Mary at the Cross', Romanos has Christ saying to her from the cross: 'Be of good courage, Mother; you will be the first to see me leave the tomb.' In a homily, George portrays Mary as waiting at her Son's tomb from Good Friday evening until he appeared to her in blazing glory on Easter morning.

In the West St Ambrose of Milan (d. 397) expressed his belief that Mary was the first to see Jesus after his resurrection. Ambrose symbolically 'justified' this belief by linking the tomb from which Jesus rose with the Virgin's womb from which he had been born. The Western author who popularized a post-resurrection encounter between Christ and his Mother was Pseudo-Bonaventura, an anonymous thirteenth-century writer. His *Mirror of the Blessed Life of Jesus Christ* touchingly described an appearance to Mary. This work influenced popular accounts of the life of Christ like those by Ludolf the Carthusian (in prose) and Guillaume de Digulleville (in verse) – both from the fourteenth century.

Ignatius read Ludolf's version of the appearance of the risen Christ to Mary. On his pilgrimage to the Holy Land, Ignatius may well have visited a chapel in Jerusalem where legend placed this appearance to Mary. At Easter in Spain, a man representing Christ and a woman representing his Mother used to come in procession to meet and re-enact the first post-resurrection appearance. Ignatius probably knew that custom.

He may also have seen artistic representations of the scene like that on the altar piece Roger van der Weyden executed around 1438 for Juan II of Castile. Various artistic expressions of Mary's role in the Easter events were already found in Spain. Roger's masterpiece influenced subsequent Spanish versions of Christ appearing to his Mother – including that found on a great altarpiece created by a group of artists for Isabella of Castile. On the popular artistic side, from the fifteenth into the sixteenth century, German woodcuts often portrayed Christ appearing and blessing his Mother, who kneels in prayer. These woodcuts, which enjoyed a wide circulation, supported the private devotion and prayer of many individuals.

In proposing for prayer an encounter with Mary as Christ's first post-resurrection appearance, Ignatius was standing in a long tradition. After the seventeenth century the episode practically disappeared from Christian art. Here and there, the appearance continues in paraliturgical practices. In the Philippines, for example, at dawn on Easter Sunday the ceremony of *Salubong* still celebrates Christ's meeting with his Mother. A child dressed like an angel removes the veil that covers Mary's face; then children throw flowers on Jesus and

Mary. Some twentieth-century writers, like Marie-Joseph Lagrange and Hans Urs von Balthasar, have defended the historical factuality of the appearance to the Blessed Virgin. In general, however, the credibility of this episode has been eroded by a deeper sensibility toward scriptural authority. How can we continue to maintain the truth of a post-resurrection encounter about which the New Testament remains silent?

The role expressed by Ignatius's proposed appearance to Mary can and should, however, be defended in the Easter week of the *Spiritual Exercises*. She certainly has her place in the total paschal mystery, which runs from the crucifixion to the outpouring of the Holy Spirit. As we have seen, John's gospel places her at the foot of the cross, where she endures an unendurable loss. When the Church is about to be formed and fashioned through the gift of the Holy Spirit, Mary is there praying with Jesus' followers as they wait for Pentecost (Acts 1:14). To deny her place in the paschal mystery would be to ignore the voices of John and Luke.

Furthermore, it is worth noting how women are to the fore in the Easter week of the *Exercises*. Ignatius recommends for meditation three appearances to women – to the Blessed Virgin, to Mary Magdalene and to the two Marys (Matt 28:9–10), before proposing for prayer the appearance to a man, Simon Peter.

Despite the Pauline and Lucan traditions, which present Peter as the first Easter witness (1 Cor 15:5; Luke 24:34), the Gospels are firmly on Ignatius's side in highlighting the holy women in their Easter narratives. We can distinguish six such narratives (in chronological order):

a) Mark 16:1–8;
b) Matt 28: 1–20;
c) Luke 23:56–24: 53;
d) John 20:1–29;
e) John 21:1–23;
f) Mark 16:9–20.

Female disciples are mentioned in five out of six of these narratives, being absent only from John 21). Mary Magdalene is the first to see and proclaim the risen Lord (John 20:11–18). Peter features explicitly in four of these narratives: a, c, d and e. According to c and d, it is Mary Magdalene's discovery of the open and empty tomb that sends Peter there. In short, the gospels encourage us to follow Ignatius in approaching the Easter mystery through women's eyes and women's experience.

Today, centuries later, during the Easter season we could do worse than follow the great themes of the fourth week of the *Spiritual Exercises*: the life-giving disclosure of the risen Christ's divinity, the resurrection as the feast of love, and the Marian and feminine face of the paschal mystery.

14

Newman's seven notes: the case of the resurrection

In *An Essay on the Development of Christian Doctrine*,[1] when expounding seven notes or tests for distinguishing between faithful development and corruption, John Henry Newman illustrates his argument by using such examples as the divinity of the Holy Spirit, Christ's real presence in the Eucharist, original sin, purgatory, and papal supremacy (for example, pp. 18, 20–7). Newman refers only in passing to the crucified Jesus' resurrection (pp. 402–3) which is classically handled by him elsewhere – in the context of justification, not in that of the development of doctrine as such.[2]

At the origin of Christianity, the appearances of the risen Lord and the discovery of his empty tomb were the two dramatic causes which first triggered Easter faith. The appearances were the primary way the disciples came to know that Jesus had been raised to new life. The discovery of the empty tomb served as a secondary, negative sign confirming his resurrection. Two books, both originally published in 1974, raise doubts about those original triggers of resurrection faith.

In *Jesus*[3] Edward Schillebeeckx explains the Easter experiences of Peter and the other disciples this way. Through the real but invisible influence of the risen Lord, they experienced a deep forgiveness and conversion which they then expressed in the model of 'appearances'. But their talk of appearances was only a means for articulating what the invisible Jesus had done for them after his death and resurrection, and did not refer to genuinely historical events.[4] In his *Interim Report on the Books 'Jesus' and 'Christ'*[5] Schillebeeckx concedes that when the first Christians spoke of appearances, this 'need not be a pure model; it can also imply a historical event'.[6] Nevertheless, he continues to play down the role of such appearances – and, for that matter, of the discovery of the empty tomb – in generating Easter faith: 'belief in the Jesus who is risen and lives with God and among us cannot be founded on an empty tomb as such, nor as such on the visual elements which there may have been in "appearances" of Jesus.'[7]

In his *On being a Christian*[8] Hans Küng clearly maintains the personal resurrection of Jesus, while throwing doubt on the historical reliability of the empty tomb story.[9] He explains: 'There can be identity of the person even without continuity between the earthly and the "heavenly", "spiritual" body ... The corporality of the resurrection does not require the tomb to be empty'.[10] Here Küng defends a corporeal resurrection, but dispenses with the need for any *bodily* continuity between the earthly and risen existence of Jesus. The totally new 'spiritual' body can come into existence without involving the former, earthly body, and yet without imperilling the continuing personal identity of the crucified Jesus. In his risen state he is identical with, and no mere substitute for, the person who died on the cross and was buried. Küng seems to locate Jesus' continuity simply at the level of soul or spirit. The new, 'heavenly' body totally replaces the one which ended in the tomb.

In this chapter I wish to apply Newman's seven notes to the proposals about the risen Lord's appearances and empty tomb made respectively by Schillebeeckx and Küng. Do their interpretations represent faithful and healthy developments, or 'corruptions' which in some way 'pervert' the truth and threaten to break up Christian life (pp. 169–71)? My argument here has to presuppose the general validity of Newman's seven notes for the genuine 'development of an idea': preservation of its type, continuity of its principles, power of assimilation, logical sequence, anticipation of its future, conservative action upon its past, and chronic vigour (pp. 171–206).[11] Schillebeeckx's and Küng's proposals have often been commented on and criticized from a biblical, exegetical point of view.[12] Here I want to examine whether, when seen in the light of Newman's criteria, those proposals represent developments or corruptions for the doctrine of Christ's resurrection.

Schillebeeckx and the appearances

Towards the end of his *Essay* Newman recognized that 'the one great topic of preaching with Apostles and Evangelists was the Resurrection of Christ and of all mankind after Him' (p. 402). Is that great 'idea' properly 'preserved' (p. 178) in Schillebeeckx's account of the resurrection? Despite some variations and novelty, this version of the first Easter maintains the 'personal-cum-bodily resurrection' of Jesus.[13] The core doctrine remains substantially identical and faithful to 'type' (p. 173).

What of Newman's second criterion for true development, 'continuity of principles' (p.178)? Does Schillebeeckx maintain or alter the principles on which the doctrine of the resurrection has developed (p. 185)? Newman admits that a real difference between principles and doctrines is not always clear (p. 179). Nevertheless, he employs the distinction, arguing that 'the life of doctrines may be said to consist in the law or principle which they embody' (p. 178). Are there principles embodied in the normal doctrine about the Easter appearances which Schillebeeckx's reductive interpretation tampers with? It seems that this may happen with one or even two important principles: the role of visible signs in generating faith and – possibly – God's freedom to make unusual interventions in the regular order of things. Let me explain.

Those who affirm that the risen Christ genuinely appeared to various individuals and groups find themselves criticized by Schillebeeckx for grounding Easter faith in a pseudo-empirical way:

Faith is emasculated if we insist on grounding it in pseudo-empiricism, thereby raising all sorts of false problems: whether, for instance, this 'Christological mode of seeing' was a sensory seeing of Jesus, whether it was 'objective' or 'subjective' seeing, a 'manifestation' or a 'vision', and things of that sort.[14]

Behind this strong language about 'emasculating' faith lies the whole question about the function of visible signs and empirical evidence as (partial) grounds for initiating and legitimating faith. If God provided appearances of the risen Christ to communicate the fact of the resurrection and invite the witnesses to a new form of faith, can and should we disdain those who accept all that as catering to a 'pseudo-empiricism' which threatens to deprive faith of its integral and virile purity? There is much to discuss and debate here. I simply want to state my concern about one principle. Schillebeeckx seems bent on denying real appearances of the risen Christ, because he is uneasy about admitting empirical grounds for the disciples' Easter faith. It leaves me with the question: Does a faulty principle (a reluctance to accept the role of visible signs and evidence in the genesis of faith) control Schillebeeckx's interpretation of the New Testament texts which report the Easter appearances?[15]

The other enduring principle which Schillebeeckx's position may also threaten is the freedom of divine interventions in the course of saving history, the appearances of the risen Christ being a major example of such interventions. Schillebeeckx asserts that 'there are always intermediary historical factors in occurrences of divine grace. The [so-called] appearances form no exception to this scheme of grace.'[16] (One must add here 'so-called', since – as we have seen – in *Jesus* Schillebeeckx denies that the risen Lord really appeared to the disciples, the appearances being merely a way of expressing the conversion they had undergone.) In Schillebeeckx's assertion that 'there are always intermediary historical factors in occurrences of divine grace', the key word is 'always'. Beyond question, there are always such intermediary historical factors. In those occurrences of divine grace which were the appearances of the risen Christ many such factors entered in: the spiritual crisis of the disciples, the places they found themselves in, the company they were keeping, and so on. Since the risen Christ encountered human beings in history, such intermediary historical factors were necessarily present. But were there *only* such factors? Schillebeeckx's doctrine of grace may be slipping from rightly

affirming that intermediary historical factors are *always* present
to implying that, at least in the realm of visible history, *nothing but* such factors are present. And that is a very different
matter. It would rule out in principle the possibility of a transhistorical factor – the special intervention in history of the risen
Christ who now transcends the normal limits of history but
freely appears to certain people within history. Thus in one or
two ways the test of principle raises difficulties against
Schillebeeckx's interpretation of the Easter appearances.

We can move to Newman's third note for faithful development, the 'power of assimilation' (pp. 185–9). According to
this criterion, doctrines develop by absorbing and incorporating
fresh elements. Since he views development as a 'process of
incorporation' (p. 187), Newman can suggest as his third test,
'the *unitive power* of faithful developments' (p. 189).

In support of Schillebeeckx's interpretation of the Easter
appearances, it might be argued that he succeeds in assimilating and incorporating new material by highlighting the themes
of forgiveness and conversion. At the same time, however, he
trims the normal teaching on Jesus' resurrection by denying or
doubting the factual status of the appearances. Newman's third
criterion does not seem to tell decisively either for or against
Schillebeeckx's position.

What then of the fourth note, 'logical sequence' (pp.
189–95)? Newman describes it not as 'a conscious reasoning
from premisses to conclusion' (p.189) but as follows: 'A doctrine ... professed in its mature years by a philosophy or religion, is likely to be a true development, not a corruption, in
proportion as it seems to be the *logical issue* of its original
teaching' (p. 195). Could Schillebeeckx claim that there is a
logical, 'natural succession of views' (p. 193) from the original
testimony to the appearances of the risen Christ to his own
explanation of what the New Testament really meant and means
by them?

Rather than offering something which seems the natural,
'logical issue' of what Paul (1 Cor 15:5–8) and the evangelists
(for example, Luke 24:34; Matt 28:16–20) proclaim and teach
about the appearances, Schillebeeckx turns them into a set of
extraordinarily incompetent and confusing writers. They really
intended to say that Peter and other disciples were converted

under the impact of grace and they had the words to say just that ($\mu\epsilon\tau\alpha\nu o\epsilon\omega$, $\chi\acute{\alpha}\rho\iota\varsigma$). Instead they verbalized their conversion and mission by talking about appearances of the risen Christ which never actually happened.

Schillebeeckx is well aware that his hypothesis about the disciples' conversion-experiences being later expressed in the form of visions 'constitutes a break with a centuries-old hermeneutical tradition'.[17] More than that, the hypothesis hardly seems to be what Newman calls 'the logical issue of the original teaching'. The ordinary conventions governing the use of language indicate that the New Testament originally meant to say that the risen Lord's appearances effected the conversion (and call) of Peter, Paul, and others. Schillebeeckx has the disciples first believing in the risen Christ and then later articulating this experience 'in the form of an appearance vision'.[18] In Newman's terms, one cannot claim here a 'natural succession of views' from the New Testament through to Schillebeeckx. There is no 'evident naturalness' which could show the process to have been 'a true development' rather than 'a perversion or corruption' (p. 191).

'Anticipation of its future' (pp. 195–9) forms Newman's fifth test. He puts it this way:

> Since developments are in great measure only aspects of the idea from which they proceed, and all of them are natural consequences of it, ... it is in no wise strange that here and there definite specimens of advanced teaching should very early occur, which in the historical course are not found till a late day.

Newman draws a reasonable conclusion from this note of faithful development: 'The fact, then, of such early or recurring intimations of tendencies which afterwards are fully realized, is a sort of evidence that those later or more systematic fulfilments are only in accordance with the original idea' (pp. 195–6).

In short, 'another evidence' of 'the faithfulness of an ultimate development is its *definite anticipation* at an early period in the history of the idea to which it belongs' (p. 199).

When tested in this way, Schillebeeckx's thesis about the genesis and articulation of Easter faith could come off reasonably well. Admittedly, his 'advanced teaching' cannot claim an 'early intimation' in the sense that we find any ancient Christian writers suggesting that the New Testament's talk of appearances was only a way of summarizing what the risen but invisible Jesus had done for the disciples and did not refer to genuinely historical events. Nevertheless, the New Testament does play down the appearances in a way which Schillebeeckx might claim as an 'early intimation' of his own approach. In early Christianity we have a shift from a situation in which certain individuals and groups testify to the appearances of the risen Lord (for example, 1 Cor 15:5-8; Luke 24:34) to the situation in which the Church directly professes her faith in his resurrection (Rom 1:4, 10:9).[19]

That becomes the standard practice in the post-New Testament creeds which, without mentioning any appearances of the risen Christ, simply confess that 'he rose again on the third day' or that 'on the third day he rose again in accordance with the Scriptures'.[20]

Apropos of the appearances, Schillebeeckx observes that as such they are 'not an *object* of Christian faith'.[21] This is to ignore two kerygmatic/credal passages where the appearances form (a secondary) part of the confession of faith (1 Cor 15:5; Luke 24:34). Schillebeeckx also slips over the fact that even if – normally – the appearances do not figure as an object in New Testament confessions of faith, nevertheless, those appearances were the primary way the disciples came to know that Jesus had been raised from the dead. In that sense the appearances were essential means for first triggering knowledge of the resurrection and faith in the risen Lord. Any adequate discussion of the Easter appearances would be usefully enriched by distinguishing between the (normal) object of New Testament faith and the (primary) means for generating the original Easter faith.

All the same, in terms of Newman's fifth test Schillebeeckx could allege an 'early intimation' for his downplaying the appearances. Pontius Pilate got into the creeds as a kind of witness to the historical reality of Jesus' death. But Peter, Paul, Mary Magdalene, 'the Twelve', and others to whom the risen Lord appeared have no place in the Church's ancient creeds which simply confess the resurrection without naming those witnesses.

Schillebeeckx's reductive interpretation of the appearances does not show up too well when confronted with Newman's sixth test for a true development (pp. 199–203), 'a *tendency conser-*

vative of what has gone before it' (p. 203). Such a development positively illustrates, corroborates, and protects its 'antecedents' (pp. 200, 202), whereas those developments 'which do but contradict and reverse the course of doctrine which has been developed before them ... are certainly corrupt' (p. 199).

It is the normative role of the apostles which Schillebeeckx's view fails to illustrate, corroborate, and protect sufficiently. He recognizes *only one* special aspect of the *first* apostles' experience: the fact that they had known Jesus before his death.[22] For the rest they 'have no [other] advantage over us than that they were there at the time'.[23] Their Easter experience of forgiveness, conversion, a renewed life, and Jesus' 'spiritual presence' in 'the gathered community'[24] can be shared by any of his followers anywhere and at any time. There is no very significant difference between the disciples' Easter experience and subsequent experiences of the risen Lord.

Once the special nature of their Easter experience gets left behind, it is hard to see why the apostolic witnesses should be regarded as normative interpreters of the risen Jesus and authoritative (rather than simply *de facto*) founders of the Christian Church. It is difficult to understand why their experience of him should remain a lasting criterion for believers and why their conversion should be the norm for Christian conversion. Schillebeeckx himself seems to draw this conclusion by remarking that it is only 'for the knowledge [but not for any normative interpretation?] of Jesus in whom we believe' that we depend on those witnesses. They 'have no [other] advantage over us than that they were there at the time'.[25]

Newman gives his seventh and final note the name of 'chronic vigour' (pp. 203–6). 'Corruption', he argues, 'cannot ... be of long standing; and thus duration is another test of a faithful development' (p. 203). The *'transitory character'* of corruption distinguishes it from true development (p. 205).

With this, as with his other note, Newman normally has in mind movements rather than the ideas of individuals which might be tested during their lifetime. However, he occasionally cites particular persons like Luther (p. 198) and Muhammad (p. 201). It seems appropriate then to raise the question: Has Schillebeeckx's interpretation of the disciples' Easter experience shown 'chronic vigour' or has it looked rather 'transitory'? He has not been winning adherents so as to guarantee the lasting 'duration' of his interpretation. Such substantial recent works on the resurrection as Pheme Perkins' *Resurrection*[26] and Hans Kessler's *Sucht den Lebenden nicht bei den Toten*[27] fail to endorse Schillebeeckx's version of the appearances. Soon after first publishing *Jesus* in 1974, Schillebeeckx himself began modifying what he had said about the appearances not referring to genuinely historical events and being only a way of expressing what the risen but invisible Jesus had done for the disciples. In *Christ* Schillebeeckx explained that he did not want to deny that the disciples to whom Jesus appeared had enjoyed some kind of sense-experience.[28] Then in *Interim Report* he admitted that when they experienced the living presence of the risen Lord, they may have seen him alive. The 'resurrection visions' may have been 'a historical reality'.[29] In other words, when the early Christians spoke of 'appearances' of Jesus, this 'need not be a pure model; it can also imply a historical event'.[30] Such modifications on the part of the author himself scarcely encourage one to acknowledge 'chronic vigour' in his original proposal about the Easter appearances.

To sum up the whole examination of Schillebeeckx's proposal. It comes off reasonably well when tested by Newman's first and (perhaps) fifth notes. The third note does not seem to tell either one way or another. Newman's second, fourth, sixth and seventh test would not encourage us to admit Schillebeeckx's proposal as a genuinely faithful development. Let me turn next to Küng's doubts about the historical reliability of the empty tomb story.

Küng and the empty tomb

As in the case of Schillebeeckx, by applying the seven 'notes' to Küng's view of the empty tomb story, I am going beyond Newman's primary intention. He originally wrote the *Essay on Development* 'to explain certain difficulties in its [the Catholic Religion's] history' (p. vii). In particular, Newman felt the need to 'account for that apparent variation and growth of doctrine, which embarrasses us when we would consult history for the true idea of Christianity' (p. 29). Nevertheless, his analogical method of arguments and the fact that he sometimes points to particular writers to exemplify his theory of development has encouraged me to try out his hypothesis (p. 30) on two contemporary writers. I take up now Küng's view that Jesus' empty tomb was unlikely and, indeed, unnecessary.

One should agree that Küng's version of the resurrection, at least substantially, meets Newman's first test. It 'preserves' the 'original idea'. 'Easter is an event primarily for Jesus himself: Jesus lives again *through God – for their* [the disciples'] *faith*'.[31] Whatever his doubts about the empty tomb, Küng refuses to merge Jesus' resurrection with the rise of faith after his crucifixion. In the first instance the resurrection personally affected Jesus himself by bringing him to new life. Secondarily, this event (made known through the Easter appearances)[32] triggered off a fresh relationship of faith for the disciples. Küng maintains the core doctrine of Jesus' personal and bodily[33] resurrection.

It is doubtful whether Küng's dismissal of the empty tomb stands up so well when confronted with Newman's second criterion for faithful development, 'continuity of principles' (p. 178). Are there principles embodied in or implied by the normal teaching about the discovery of the empty tomb that Küng's position tampers with? This may be happening in two ways which concern, respectively, the divine identity and the saving role of the man whom Joseph of Arimathea buried.

First, the matter of identity. From the time of the Book of Acts the emptiness of Jesus' grave has been understood to reflect the holiness of what it once held, the corpse of him who was 'exalted at the right hand of God' and known to be both 'Lord and Christ' (Acts 2:33, 36). This 'Holy One' could not 'see corruption' (Acts 2:27). Küng's view means that this 'Holy One' could and did 'see corruption'.

Second, the empty tomb expresses something vital about the nature of redemption which Jesus effected – namely that redemption is much than a mere escape from our scene of suffering and death. Rather it means the transformation of this material, bodily world with its whole history of sin and suffering. The first Easter began the work of finally bringing our universe home to its ultimate destiny. God did not discard Jesus' earthly corpse but mysteriously raised and transfigured it so as to reveal what lies ahead for human beings and their world. In short, that empty tomb in Jerusalem is God's radical sign that redemption is not an escape to a better world but a wonderful transformation of our world. Seen that way, the open and empty grave of Jesus is highly significant for our appreciation of what redemption means.

The nature of redemption is then a second principle expressed by Jesus' empty tomb. Küng's dissent from this normal doctrine threatens a highly significant sign of redemption as transformation, and risks turning redemption into an escape to another and better situation of totally new heavenly and spiritual bodies.

As was the case with Schillebeeckx, it is hard to decide whether Newman's third note for faithful development, the 'power of assimilation' speaks for or against Küng's downplaying the empty tomb. On the one hand, it can look as if he incorporates new material from biblical exegesis and modern science: 'Historical criticism', he concludes, 'has made the empty tomb a dubious factor and the conclusions of natural science have rendered it suspect.'[34] On the other hand, however, Küng himself knows that contemporary biblical criticism is by no means unanimous in rejecting the fact of the empty tomb: 'There are ... a number of influential exegetes even today who hold that the empty tomb is historically probable.'[35] He might have added also that 'natural science' does not necessarily render the empty tomb suspect. Wolfhart Pannenberg and Xavier Léon-Dufour, for example, respect the findings of modern science and maintain the fact of Jesus' empty tomb.[36] All the same, it remains difficult to judge whether or not Küng's view on the empty tomb successfully exemplifies Newman's third note, 'the unitive power of faithful development'.

Could Küng claim that he satisfies Newman's fourth criterion of 'logical sequence' and presents 'a faithful development of the original idea' (p. 149) of Christ's resurrection? Newman puts the test in these terms:

> There is a certain continuous advance and determinate path which belong to the history of a doctrine, policy or institution, and which impress upon the common sense of mankind, that what it ultimately becomes is the issue of what it was at first. (p. 195)

Küng doubts the historical reliability of the empty tomb story. Is that the natural 'issue' of what the doctrine of Christ's resurrection 'was at first'?

As regards the fate of Jesus' body, both the tradition behind the Synoptic gospels and that which entered John's gospel testified to one (Mary Magdalene) or more women finding Jesus' grave to be open and empty. Early polemic against the message of his resurrection supposed that the tomb was known to be empty. Naturally the opponents of the Christian movement explained away the missing body as a plain case of theft (Matt 28:11-15). But we have no early evidence that anyone, either Christian or non-Christian, ever alleged that Jesus' tomb still contained his remains.

During the succeeding centuries it was only such outsiders as Celsus in the second century or Reimarus in the eighteenth who either denied the empty tomb or explained it away on merely natural grounds (as, for example, a case of body-snatching). Küng would argue that the historical and natural sciences require us to modify radically two thousand years of thinking about Jesus' empty tomb'. It should now be seen not as a fact but as a 'legendary' elaboration of the message about Jesus' resurrection, a pictorial embellishment of the Easter kerygma and the statements about appearances that we find in places like 1 Corinthians 15:3b-5, 7-8.[37]

However, Perkins among others shows the flimsiness of the hypothesis that kerygmatic traditions about the risen Jesus' appearances produced empty tomb stories.[38] Careful exegesis indicates that the two traditions have independent origins. The differences are such that it is hard to interpret Mark 16:1-8 as embodying some legendary elaboration of the statements about Jesus' resurrection and appearances found in 1 Corinthians 15:3-5, 7-8. Further, as we have seen, there are those like Pannenberg and Léon-Dufour who do not agree that modern science necessarily casts doubt on the empty tomb story. In brief, neither contemporary exegesis nor the natural sciences compel us to alter radically the original teaching about Jesus' empty tomb and flout the logical sequence which Newman's fourth test expects to find in the faithful development of an idea.

Could Küng find some early anticipation for his reductive interpretation of the empty tomb story, thus satisfying Newman's fifth criterion? He might note two 'tendencies' that 'show themselves early' (p. 195) and lend some support to his case. First of all, with one exception, Küng's assertion is true:

'Even according to the New Testament, the empty tomb never led anyone to faith in the risen Christ.'[39] The one exception comes in John 20:8 where the beloved disciple sees only the sign of the empty tomb and yet believes.[40] Elsewhere the Gospels never report that the mere discovery of the empty tomb leads anyone to Easter faith. Second, unlike the burial of Jesus (1 Cor 15:4), the discovery of the empty tomb as such never entered any kerygmatic/credal passages preserved in the New Testament. Likewise it did not find a place in the Apostles' Creed and Nicene Creed, which confess Jesus' resurrection from the dead without explicit reference to the women finding his tomb to be empty. In this way two early 'tendencies' might be alleged in support of Küng's minimalizing approach to the empty tomb tradition.

Newman's sixth note, 'a *tendency conservative* of what has gone before it', is not verified in Küng's view. The main antecedent to be illustrated and corroborated here is surely the common Easter faith of Christians. Does Küng manage to do this? He argues that 'even if the narrative of the empty tomb had a historical core, faith in the risen Christ would not be made any easier and for some people today it would even become more difficult'.[41] It is interesting that Küng speaks only of 'some people'. I doubt whether this would be so for the vast majority. For them to deny the historicity of the empty tomb is to deny the resurrection itself. To judge from what I have heard over and over again in different parts of the world, ordinary believers' faith in Jesus' resurrection does involve his grave being empty. They would not believe in his resurrection from the dead unless his tomb had been found open and the corpse gone. For very many people today faith in the risen Christ would be made difficult and even impossible if the narrative of the empty tomb did not have a historical core. In that sense Küng's doubts about the empty tomb do not exemplify Newman's *'tendency conservative* of what has gone before'.

Küng might do better when tested by the seventh note, 'chronic vigour'. Both before and after the publication of *On Being a Christian*, some have doubted or denied the empty tomb, while maintaining the true personal resurrection of Jesus himself.[42] Küng's reductive interpretation of the empty tomb story, while not 'vigorous' in the sense of commanding great support among Christian theologians and exegetes,[43] does not look 'transitory'. My guess is that it will continue to prove 'chronic', inasmuch as a small group will continue to uphold Jesus' personal resurrection while dispensing with the fact of the empty tomb. The seventh and last note does not appear to tell decisively against Küng.

Testing Küng's position on the basis of Newman's seven notes yields the following results. Küng's view of Jesus' tomb could show up fairly well in the light of the first and fifth criteria. The third and the seventh fail to tell clearly for or against his view, whereas the second, fourth, and sixth notes point to a 'corruption' rather than a truly faithful development.

If one were allowed to enlarge and improve Newman's seven tests for distinguishing real development from corruption, one new test could well be worship – what Newman himself calls the 'development of doctrine into worship' (p. 48). Do the views of Schillebeeckx and Küng on, respectively, the appearances of the risen Christ and his empty tomb help believers to worship better? This chapter, however, has not pressed that question but has simply applied to the two cases the seven tests as Newman presented them.

Newman's central purpose in his *Essay on Development* was to scrutinize eighteen hundred years of history and to explain 'certain apparent variations' in the teaching of Catholic Christianity (p. 7). If he succeeded in so dealing with a sufficient number 'of the reputed corruptions, doctrinal and practical, of Rome', that might 'serve as a fair ground for trusting her in parallel cases where the investigation had not been pursued' (p. 32). But the fact that he also exemplified his argument from the good and bad practice of individuals has encouraged me to try out his seven tests on two contemporary writers. In any case, unless and until Newman's notes prove themselves to be serviceable today, they will remain a matter for historical study and have no enduring value for the living doctrine and worship of the Church.

This chapter aimed at illustrating the enduring value of Newman's seven criteria by taking up two modern cases. Tested in that way, Küng's interpretation of the empty tomb tradition and, even more clearly, Schillebeeckx's original proposal about the risen Jesus' appearances look like 'corruptions' rather than faithful developments of the 'idea' of the resurrection.

15

Christ's resurrection
and ascension

The story of Christ's ascension at the beginning of the Book of
Acts can come across as embarrassingly mythological. Jesus
takes off into the sky and disappears behind a cloud. Two
angels in white robes show up and speak with one voice, telling
the disciples not to stand around any more gazing open-
mouthed into heaven. 'This Jesus, who was taken away from
you up into heaven, will come in the same way as you have
seen him go' (Acts 1:11).

One turns with relief to the end of Luke's gospel where the
same author reports in a much simpler way how the post-resurrection appearances to the original disciples ended. While
blessing his disciples, the risen Jesus 'parted from them' (Luke
24:51). At that point some ancient copies of the gospel add:
'and was carried up into heaven'. Even if those words actually
come from Luke himself and are not added by a later hand, it
is still a less vivid and embarrassing scenario than we find at
the start of Acts. There are no angels and no cloud. If we agree
with many scholars that the words 'and was carried up into
heaven' are slipped in by a later copyist, Luke's gospel does
not speak at all of Jesus' going up into the sky.

In this way we can play the end of Luke's gospel off against
the beginning of his Acts of the Apostles, so as to demytholo-
gize the vivid scenario of the ascension. This means under-

scoring the resurrection and downplaying the importance of the feast we celebrate between Easter and Pentecost.

After all, in the eucharistic acclamations that follow the consecration we say: 'Dying you destroyed our death; rising you restored our life, Lord Jesus, come in glory.' We do not say, 'ascending you restored our life'. The fourth acclamation reads: 'Lord, by your cross and resurrection you have set us free. You are the Saviour of the world.' There is no talk about 'your cross and ascension' setting us free.

Can we be satisfied with reducing the ascension to the status of a minor feast, a small peak between the towering mountains of Easter and Pentecost? May we explain the ascension as the close of the risen Jesus' appearances to his original disciples and leave it at that?

This treatment of the ascension becomes more difficult, once we begin to notice other passages in the New Testament that speak of Jesus being 'exalted to the right hand' of God the Father (Acts 2:33; Acts 7:55–56; Rom 8:34; Col 3:1). In confessing that 'he ascended into heaven and is seated at the right hand of the Father', the Creed reflects the biblical pictures of Jesus going up from our world to assume his rightful place alongside his heavenly Father.

One New Testament hymn speaks of Christ being 'taken up in glory' (1 Tim 3:16). Another hymn expresses his exaltation in terms of his universal authority and divine identity being now revealed: 'God has highly exalted him and bestowed on him the name which is above every name, that at the name of Jesus every knee should bow, in heaven and on earth and under the earth, and every tongue confess that Jesus Christ is Lord, to the glory of God the Father' (Phil 2:9–11).

The pictorial counterpart for this hymn, which St Paul quotes in his letter to the Philippians, can be found in the twelfth-century Church of St Clement in Rome. When you enter from the street and stand in the aisle, you can lift your eyes high above the altar to a majestic mosaic. It represents Christ ruling in divine glory over the whole universe. At a lower level beneath your feet are the ruins of a fifth-century church. You can go down even further to visit a first-century alley and the traditional site of the home of St Clement of Rome. From under the earth and on the street level this remarkable church invites visitors to look up at Christ surrounded by the stars of heaven and acknowledge him to be the glorious Lord of the whole world. Unquestionably the early Church speaks more of his resurrection than of his ascension when stating what happened to Christ himself after his death and burial. Nevertheless, the New Testament *does* talk of his going up into heaven. Christians are faithful to the Scriptures when they follow up Easter by celebrating the Feast of the Ascension. In the Creed they confess that Jesus not only 'rose again' but also that he 'ascended into heaven'.

In what ways do these two beliefs relate to each other or else differ? The thrust of the first is more 'horizontal', that of the second more 'vertical'. Let me explain. Even if Christ's resurrection bursts the normal bounds of history, there is still something unmistakably 'horizontal' about it – a 'before' and 'after' to it. Before the resurrection he first died and then was buried. After that Christ rose again on the third day. The movement suggested by the ascension is not so much horizontal (and historical) as it is vertical. From the depths of humiliation entailed by his death on the cross, Christ has gone up into the glory of heaven.

We human beings absorb and express events in terms of time and space. The first Christians took in and stated what had happened to the person of Jesus in terms of time (the resurrection) and space (the ascension). He had risen again on the third day and ascended into heaven. Inevitably the earliest Christians reached for this language of time and space when communicating what they knew to have happened to Jesus after his crucifixion.

Admittedly Jesus' resurrection from the dead remains the central claim. Defenders of Christianity write books with such titles as *Who Moved the Stone?* I have not yet heard of any book of Christian apologetics entitled *Did He Ascend?* Nevertheless, belief in Jesus' ascension has its own special function.

One way of establishing this point could be to compare the mosaic of St Clement's with Michelangelo's statue of the risen Christ to be found in another church in Rome, that of Santa Maria sopra Minerva. As in so many Western paintings and statues of the risen Jesus, he is triumphantly alive again, but there is not much sense of his new, transformed existence. He has returned to life and, if one may put it this way, looks a

splendid athlete. But he does not come across as living now in
transfigured glory.

Like Christian art, the very language of 're-surrection' itself
can wrongly be taken to imply a mere 'return' or 'coming back'
to life, as if Jesus were simply resuscitated or reanimated after
his death and burial. That would be to forget how his resurrection meant his entering into an awesome new state of glory
(Luke 24:26).

We need St Clement's majestic mosaic of the gloriously
transformed Christ to remind us that his resurrection was much
more than a mere coming back to life under the normal conditions of our present existence. We need also the language of the
Feast of the Ascension. Jesus went up into heavenly glory to sit
at the right hand of the Father.

That language and those images speak of Jesus sitting, not
near God's throne, but at the Father's very right hand. He has
now assumed his true place. During his earthly life Jesus spoke
to God and of God with astonishing familiarity and scandalous
intimacy. He had every right to do so. He is now vindicated
and shown to be truly the divine Son of God at the right hand
of the eternal Father.

To be sure, the beliefs in Christ's resurrection and in his
ascension converge in maintaining that even death did not
finally defeat him. But these two beliefs differ or at least sepa-
rately fill out the total picture for us, just as the statue in Santa
Maria sopra Minerva and the mosaic in St Clement's do. As a
sign of victory over death, Michelangelo's risen Christ carries
his cross. That is a useful reminder of the before and the after
– of the horizontal, historical level. Jesus died and was buried
and then rose victoriously from the dead. The mosaic in St
Clement's reminds us that Jesus' victory was much more than
the mere reanimation of a corpse. He has entered into his final
glory to be acknowledged for what he truly is, the only Son of
God and divine ruler of the universe.

In brief, Easter remains the major feast of the year. But it is
at our peril that we ignore the ascension and what it clarifies
about Christ's true and final state.

16

On reissuing Venturini

Mainline Christian belief has always understood the New Testament to maintain that the historical Jesus of Nazareth was put to death by crucifixion, was buried, and then rose from the dead. For the resurrection the New Testament offers as primary evidence the appearances of Jesus, encountered alive after a period of time in the tomb; the secondary evidence is the empty tomb itself.

From the start of Christianity various arguments were raised against the reality of Jesus' resurrection, and even against that of his death. Matthew's gospel reports how some opponents alleged that the body of Jesus had been stolen from the tomb (28:15). In the second and third centuries Gnostic Christianity claimed that the powers of this lower world failed to harm the heavenly Revealer and Saviour. They merely succeeded in crucifying a substitute, an image or the fleshly part of Christ, while the spiritual Jesus remained alive, laughing at their mistake.[1] In the seventh-century Koran we read that the people did not crucify him and kill him, though they thought they did.[2] This is to assert that Jesus did not die on the cross as reported by the gospels.

The rise of modern historical consciousness produced by the end of the eighteenth century, what Albert Schweitzer called 'the earliest fictitious lives of Jesus'[3] – those by Carl Friedrich Bahrdt (1741–92) and Karl Heinrich Venturini (1768–1849), the former's work being 'the sketch' and the latter's 'the finished picture' (p. 44). Both authors denied that Jesus died on the cross. According to Bahrdt, the Essenes stage-managed a sham death. According to Venturini, by accident or good fortune Jesus was taken down from the cross unconscious but still alive: with the help of Essene brethren he revived, lived on and took leave of his disciples in a scene which they mistakenly interpreted as his ascension into heaven. Schweitzer reports others like H. E. G. Paulus (pp. 53–55) and F. E. D. Schleiermacher (pp. 64–65)[4] who portrayed Jesus as recovering from a death-like trance after he was taken down from the cross. At the end of a section on Venturini Schweitzer remarks that his life of Jesus 'may almost be said to be reissued annually down to the present day, for all the fictitious "lives" go back to the style which he created. It is plagiarized more freely than any other Life of Jesus, although practically unknown by name' (p. 47; see pp. 326–29).

This perceptive observation Schweitzer published in 1906 has proved truly prophetic for our century. The latest major 'reissue' of Venturini came in 1992 with Barbara Thiering's *Jesus and the Riddle of the Dead Sea Scrolls*.[5] Before evaluating her book, this article will look at nine variants on Venturini which have appeared between 1916 and 1987. In examining our authors (in greater or lesser detail) we will keep in mind several basic questions:

1.   How do they think Jesus survived crucifixion?
2.   What do they imagine that he subsequently did?
3.   What sources do they appeal to in support of their claims?
4.   Do they show any awareness of other works which argue for the survival hypothesis? Or is this a case of Venturini being reissued, although 'unknown by name'?
5.   What do they think their hypothesis does to reinterpret, perhaps enhance or else destroy Christian belief and practice?

Moore, Lawrence, Graves

The first 'reissue' of Venturini's 'life' of Jesus to be recalled is a substantial novel by George Moore (1852–1933), *The Brook Kerith: a Syrian Story*.[6] This Irish writer presents Jesus as 'a pious Essene' (p. ix), a 'rough shepherd philosopher' (p. x), who left his sheep to preach, work miracles and allow himself to believe that he was the Messiah and even the Son of God. His survival from crucifixion runs as follows:

> The man is put on the cross and is lifted from it apparently dead, but is not dead, and when he wakens from his swoon he perceives that he was mistaken in all things: angels did not come down from Heaven to lift him from the cross and bear him back to his father, and the world still subsists the same as before. (p. ix).

After he revives in the tomb, Joseph of Arimathea carries him out and cares for him in secret, while allowing a story of Jesus' resurrection from the dead to spread unchallenged. When he recovers, Jesus returns to his former work as a shepherd with the Essene community on the brook Kerith. Converted by a vision on the Damascus road, Paul of Tarsus meanwhile travels around the Mediterranean world and preaches salvation through the crucified Jesus.

Moore alters the story of Paul's arrest in Jerusalem and subsequent imprisonment (Acts 21-26) by having the apostle escape and flee into the wilderness beyond Jericho. He is rescued by Jesus who then takes him to the coast; Paul travels to Rome (Acts 27-28) and continues to preach the Jesus of his own imagination. The real Jesus, who has come to believe in a form of pantheism, meets a group of monks from India. The book ends with a strong hint that the ageing Jesus will travel to the Indian subcontinent for a stint of preaching there.

In developing his story Moore uses all four gospels, the Acts of the Apostles and Paul's letters as reliable and straightforward historical sources. Supernatural events, above all the Easter appearances, get explored and explained naturalistically. The appearance of the risen Jesus on the Emmaus road, for instance, turns into a dream and a case of mistaken identity.

The second book which we will examine is *The Man Who Died* by D. H. Lawrence (1885-1930).[7] As a novella, this work of fiction naturally has no footnotes. It portrays Jesus as saying to some peasants after he had supposedly died, 'I am not dead. They took me down too soon.'[8] He had awakened in the tomb and had simply walked out (p. 10). Some peasants took care of him in the days which followed. In the meantime the rumour spread that the body had been stolen (p. 22). After being a guest of the peasants for a few days, Jesus returned to the area of the tomb where he encountered Mary Magdalene. He told her: 'Do not be afraid. I am alive. They took me down too soon, so I came back to life. Then I was sheltered in a house.' He added that she should not touch him because he was 'not yet healed and in touch with men'.[9] His triumph was that he was not dead, but that he had outlived his mission (p. 25). Jesus continued: 'The teacher and the saviour are dead in me; now I can go about my business, into my own single life.'[10] He attributed the fact that he was still alive to Judas and the high priest. They had shown him his limits and had saved him from his own 'excessive salvation'.[11]

Jesus feared encountering his followers because he had 'risen' differently from what they had expected (p. 28). He had, however, instructed Magdalene beforehand to return on the third day (p. 30). This she did, though other women insisted upon accompanying her (pp. 35–36). Jesus met the group in the garden but left quickly so that he could 'ascend' to his father (p. 36). He returned to the peasants' house until he was cured of all his wounds. Later, when he was departing the area he came upon some of his old companions on the road. When they finally recognized him he disappeared down a side lane and under a wall (p. 44).

Jesus then went to a temple of Isis in Lebanon where he was befriended by a woman who owned the temple. She believed that he was Osiris. With her help he tried to discover the meaning of earthly existence. He learned (with her) what love really was since he had previously denied himself sex. When she became pregnant he abandoned her with the words: 'I have sowed the seed of my life and my resurrection, and put my touch forever upon the choice woman of this day, and I carry her perfume in my flesh like essence of roses.' He then concluded: 'So let the boat carry me. To-morrow is another day.'[12]

Typical reactions to Lawrence's work written at the time of its publication were: 'If one forgets the impossibility of the book's postulate, there is much in it that is poignant and beautiful;'[13] 'So far as Lawrence's attitude to it [reality] is concerned, he seems to have come to the brink and turned away.

He has not evaded himself, but he evades Jesus.'[14]

Our third author, Robert Graves (1895–1985), is best known as a poet and novelist. But (with Joshua Podro) he published his reconstruction of how Jesus survived crucifixion as a factual, historical account. Yet in doing so he succumbed to the temptation to conjecture, fabricate and fill in details that the real evidence does not support. In their variant of the 'swoon theory', he and Podro generously supply information about the 'extreme sultriness of the weather' (which, together with the spikenard ointment smeared on the shroud, helped to keep Jesus alive in the tomb), and about the way he escaped:

> The Roman soldiers, hired to stand guard, rolled back the stone at night while their sergeant was asleep and tried to steal the ointment – which was worth several years' army pay and could easily be sold in the brothels of Caesarea. They found Jesus still alive, and the sergeant, when acquainted with the surprising news, let him go; being subsequently bribed by Bunni [the name Graves and Podro give to Nicodemus] to say that the disciples had removed the body.[15]

All of this suggests a novelist's anxiety to reconstruct a well-rounded story, although one must be grateful that Graves and Podro do not indulge a taste for *cherchez la femme* and arrange for Jesus to have a sexual rendezvous with a priestess of Isis (as does Lawrence) or Mary Magdalene (as we will see others doing). What is remarkable is the lack of reviews of this book as well as of the earlier and much longer book by Graves and Podro, *The Nazarene Gospel Restored*. C. F. Nesbitt, in evaluating this earlier book, said: 'One eminent scholar has summarized it as "misguided ingenuity unchecked by the faintest trace of common sense". It is difficult, if not impossible, to improve on that judgement.'[16] Nesbitt concluded:

> Devout Christian people, approaching this book with hopes of enlightenment and enrichment of spirit, will be completely disappointed, and students or scholars who come to it with expectations of help in the endless search for the real gospel will find little to reward their persistence. The general public

will probably brush it aside, if it ever notices it at all, with a shrug of complacency as just another book on the Gospels – and why so many of them anyway? Someone will perhaps lose money on the investment and it will soon pass into the limbo of forgotten efforts. It probably deserves just such a fate![17]

H. H. Hoskins, in commenting on Graves' and Podro's *Jesus in Rome*,[18] concludes his remarks by saying:

What drives informed and ingenuous men to lengths of ingenuity? Chiefly, it seems, the absence of a reasonable alternative. The gospel cannot be true. We Christians are dishonest or naïve. Supernatural events are *a priori* impossible, and orthodox belief is blindly opposed to the findings of modern science. (Now it is not geology or anthropology but, of course, nuclear physics, which proves that if Jesus had dematerialized at the Ascension, there would have been a shocking explosion!) The inquisitive can read all about it on page 5. But it seems a pity that in spite of all the modern means of communication between intelligent beings, such Pseudodoxia Epidemica should continue to bedevil us.[19]

Schonfield, Updike, Joyce

Hugh Schonfield caused a sensation in 1966 with the publication of his book, *The Passover Plot*.[20] He wrote as a devout Jew (p. 10). When Schonfield read the New Testament he admits that he used his own translation (p. 15). This leads him to some interesting assertions such as: Jesus was the first-born in his family with four younger brothers (Jacob [James], Joseph, Simeon, Judah) and two younger sisters (p. 52), and the Cleophas of the Emmaus story was the brother of Joseph, the father of Jesus (p. 182); Cleophas' son, Simeon, was therefore a cousin of Jesus (p. 245). Schonfield dates the gospels as having been written between AD 75 and 115, outside Palestine in a substantially Gentile-Christian environment (p. 228). Because of this late date they are dependent for some details on such writers as Josephus (p. 253).

At the very beginning of the book Schonfield explains to his readers the viewpoint from which he is writing: 'the main dilemma of Christianity is patent and stems from a creed which down through the centuries has so insisted on seeing God in Jesus Christ that it is in danger of being unable to comprehend the existence of God without him.'[21] A few pages later he also states that the 'fundamental teaching of Christianity ... was that in Jesus the Messiah (the Christ) had come.'[22]

According to Schonfield, Jesus accepted the title of Messiah and believed it to express his calling (p. 21). The title went back to the time of his baptism in the Jordan (p. 245). Jesus read the Old Testament to look for messianic passages, since he believed that it was incumbent on him to fulfil the messianic predictions (p. 43). He embarked on a programme calculated to fulfil what he believed the prophecies demanded of the Messiah (p. 131). These included facing a conspiracy of rulers to destroy him, and being saved from death by the mercy of God (p. 161).

In setting his agenda Jesus was aided by the Jewish belief in a resurrection that would entail a reanimation of the body to be in some way immortalized (p. 158). Given all that, his plan consisted in the following items:

1. singling out a particular Passover as the season when he would suffer, taking care not to be arrested beforehand;
2. arranging (with Judas) to be arrested on a Thursday, so that he would be crucified on a Friday (the eve of the Sabbath);
3. devising to be taken down before the Passover began (pp. 160–61).

Part of the plot involved taking a drug to give the impression of a premature death and having Joseph of Arimathea ask for the 'body' (p. 166). Jesus was taken down and 'buried' alive (p. 168). At the earliest possible moment someone went to the tomb to revive him. He regained consciousness temporarily but finally succumbed (p. 172). Later Mary Magdalene, who was unbalanced, went to the tomb. She was deluded in thinking that whoever spoke to her was Jesus himself (p. 176). Schonfield does not accept Luke's account of Jesus' appearance to the disciples on the road to Emmaus; the man who 'appeared' in John 21 was simply the stranger whom Mary met at the tomb and who had also 'appeared' to the disciples on the road to Emmaus (pp. 178–79).

Schonfield draws from (a) Robert Graves to assert that Luke's gospel depended on Lucius Apuleius for material about the disciples on the road to Emmaus (p. 177), and from (b) Tertullian to assert that Jesus' body was stolen (p. 171). Naturally, apocryphal sources such as the *Gospel of Peter* and *The Book of the Resurrection of Jesus Christ, by Bartholomew the Apostle*) are included as supporting evidence to construct a version of the events which happened after Jesus' 'burial'.

A Jewish reviewer, Samuel Sandmel, summed up the 'value' of the book thus:

> Schonfield's imaginative reconstruction is devoid of a scintilla of proof, and rests on dubious inferences from passages in the Gospels whose historical reliability he himself has antecedently rejected on page after page. In my view, the book should be dismissed as the mere curiosity it is.[23]

Schonfield's book occasioned a sharply critical commentary, entitled 'The Gospels Re-Written,' in the *Tablet*. Then followed an exchange of letters between Schonfield and the reviewer which were also printed in the same journal.[24] Other scholars like Herbert Musurillo concentrated on the factual errors found in the book (such as Luke's alleged dependence on Apuleius' *Golden Ass* which in fact appeared later than the third gospel).[25] John L. McKenzie noted a gross internal contradiction: '[The] Jesus of Schonfield is not the Jesus of the Gospels. In Schonfield's view, of course, the Jesus of the Gospels is entirely unhistorical anyway. In spite of this, whatever Schonfield knows about Jesus he has drawn from the Gospel.'[26]

George Moore ended his book, as we saw, with a firm hint that Jesus spent his last years in India. A variation on this *Jesus-lived-in-the-East* theme comes from none other than John Updike. In a 1971 work John Updike added to the stories that Jesus died far from the Palestinian area.[27] According to Updike, Jesus did not die on the cross but 'lived in a remote village on the northern part of the Japanese island of Honshu until his death at 106 years of age' (p. 213). He had arrived in Japan when he was twenty-one years old around the year AD 27. He came under the influence of the sage of Etchu who took him in and taught him many things. One teaching of the sage was that 'dual consciousness was not to be avoided but desired: only duality reflected the universe' (pp. 214–15). After eleven years Jesus returned to Jerusalem. There he selected the Twelve. Judas was one of the Twelve and had hysterically attached himself to Jesus (p. 215).

The kiss in the garden was typical – all showmanship and symbolism. Then, the priesthood proving obdurate (and why not? any Messiah at all would put them out of a job), Judas had offered to be crucified instead, as if we were dealing with some Moloch that had a simple body quota to meet. The poor Romans were out of their depth; eventually they hanged Judas, as they generally hanged informers – a straightforward policy of prudence. For Him, there had been nails in the palms, and a crying-out, and then dark coolness, a scuffle in which He overheard women's voices, and a scarlet dawn near the borders of Palestine. For the first days eastward, until the wounds in His feet healed, He had had an escort, He dimly remembered. Gruff men, officials of some sort.[28]

After escaping, Updike continues, Jesus returned to Japan via Siberia. He then settled in Hachinoe where he married and became the father of three daughters (p. 216). Jesus' grandson was 'the very image of old Joseph of Bethlehem' (p. 217).

Updike concludes his short story by contending that Jesus spent his remaining years as a healer. He never doubted that he was unique, the only son of God.

One family in the village says it is descended from Jesus. Many of the children have the star of David sewn on their clothes, and parents sometimes mark the sign of the cross in ink on the foreheads of children to exorcise evil spirits ... An annual 'Christ festival,' held on June 10, attracts many visitors.[29]

In the making of his story, Updike seems to have drawn on the Mahikari devotees, a twentieth-century group, who postulate a Honshu-connection for Jesus. The historical roots for this belief are probably to be found in the activity of Nestorian Christians in the East. But we are unable to find any scientific studies of the Mahikari or the related Mahikari Sukyo groups.

Donovan Joyce gives the survival hypothesis a new twist by linking Jesus to those who perished at Masada in AD 73.[30]

Like Baigent, Leigh and Lincoln, who wrote later, he disputes the accuracy of the canonical gospel stories since their accounts are sometimes incompatible with each other. According to Joyce:

> Once the Gospels are shorn of all the supernatural non-sense, theological posturings and vanities, philosophical speculations and historical and procedural errors which obscure them – thereby greatly impressing the ignorant and keeping the superstitious cowering in fear – the true facts of the tragic drama emerge with crystal clarity.
>
> The three most important [gospels] reveal that: 1) the historical Jesus was engaged upon an enterprise – the penalty for which was death – far different from his never defined 'mission', which apparently consisted of nothing more than a dash to the Cross; 2) Jesus was not betrayed but surrendered himself to the Roman authorities in a deal – made through an intermediary – in which Pilate released the 'notable prisoner', Barabbas, in exchange for him; 3) the extremely suspicious circumstances surrounding the entire 'execution' proceedings not only ensured that a living Jesus would emerge from the tomb, but demanded it.[31]

To support these assertions Joyce claims that he was asked to smuggle out of Israel a document from Masada – a document written on the night of 15 April 73. We are told that it was written by a 'Jesus of Gennesareth, son of Jacob' (pp. 10–11). A Professor Grosset allegedly asked Joyce to smuggle out the scroll, and supplied the 'information' that Jesus had a son (p. 12).

To discredit the passion narratives of the Synoptic gospels, Joyce asserts that the last 12 verses of Mark's gospel (16:9–20) are bogus. Since the other two gospels relied on Mark, they also stole the resurrection story (p. 19). Joyce claims that the Romans had two different methods of crucifixion which were never combined – the gospels conflated them in the case of Jesus (pp. 20–22). The Easter appearance reported by John 20:19–31 illustrates this false combining of forms of crucifixion, and constitutes the most flagrant example of gospel falsification (pp. 21–22).

Like Schonfield and others, Joyce places much credence in the non-canonical 'gospels'. He believes that many were as authentic as the canonical gospels (p. 23), but were purposely 'lost' after the Council of Nicea in 325 (p. 25).

Joyce notes that controversies have arisen over the years concerning Jesus' conception, and that people claimed that Mary was pregnant by a man other than Joseph (p. 41). In fact, Joyce asserts, we know quite clearly that Alpheus is the father of Jesus' brothers and sisters (p. 44), who number four brothers and at least two sisters. Alpheus is Jesus' real father (p. 47). Even the gospels identify Alpheus (the Jewish rendering of Jacob) as the husband of Mary (pp. 48–50).

To establish the motivation for Jesus' lifestyle, Joyce examines his links to John the Baptist. John's father was a Hasmonean, therefore Alpheus and his brother, Joseph, were also Hasmoneans (pp. 67–68). John the Baptist, Joyce continues, was killed by Herod Antipas for being a heir to the Hasmonean 'throne'. With John out of the way, Jesus would be next in line for the throne (pp. 82–83). Such a fact accounts for Jesus being called 'King of the Jews'. Thus we know why Herod was hostile toward John, and why later on the Romans were upset with Jesus.

According to Joyce who cites the *Gospel of Philip* as his source for the information, Jesus was married to Mary Magdalene (p. 94). Right before his crucifixion she anointed him with 'spikenard', which was reserved to Israel's kings (p. 101). As a king, therefore, Jesus made his (triumphant) entry into Jerusalem and went to the Temple to clear out the moneylenders. This action caused the Romans to react and kill some people, but Jesus escaped (p. 104). One of those arrested was Barabbas, who in reality was the son of Jesus (p. 107). Jesus' whole purpose was to reestablish the Hasmonean monarchy (p. 112).

At the Last Supper a plan was contrived so that Jesus would not die on the cross (p. 117). Before the Last Supper, Jesus hatched a plot with Judas to be 'betrayed' (p. 125). As events went forward Jesus was so scared that his plans would not work that he actually sweated blood (p. 127). He was then arrested and condemned to crucifixion for attempting to restore the Hasmonean throne (p. 130). While he was on the cross he was given opium (p. 121). The actual crucifixion was semi-public so that Jesus could be resuscitated (p. 131). This involved the cooperation of the bribed Pilate (p. 129).

Jesus was taken down from the cross while still living, and was buried in the tomb of a close relative, Joseph of Arimathea (p. 143). He remained in the tomb for two days. Once out of the tomb, he was discovered by his wife, Mary Magdalene. After being seen by a few followers he went to the monastery at Qumran (p. 156).

When the Romans began pursuing the Zealots after AD 66, Jesus fled to Masada. Accompanying him were his wife and a few bodyguards (p. 171). It was at Masada, where they all died, that Jesus wrote the scroll (p. 174).

Joyce's book rarely gives citations from or references to Scripture, early Church fathers, or other sources. He cites as authorities the already mentioned Professor Grosset as the one who possesses the 'Fifteenth Scroll', John Allegro's book *The Dead Sea Scrolls* (p. 137), and an obscure English theologian, John Bezzant, who asserts that uneducated and unreflective people often feel they are being put off when they hear talk of life after death (p. 148).

Joyce fared badly at the hands of reviewers (the few that thought his book was worth commenting on). *Time* magazine spoke of his publishing a 'preposterous pseudostudy'.[32] *Publishers Weekly* called Joyce an amateur biblical scholar, and wondered if the book was not just 'nonsense, breathless fantasy'.[33] John Breslin remarked in *America* magazine that a 'more ignorant or tendentious attempt to debunk the New Testament could hardly be imagined, but it will sell'.[34]

Baigent, Leigh, Lincoln

Almost a decade after Joyce, Michael Baigent, Richard Leigh and Henry Lincoln authored a book entitled *Holy Blood, Holy Grail*.[35] These writers claim that, since there are major discrepancies between the gospel writers, 'the Gospels can only be accepted as a highly questionable authority, and certainly not as definitive'.[36] They go on to say that the Bible is 'only a selection of works and in many respects a somewhat arbitrary one'.[37] 'The New Testament as it exists today is essentially a product of fourth century editors and writers – custodians of orthodoxy, "adherents of the message", with vested interests to protect.'[38] Basing themselves on a supposed letter of Clement of Alexandria, Baigent and his associates assert that the Gospel of Mark has been purged (p. 290). This is specially seen in the ending of that gospel where there is no resurrection scene, no reunion with the disciples (p. 293). They appeal to Morton Smith[39] who had claimed to have discovered fragments of a missing esoteric version of Mark's gospel in a monastery near Jerusalem (pp. 289–90).

The general theme of their book is that Jesus was the bridegroom at the marriage feast of Cana, the bride being Mary Magdalene (who is identified with Mary of Bethany and the anonymous woman who anointed Jesus according to Mark's gospel). They subsequently had a number of children (p. 285), including Barabbas (p. 324). Evidence that Mary Magdalene was married comes from the fact that unmarried women did not travel unaccompanied; therefore she must have been married to Jesus (p. 305). She was probably a devotée of Ishtar or Astarte (p. 305). A Pharisee with Essene connections, Jesus was not really from Nazareth since that place did not appear as a town until sometime after the revolt of AD 68–72 (p. 318). Jesus was, however, an aristocrat since the marriage feast of Cana was not that of the 'common people' (pp. 318–19). This is substantiated by Pilate calling him a 'King' (p. 320). Jesus must have done something to have incurred Roman wrath – that is why he underwent a Roman-style execution.

Jesus hung on the cross for three hours. Because of exhaustion and general debilitation he appeared to have died, but like others he probably could have hung on the cross for three days before dying (p. 326) In addition the crucifixion took place on private property with few witnesses (p. 328). What really happened was that his family had bribed Pilate (p. 328–9) who instead of denying burial to Jesus – the Roman custom was to deny burial to crucified criminals – gave the body to Joseph of Arimathea (p. 329). Joseph was related to Jesus by blood (p. 330). The authors describe the execution thus:

> With the general populace kept at a convenient distance, an execution was then staged – in which a substitute took the priest-king's place on the cross or in which the priest-king himself did not actually die. Toward dusk – which would

have further impeded visibility – a 'body' was removed to an opportunely adjacent tomb, from which, a day or two later, it 'miraculously' disappeared.[40]

Another explanation is that Simon of Cyrene took Jesus' place on the cross, as Basilides (a second-century Alexandrian Gnostic) claimed (p. 353) and Nag Hammadi scrolls (e.g. *The Second Treatise of the Great Seth*) attest (p. 355).

In the end our three authors do not want to make firm claims about where Jesus went in the years that followed his 'mock' crucifixion. Why was his 'resurrection' mentioned at all in the Bible? Its purpose was 'to place Jesus on a par with Tammuz, Adonis, Attis, Osiris, and all the other dying and reviving gods who populated both the world and consciousness of their time'.[41]

While Baigent and his associates are modestly careful about telling us where Jesus went after the 'crucifixion', they 'know' that his wife, Mary Magdalene, got away with the children to southern France (p. 373). There the Jesus bloodline continued through the Merovingians, the Carolingians and the House of Lorraine right down to the Habsburgs and other noble, royal or imperial families of today (pp. 373–8). Alongside this uniquely snobbish claim, our trio are confident that they have not 'compromised or belittled Jesus'. Their 'investigations' serve to replace the 'incomplete' figure of 'established Christianity' with 'a living and plausible Jesus – a Jesus whose life is both meaningful and comprehensible to modern man' (pp. 383–4).

Besides the people mentioned above, others whom our authors referred to in order to substantiate their claims were Robert Graves (an alleged expert on the tribe of Benjamin),[42] and Ernest Renan (who supposedly embarrassed the Catholic Church by his application of German methodology to the New Testament).[43] As regards those who had explored the Jesus-survived-crucifixion theory prior to them, our trio revealed that they knew the work of Graves, Donovan Joyce, Hugh Schonfield and those (whom we will discuss later) who alleged that Jesus spent his last years in northern India (the legend of the Kashmir connection).

Derrett, Divyanand

While the work by Baigent, Leigh and Lincoln won great notoriety,[44] another book, which was published in the same year and developed its own particular variant on the survival-of-crucifixion theory, created few waves. This was J. Duncan M. Derrett's *The Anastasis: The Resurrection of Jesus as an Historical Event*.[45] Essentially Derrett's 'conjecture', as he calls it, comes to this. Jesus 'entered into a self-induced trance after the crucifixion' (p. 45). Those who buried him took him to be dead but his clinical death was reversible and, in fact, was briefly reversed before irreversible brain-death finally occurred. But he had made significant use of his short-lived recovery. For after he revived in the cold tomb and had been helped out (apparently by the watchers at the tomb and the young man of Mark 16:5-7), he was able to commission his disciples. Shortly thereafter as a result of his sufferings and crucifixion he underwent final brain-death. He had authorized his disciples to dispose of his corpse by cremation and they burnt it outside the walls of Jerusalem. The ascension was a 'euphemism' for that cremation (pp. 83, 90).

In supporting this reconstruction Derrett appeals to an irony which he repeatedly finds in that 'artful' evangelist Mark (p. 63), who wrote around AD 50 (p. 10). His gospel was to be sung (p. 135), and received its first recitation around AD 55-60. (Why the delay in the first performance?) The crucifixion is seemingly dated to AD 40 (p. x).

Behind the New Testament words for resurrection, *anastasis* and *anistēmi*, Derrett detects Jesus' temporary revival from clinical death. Subsequently 'as a second thought' the Church applied the verb *egeirō* to Jesus (p. 1). Then the sense of *anastasis* as Jesus' brief revival got reclassified as his glorious and lasting resurrection from the dead. Here, of course, Derrett's argument simply passes over the traditional, *pre*-Pauline formulations which use *egeirō* rather than *anistēmi* and which go back to the first stages of Christianity (1 Thess 1:10; 1 Cor 15:4; Rom 4:25). The same is true of what may be early formulations embedded in Peter's speeches in Acts (3:15; 4:10; 5:30). It seems clear that *egeirō* is at least as old as *anistēmi* in its application to Jesus' destiny and no 'second thought'. Furthermore,

Derrett evidently holds that the announcement 'he was raised, *ēgerthē*' (p. 64; Mark 16:6) belongs to a pre-Marcan, perhaps long pre-Marcan formula for recitation at Jesus' tomb (p. 60). If so, *egeirō* was there in Christian language at the very outset.

In putting his case Derrett dismisses the appearance stories of a genuinely risen Christ reported by Matthew, Luke and John as 'almost entirely secondary' (p. 5). Their minimal facticity derives from the effect on Jesus' followers when rumours of his revival from clinical death spread: 'they began to have ecstatic visions of him ... That such a shock could cause visions, especially amongst adepts at ecstasies ... no one need doubt' (p. 109). (How does Derrett know that the disciples were adepts at ecstasies? The footnote reference he gives to Plutarch establishes nothing.) According to our author, the appearances reported in 1 Cor 15:5-8 were simply (later) ways of expressing belief in Jesus (pp. 97-9). He assures his readers that 'the earliest form of the Christian message was centred on the tomb' (p. 102). This simply glosses over the fact that the kerygmatic material on which Paul draws in 1 Cor 15:3b-5, 7 and elsewhere, as well as early formulations which Luke seems to have incorporated into the opening speeches in Acts, do not proclaim the empty tomb. At best it is only hinted at (1 Cor 15:4; Acts 2:29ff.). Mark 3:21, 31-33 allows him to speak of 'trances' (p. 55) which prepared Jesus for his climactic 'self-induced trance' on the cross. Derrett knows a great deal about what went on the in mind of Mark, Luke and the young man at the tomb (pp. 64-6). He knows, for instance, just how Mark saw the link with Moses and Jacob in the women's experience at the grave (pp. 102-3).

Derrett finds a hint in Mark's narrative that Jesus was not yet irreversibly dead when taken down from the cross and buried. According to that evangelist, Joseph asked Pilate for the *sōma* (neuter noun) of Jesus, 'but taking him (*auton*) down, buried *him* in a tomb' (p. 60). Our author sees something significant in the fact that Mark uses *auton* and not *auto* (*it*). Yet a few pages on, Derrett himself, when speculating about what happened to 'it' – namely, Jesus' corpse when brain-death finally intervened – repeatedly speaks of 'burying him', 'burying Jesus', and 'reburying Jesus' (pp. 77-80). Presumably Derrett does not mean us to find a suggestion in *his* text that even after irreversible brain-death Jesus was not really dead.

In short, Derrett misuses what data we have to support a conjecture for which there is not a shred of hard evidence. He practically admits as much when he writes of 'the loud silence of the gospels and epistles' about Jesus' life after his brief revival from clinical death (p. 71). Derrett himself points out how the ancient world knew cases of revival from apparent death. But that is certainly not what the New Testament reported the resurrection of Jesus to have been and to mean. Derrett suggests that the mortally injured Jesus, while dying of gangrene, 'in some way we do not know', gave the disciples the theological ideas (p. 128), which got Christianity going and founded belief in him as the divine Saviour. Derrett's 'conjecture' leads him to what can politely be described as a quite implausible suggestion.

To complete our run-up to Thiering's version of how Jesus survived crucifixion, we will look briefly at one recent exponent of the Jesus-in-India legend. With his 1894 book, *The Unknown Life of Jesus Christ*, Nicolas Notovitch fashioned the first part of the legend: Jesus, it was alleged, spent some pre-ministry years in India.[46] The second half of the legend was created by Mirza Ghulam Ahmad (1839–1908); in an 1899 work (in Urdu) he asserted that Jesus was saved from the cross, went to Kashmir and eventually died there at the age of 120 years in Srinagar, where today tourists are still shown his 'grave'. The whole story of how this legend was simply created (without a shred of evidence in its support), spread widely among a gullible public and still finds such latter-day exponents as Holger Kersten is splendidly told by Günter Grönbold.[47]

In *Jesus Survived Crucifixion*[48] Soami Divyanand offers a recent repetition of the legend originally fashioned by Ghulam Ahmad. Divyanand draws on Kersten's discredited book, *Jesus Lived in India*.[49] To assure us that for many years after the bungled crucifixion Jesus continued his mission in India (pp. 2–3, 103), he reprints a forged document that first turned up in Leipzig in 1849; a long 'letter' allegedly written to his brethren in Alexandria by a Jerusalem Essene, who 'reports' how Jesus, his fellow Essene, survived crucifixion (pp. 127–69).[50] For good measure Divyanand adds two further astonishing 'documents': a 'description' of Jesus by Pilate's predecessor as governor of Judea (pp. 123–24), and Jesus' death-warrant 'issued' by Pilate himself (pp. 125–26).

Like Baigent, Leigh and Lincoln, Divyanand (p. 35) also appeals to Morton Smith's edition of the *Secret Gospel of Mark*, a text which Smith alleged to have found and copied in 1958 (when visiting a monastery out in the Judean desert).[51] In recent years more and more scholars have concluded that the text, which no one else has seen, could have been simply a hoax perpetrated by the late Morton Smith.

Divyanand could be setting a record by including in his work three forged documents and relying on what is possibly a fourth forgery. Yet his *Jesus Survived Crucifixion* has been on sale at what has been reckoned England's most prestigious scholarly bookstore: B. H. Blackwell's of Oxford. Divyanand has, however, the merit of putting his finger clearly on a dramatic theological consequence of the thesis about Jesus' survival; it would 'leave no room' for Christianity's 'central doctrine according to which he died on the cross for the atonement of our sins' (pp. 2–3). In passing, George Moore drew attention to the same thesis in a dialogue about Jesus between Joseph of Arimathea and his servant:

> But Esora, thy face wears a puzzled look. One thing puzzles me, she answered, I cannot think what would have put it into his head that he was sent into the world to suffer for others. For are we not all suffering for others?
>
> The simplicity of her question took Joseph aback, and he replied: I suppose thou'rt right in a way, Esora. Thou hast no doubt suffered for thy parents; I have suffered for my father.[52]

The sense of what is theologically at stake, the link with India and even the connection with the Essenes, bring Moore, Baigent/Leigh/Lincoln and Divyanand together. But it is above all Barbara Thiering who forces everything through the eye of the Essene needle of Qumran. To her we now turn.

Thiering

The 1992 book that made Thiering famous or simply notorious rested upon and quoted liberally from an earlier trilogy, which purported to be scholarly but which has won no real acceptance from fellow academics. In *Redating the Teacher of Righteousness*[53] she wanted to identify John the Baptist with the Teacher of Righteousness of the Qumran Scrolls, in particular by reinterpreting palaeographical evidence and dating the relevant texts not from 150–100 BC but to the middle of the first century AD. In his review, Ben Zion Wacholder characterized her thesis as 'utterly implausible.[54] In the *Anchor Bible Dictionary* Jerome Murphy-O'Connor has summed up the scholarly consensus about the Teacher of Righteousness: he cannot be dated after the middle of the first century BC; any later identifications 'are excluded by the paleography of the Scroll'.[55] We ourselves have not found even one recognized authority on the Qumran Scrolls who has followed Thiering in identifying John the Baptist with the Teacher of Righteousness.

The second book in Thiering's trilogy, *The Gospels and Qumran. A New Hypothesis*,[56] took the further steps of identifying the Wicked Priest of the Qumran Scrolls with Jesus and of claiming that the New Testament people were written in pesher code (reading an ancient text as being directly addressed to the future generations rather than to those persons living at the time of its author) to record the ongoing history of the Essene/Christian community.[57] In a review A. R. C. Leaney described the 'theory' and her decoding efforts as 'fantasy. It all depends on unproven and improbable identifications, especially esoteric vocabularies, and the like. The author ... must abandon her dream world for ... historical investigation.'[58]

Instead of following Leaney's advice, Thiering pressed on to publish *The Qumran Origins of the Christian Church*,[59] which she believed to have 'proved beyond doubt' that the history of the Qumran community and that of Christianity's origins 'perfectly fitted together' (p. 13). As regards Jesus, she argued that he was crucified at Qumran but was taken down alive to survive for many years and travel around the Mediterranean before finally dying some time in the 60s. In a contemporary review F. F. Bruce commented that in reading the book he 'was asked to believe too many impossible things all at once'.[60] Nearly a decade latter, N. T. Wright of Oxford University summed up the common reaction to the final work in Thiering's trilogy: 'no serious scholar has given this elaborate and fantastic theory any credence whatsoever'.[61] Florentino García Martínez, now secretary of the editorial board for the *Revue de Qumran*, has described it as 'science fiction' and believed that the writer had 'completely lost contact with all historical and literary reality'.[62]

In her 1992 book, *Jesus and the Riddle of the Dead Sea Scrolls*, which Doubleday retitled for the British edition as *Jesus the Man: A New Interpretation from the Dead Sea Scrolls*,[63] the only substantial items added to Thiering's earlier trilogy are the claims that Jesus married Mary Magdalene, had three children, divorced her, got remarried to Lydia of Acts 16, and passed his old age in Rome. (Thiering's 'exegesis' of the Lydia story has to be read to be believed!) As we have seen, a marriage or liaison with Mary Magdalene was already endorsed by Joyce and Baigent/Leigh/Lincoln. In *The Nazarene Gospel Restored* Graves and Podro turned Jesus into the adopted son of Mary Magdalene (p. 98). Their *Jesus in Rome* has Jesus visiting Rome some years after his escape from the tomb. In short, Thiering's latest book, when compared with earlier works in the field, adds only one *new* item of 'interpretation' in that it asserts that a number of years after surviving crucifixion Jesus divorced his first wife and remarried. This book also stands alone, of course, for its 'method' by forcibly lining the New Testament up with the Qumran documents.

By using the 'pesher method', Thiering maintains, the Qumran community left us in code their story and, in particular, the story of Jesus – both before and after his near brush with death by crucifixion. As we saw, Venturini, Moore and, in fact many others, have theorized about the link between Jesus and the Essene community. Thiering is alone in claiming that this community left us in the New Testament an encoded version of their story. We saw how Joyce asserts that if we follow his lead 'the true facts' will 'emerge with crystal clarity'. Thiering is similarly optimistic about her 'rigorous, logical methods'; she is convinced that anyone using them 'must arrive at the same answer' (p. 3). But, in fact, her hypothesis about this coded community history, as Wright remarks, 'has convinced no one, whether Jewish, Christian or agnostic, with any pretensions to Scrolls scholarship' (p. 21). What we find in these Scrolls which use the pesher method (a way of interpreting ancient prophecies) does not 'correspond in any way to what we find in the gospels' (Wright p. 27).[64]

In the introduction to her Jesus-book Thiering expresses the hope that by decoding the New Testament and giving us Jesus' real story in all its chronological detail, she will help readers strip away the mystery and see him as 'a real, human, fallible figure' (p. 3). 'Fallible' presumably refers to the breakdown of his first marriage, the divorce and the subsequent union with Lydia. Thiering's account of what really happened, she promises, will open up 'a whole new understanding of historical Christianity' (p. 4).

In this article we have looked at ten twentieth-century variants on Venturini's original version of the Jesus-survived-crucifixion hypothesis. Several of them join Venturini by introducing the Essene connection (Moore, Joyce, Divyanand and, in her own spectacular way, Thiering). Most of our latter-day reissues of Venturini represent Jesus as living on for years after his brush with violent death (Moore, Graves/Podro, Updike, Joyce, Baigent/Leigh/Lincoln, Divyanand and Thiering); two argue that, although he escaped dying on the cross, Jesus passed away shortly afterwards (Schonfield and Derrett). As we saw, some of our authors despatch Jesus to Japan, Italy, or India, while Joyce lets us lose sight of him in the last days of desperate resistance at Masada.

In one way or another they all use or rather misuse New Testament books as sources. They also often draw on 'special' documents: on apocryphal works which do exist (Schonfield, Joyce and Baigent/Leigh/Lincoln), on forged documents (Divyanand) and on shadowy works which may never have existed at all (Joyce and Baigent/Leigh/Lincoln). Or else they claim to possess 'special' insight about the interpretation of well-known documents: thus Thiering turns her own peculiar decoding approach loose on valuable Jewish sources in a way which can only embarrass the real experts on the Dead Sea Scrolls.

Other sources show up in our new versions of Venturini. By popularizing concepts of the dying god and the divine king, Sir James Frazer and his followers supplied the mythological background for Lawrence to despatch Jesus to the temple of Isis and have him thought of as Osiris come back from the dead.[65] The shadow of Frazer's golden bough stretches out towards Graves, Schonfield and Baigent/Leigh/Lincoln. An old cultural connection, a fascination with the Essene community and the attempt to 'prove' that Jesus was one of them, lives on in the works of Moore, Joyce, Divyanand and Thiering. The view that Jesus was an Essene goes back through Venturini at least to Frederick the Great of Prussia (1712–86) (Grönbold pp. 112–16). A rather contemporary theme shows up in Derrett's 'conjecture' about Jesus briefly surviving crucifixion: the distinction between clinical death and brain death. Had Derrett been watching a medical programme on TV and so got the 'bright' idea of applying that distinction to the case of Jesus?

Among possible sources for these twentieth-century editions of Venturini one might have imagined later authors drawing on, correcting and expanding earlier ones. But from Moore right through to Thiering, except for Baigent/Leigh/Lincoln, none of them seems to have mentioned predecessors who had already developed the Jesus-survived-crucifixion theory. Were they all really ignorant about the fact that others had already been busy at this thesis? Or did they know that but refrained from making comments out of a concern to claim a 'new' interpretation of what had happened to Jesus?

Murphy-O'Connor comments on Thiering's *Redating the Teacher of Righteousness*: 'I cannot see that any of the canons of sane historical exegesis are respected' (p. 429). She and Derrett have held university positions. But those two are simply no better than the others in blatantly subjective appeals to 'evidence' or use of 'methods'. As wonderful pieces of literature, Lawrence's novella, Moore's novel or Updike's short story tower above the pack. Writers of fiction, especially great ones, have their own mysterious motives and agenda. But what prompted the others to reissue Venturini? The desire to produce a megaseller? Some of these reissues have reached the best-seller list (e.g. those by Schonfield, Baigent/Leigh/Lincoln and Thiering). Or, to echo Hodgart's remarks about Graves, was it their 'rich and steaming imagination' that led them to show 'contempt for normal processes of scholarship'? Should we discern in Venturini and his followers something of the same attempt to fill up the gaps that shines through the ancient apocryphal gospels?

Or dare we think that a dislike for mainline Christian faith or a straight desire to debunk the resurrection message fuelled the willingness to abandon common sense and sacrifice intellectual integrity? Some of our authors are clear that their thesis could destroy faith in a Jesus who truly died for us sinners (Moore and Divyanand). Derrett tries to salvage some credibility for the Christianity which emerged after Jesus died by gangrene and was cremated. Baigent/Leigh/Lincoln and Thiering vaguely hope that their stories about Jesus will convince people to accept more readily his genuine humanity and might even improve Christianity. But these and the other authors stretch the limits of historical and theological credulity much too far for anyone who has serious and scholarly interests in the fate of Jesus and the origins of Christianity. Williams' criticism of Derrett touches them all: 'That Christianity is the outcome of a freak turn of events after Jesus' burial, rather than the fruit of his whole life sealed by his death on the cross [and his resurrection], is hard to swallow' (p. 446).

Sandmel labelled Schonfield a 'mere curiosity'. *Time* magazine called Joyce's book a 'preposterous pseudo-study'. Wright dismisses Thiering's latest as 'farcical', 'fantastic' and an 'exegetical circus stunt' (pp. 28, 29, 31). But such books are probably review-proof. Schweitzer was right. Every year or so Venturini will continue to be plagiarized. Given venal publishers and a gullible public, there is nothing to stop this 'cultural' and commercial phenomenon – the perennial reissue of Venturini.

17

Why do we need to be saved and who saves us? – a Catholic perspective

I

In a Jewish–Christian dialogue on redemption or salvation it seems that one can begin with substantial agreement but will end with utter disagreement. On the human need for redemption or salvation, one can accumulate Jewish and Christian perspectives which look very similar.[1] But then the Christian account of how redemption takes place seems to imply that there will be little or no common ground with Jews about the divine response to the human condition.

First of all, how have Christians understood our common human need for redemption or salvation?[2] Right from the beginning of Christianity the problem has been defined in three ways. Human beings are oppressed by various forces beyond their control; they are guilty and contaminated; they are closed in on themselves and need the healing power of love.

Let me state in parenthesis that I am using 'redemption' and 'salvation' interchangeably. The terms had different origins and developments. But, despite those etymological differences, in common usage today their meanings largely coincide.

Oppression

From the first century and down through the ages Christians' need for salvation has been seen in terms of sin, death, and diabolic forces of evil as the primeval forces which hold human beings in bondage. In his letter to the Romans, especially in chapters 5 to 8, Paul presented classically this vision of humanity and indeed of the whole created universe groaning to be freed from the slavery of death, decay and sin. Chapter 7 contains the vivid passage on the person who wants to do good but feels helplessly imprisoned by the power of evil (Rom 7:13–25).

The Christian Bible ends with the Revelation of John, a book that perpetuates Hebrew apocalyptic imagery and envisions human life as constantly threatened by satanic forces of evil and death. Full salvation will come when the old order passes away and death shall be no more (Rev 21:4).

In the centuries that followed, Christians maintained and expanded this perspective on human life. Redemption meant an exodus from the bondage of evil, a journey of liberation, a new Passover which they experienced above all in their baptism. In his homily *On the Pasch* (composed between 166 and 180) Melito of Sardis left a brilliant testimony to this view of things which has its roots in the New Testament (for example, 1 Cor 5:7; 10:1–2). Melito confronted the experience of being enslaved by death and the forces of evil to proclaim salvation in terms of an exodus from that state (*On the Pasch*, 18, 102). In Christian worship this ancient perspective finds its permanent witness in the *Exsultet* or Paschal Proclamation which represents redemption as deliverance from slavery and the chains of death.

One can accumulate many examples of this version of why humanity needs to be saved. Christian art, prayer, literature and theology added images from warfare, medieval tournaments and journeys to articulate the human hope for victory over the forces of evil.[3] One thinks of the gallery of oppressive forces in John Bunyan's *Grace Abounding* (1666), *The Pilgrim's Progress* (1678) and *The Holy War* (1682). Earlier in the seventeenth century Sir Walter Raleigh (c. 1552–1618), apparently the night before he

died, wrote an epitaph which superbly expresses what it is
to live our days under the menacing shadow of death:

> Even such is Time, which takes in trust
> Our youth, our joys, and all we have,
> And pays us but with age and dust;
> Who in the dark and silent grave,
> When we have wandered all our ways,
> Shuts up the story of our days.

In our own time the Christian poet David Gascoyne (b.
1916) brilliantly redefined the oppressive forces which constantly threaten 'man's long journey through the night'. We
exist in a world where 'fear and greed are sovereign lords'.[4]

Whether we look at our homes, our places of work, our cities,
our countries or the international order of things, 'fear and greed
are sovereign lords'. Fear of the bomb, fear of war, fear of geno-
cide, fear of debilitating illness, fear of poverty – that fear merely
writes large the fear which can drive people to destroy themselves and others in the quiet desperation of their private lives. It
is the same with the greed that inspires the international drug
trade. It writes large the greed which can wreck families, break
communities and produce pervasive injustice.

This is the first reason Christians and many others have
given to explain why human beings need and know they need
salvation. Sin, death and other forces of evil imprison them
and threaten them with disintegration. They can feel themselves dehumanized, psychologically and religiously, locked
into a seemingly senseless cycle of birth, poverty and death,
or else affluent but imprisoned by the false standards of con-
sumer society.

A sense of guilt

A second reason why men and women are candidates for
redemption is their guilt. Sin turns them away from God and
from one another. They become guilty, and need forgiveness
and some kind of expiation for their sin.

To be sure, a sense of guilt and the need for forgiveness and
reparation can be dismissed as signs of psychological weakness and immaturity. They can be written off as hangovers

from a religious past or at least as signs of an underdeveloped personality. It is tempting to read the language of sin and expiation this way. This would be to belittle a central theme in the Hebrew and Christian Scriptures.

In a psalm traditionally connected with King David's double sin of murder and adultery, the king prays: 'Wash me from my guilt, cleanse me from my sin' (Psalm 51:2). The imagery from the ritual of Yom Kippur gets taken over in Christian Scriptures by the Letter to the Hebrews. The most memorable parable which comes from Jesus is the story of the prodigal son (Luke 15:11–32). Among other things it offers a superbly simple statement of real guilt and repentance. The young man does not say 'I've made some mistakes, but I'm back.' Rather he says: 'Father, I have sinned against heaven and before you' (Luke 15:21).

The lack of love

The lack of love, both given and received, keeps human beings in need of salvation. This is the third major reason why men and women require to be redeemed from their present state.

In the phenomenology of human conduct with which he opens his letter to the Romans, Paul speaks of people being 'without natural affection and pity' (Rom 1:31), or 'heartless' and 'ruthless' as the Revised Standard Version translates the phrase. Long before Paul, the prophets and others grieved over a lack of loving fidelity to a God who cared so deeply for his own. The law could be summed up by a wholehearted love for God and the call to love one's neighbour as oneself.[5]

Insofar as people lacked this vertical and horizontal love, the Hebrew and Christian Scriptures understood them to be leading unredeemed lives.

Two thousand years later, we still know – in all its new manifestations – the same problem. Personally we can be aware of how tempting it is to be closed to others and become preoccupied with ourselves by indulging a self-concern or self-satisfaction that perhaps fails to respect anyone. We experience even on a quite regular basis a Kafkaesque, nightmarish world of people who take our money and never fulfil the contract, of records lost by officials who do not care, of hospitals that do not deserve the name and so forth. How many societies are permeated with real social solidarity and responsibility? Then there is the even larger scene. Whole groups of people and nations can be fiercely, even murderously alienated from each other. A lack of understanding and love constantly endangers the very existence of the human race. At every level there is clear and manifest need for a love which can heal our deep and heartless alienations.

Such then is the triple classification with which one can put together the way Christians and so many others think about the human need and the human search for salvation. We face here an all-pervasive theme. One can hardly read a worthwhile novel, see a quality film, visit an art gallery or attend any religious service without being confronted with our radical need to be redeemed. To an extent we are enslaved, guilty and unloving beings. That state sets up expectations of salvation.

The Second Vatican Council took up the three traditional ways of viewing the human predicament, paying more attention to the first and third.[6] Not surprisingly we find this teaching in the very first document to be solemnly approved by the Council (the 'Constitution on the Sacred Liturgy' of 4 December 1963) and in the last document (*Gaudium et Spes* or the 'Pastoral Constitution on the Church in the Modern World' of 7 December 1965).[7] Whether reflecting on Christians worshipping together in various ceremonial ways or on a whole range of our common experiences today, the bishops knew one thing to be blindingly obvious: human beings need to be delivered from evil.

Gaudium et Spes noted 'the new forms of slavery' people face in our century and did not overstate the threatening presence of hatred in our world: 'We have not yet seen the last of bitter political, social and economic hostility, as well as racial and ideological antagonism, nor are we free from the spectre of a war of total destruction' (no. 4). Where that is the distressing prospect 'out there', the scene within the human 'heart' looks no more comforting. The same document, *Gaudium et Spes*, sketched vividly what 'the bondage of sin' entails – that sense of being 'bound by chains' and unable by oneself 'to overcome the assaults of evil successfully' (no. 13).[8]

II

Thus far I have focused on the *question* of salvation. What is the Christian answer to the question? Christian faith and theology have acknowledged the *answer* in the life, death and resurrection of Jesus of Nazareth. The three ways of articulating the redemption he brought correspond to the triple typology of the human predicament.

Human beings find themselves imprisoned and oppressed by evil. Jesus is the victorious king who delivers them. They are guilty and contaminated by sin. He is the priest and victim who brings them forgiveness and expiation. Both within themselves and in society they suffer from the lack of love. Jesus reveals and brings the power and presence of divine love.

These then are the three classical models used by Christians to express what Jesus has done as king, priest (and victim) and prophet. His redemptive achievement can be articulated in terms of victory, expiation and love.

In the history of Christianity sometimes one model of redemption has proved more prominent than another. The theme of victorious deliverance showed up strongly until the Middle Ages and has come again to the fore in our century. See, for example, Gustav Aulen's *Christus Victor* (1931) and the approach of contemporary liberation theology. The model of expiation, under the particular form of satisfaction, had enormous success in the centuries which followed the classic work by Anselm of Canterbury *Cur Deus Homo* (1098). Peter Abelard (1079–1142) classically expounded redemption in terms of love, even if he tended to reduce matters to the (supreme) example of love provided by Jesus.

In *Gaudium et Spes* the Second Vatican Council conveniently gathers together the three models for the redemption effected by Jesus.

> As an innocent lamb he merited life for us by his blood which he freely shed [model two]. In him God reconciled us to himself and to one another [model three], freeing us from the bondage of the devil and of sin [model one], so that each one of us could say with the apostle: the Son of God 'loved me and gave himself for me' [model three] (no. 22).

In general, *Gaudium et Spes*, the longest document from the Second Vatican Council, gives more attention to the redemptive struggle for victory (for example, no. 37) and the love that can transform the world (for example, no. 38).

Referring again to the *Exsultet* or Paschal Proclamation (a prayer of praise sung on Holy Saturday which in its present form goes back at least to the seventh century), the three models of salvation in proclaiming what Jesus' death and resurrection has effected are gathered together here.

This is the night when Christians everywhere,
washed clean of sin
and freed of all defilement,
are restored to grace and grow together in holiness [model
   two].
This is the night when Jesus Christ
broke the chains of death
and rose triumphant from the grave [model one].
Father, how wonderful your care for us!
How boundless your merciful love!
To ransom a slave
you gave away your Son [model three] ...
The power of this holy night
dispels all evil [model one], washes guilt away,
restores lost innocence [model two], brings mourners joy.
Night truly blessed when heaven is wedded to earth
and man is reconciled to God [model three]!

Like the great prayers of Christian worship, the Christian Scriptures endorse three models in expounding the salvation Jesus has brought. Even individual books such as John's gospel or Paul's letter to the Romans make use of all three models of redemption. In John's gospel Jesus assures his disciples 'Fear not, I have overcome the world' (16:33). He is 'the Lamb of God, who takes away the sin of the world' (1:29), the one who through love 'lays down his life' (15:33). Redemption understood either as victorious liberation or expiation or reconciling love turns up in the letter to the Romans. First, Paul praises God who through Jesus rescues us from being enslaved to sin and death (Rom 7:24–25). Second, Jesus' sacrificial death has been 'the means of expiating sin'

(Rom 3:25). Third, through the death of Jesus God has shown a uniquely reconciling love (Rom 5:6–11).

III

Here I have set out to define three fundamental perspectives on the human predicament (oppression, guilt, and lack of love), and the three models of redemption through Jesus which recur in Christianity right from its origins (victorious liberation, expiation, and reconciling love). To conclude I would like to sketch the disconcerting and even decadent ways in which some Christians have wrongly redefined the three models of redemption.

1) At times the victorious deliverance through Jesus' death and resurrection has been taken up in two wrong ways. Many Christians have turned this redemptive model into a conviction that such a deliverance comes only through literal membership in the Church and participation in her sacramental life. A faith in a universal liberation could shift its primary focus from Jesus to his Church.[9]

Faith in Jesus' victory has also fostered in some a convenient illusion of passivity. Such an attitude, however, does not tally with the call of the Christian Scriptures to express one's gratitude for the gift of redemption by sharing in the ongoing struggle against the powers of evil. No one could accuse the letter to the Ephesians of playing down the deliverance effected through Jesus. Yet that letter ends with a stirring call to spiritual combat against all the forces of evil (Eph 6:10–20). In our own century the Second Vatican Council reaffirmed that so far from encouraging passivity, faith in Jesus' redemption entails active engagement (see, for example, *Gaudium et Spes*, 37, 38).[10]

2) Then the pardon and expiation brought through Jesus' death and resurrection have been often misinterpreted to mean propitiating an angry God. The Christian Scriptures do not support the thesis of penal substitution, according to which the innocent Jesus literally took on himself the personal guilt of all human beings, was punished by a vindictive God (even to

the point of suffering the torments of hell) and so propitiated the divine anger against the human race. A tradition (which began *after* Anselm) misrepresented in such a way redemption understood as pardon for the guilty and expiation for sin. That tradition of penal substitution, however, has no basis in early Christianity and offers a monstrous view of God.[11]

3) Lastly, the third model of redemption can be altered by sentimentalizing the redemptive love exercised through Jesus, or by reducing matters merely to the example of generous love he showed in life and death. In such versions he becomes simply an heroic 'man-for-others.' The true Christian account of the transforming power of divine love talks rather of the 'new creation' brought about by God's reconciling love displayed in Jesus' death and resurrection (2 Cor 5:14–21). We find that fuller account in Dante's *Divine Comedy* which ends by praising the divine love that 'moves the sun and the other stars'.

Summary

Christians have used three models in describing and explaining the universal salvation which came and comes through Jesus of Nazareth. It is hard to believe how often that victorious liberation, expiation, and transforming love have been misrepresented. Yet what is even sadder is the truth of Nietzsche's gibe: 'His disciples should look more redeemed.' Saints are remarkably liberated, purified and loving men and women. Christianity needs more saints if its faith in the salvation brought by Jesus is to prove more credible. Whenever his disciples do look redeemed, then their version of Jesus' answer to the suffering human condition can be heard and believed. At the end of the day, it can only be the presence of true holiness that lends real credibility to the Christian account of salvation.

18

Power made perfect in weakness: 2 Corinthians 12:9-10

In his form-critical and *religionsgeschichtlich* analysis of 2 Corinthians 12:7-10 Hans Dieter Betz shows how this key passage can affect and even determine one's interpretation of the whole letter.[1] Within these four verses the apostle's references to 'power' and 'weakness', while obviously touching the substance of his meaning, may leave our exegetical heads spinning. Let us look first at the basic options open to exegetes in dealing with these notions.

I

What does Paul intend by the 'power' which coincides with his 'weakness' (v. 10) or – as he puts it a verse earlier – the 'power' which 'is made perfect' in 'weakness'? Does he simply mean that the situation of 'weakness' brings some previously hidden power to his own notice and that of others? In other words, is he alerting us to the (personal and public) *revelatory function* of 'weakness'? Or does Paul understand this 'power' to increase or even first become available in the face of 'weakness'? In that case the apostle would be affirming something about the order of *ontological reality*. In brief, is Paul speaking primarily about the order of knowledge (his own knowledge and that of others) or

about the order of reality? A third possibility is that he thinks of
both orders. Under circumstances of 'weakness' something happens (power intervenes), and both Paul and others become aware
of this new development.

Among exegetes Alfred Plummer in the *International
Criticial Commentary* stands out by his insistence on the revelatory function of 'weakness' – to the explicit exclusion of
any 'ontological' explanation. His interpretation reflects a
dialectic between hiddenness and revelation, between superficial appearances and what man must be 'taught'. He comments on v. 9 as follows: 'Where human strength abounds, the
effects of Divine power may be *overlooked* ... Where it is
manifest that man was powerless, God's power becomes, *not
more real, but more evident.*' His exegesis of v. 10 continues
to expound this notion of Christ's power becoming 'conspicu-
ous' in weaknesses: 'Experience has *taught* him [sc. Paul],
and has *taught* those who have been witnesses of his work,
how much he can accomplish when he is *apparently* disabled
by his infirmities and afflictions' (italics mine).[2]

Rudolf Bultmann in his *Theology of the New Testament*
apparently favours such as 'revelatory' interpretation for 2
Cor 12:9. When discussing 'the origins of righteousness' he
invokes this verse and explains that God's grace does not
come to man as 'a prop for his failing strength, but as the
decisive question: Will you surrender, utterly surrender, to
God's dealing – will you know yourself to be a sinner before
God?'[3] This searching question intervenes to make man aware
of his real situation. Later Bultmann argues that 'Paul's dictum "for power comes in weakness to perfection" (II Cor 12:9)
is spoken as a basic principle and holds true for any "weakness".' Through 'the understanding of suffering learned
beneath the cross ... the believer's sufferings have become
transparent to him'.[4] In the encounter with suffering the
believer becomes 'aware of his weakness and insignificance'
and 'learns' the truth of man's reliance upon God.[5]

In opposition to such a revelatory explanation other scholars
adopt a more or less 'ontological' view of 2 Cor 12:9f. Thus in
his paper on 'God's Righteousness in Paul' Ernst Käsemann
maintains: 'According to II Cor 12:9 and 13:3f., God's *power*
operates at the same time as a *gift* within us.'[6] We will return

later to other aspects of Käsemann's exegesis. For the moment, I wish simply to draw attention to the fact that here its trend is heavily 'ontological'. In the ninth edition of the Meyer commentary on 2 Corinthians, H. Windisch shows himself partial to a basically similar view. He comments on 12:9b, 'At the cost of his own weakness Paul draws down upon himself Christ's power. The renunciation of his own worth, the humble and open confessions of his own helplessness is thus the pre-condition for the entrance of this heavenly reality into him.'[7] Windisch's interpretation carries him beyond Käsemann: the humble admission of weakness constitutes both a moral duty and a pre-condition for the communication of divine power. We will come back to this point. It is enough here to note that for Windisch the 'power' which comes to fulfilment in 'weakness' forms an actual force communicated in different degrees. In his *Paulus und Christus* he draws the conclusion that the 'power increases proportionate to the suffering (*je mehr Leiden, desto mehr Kraft*)'.[8] A further comment on 2 Cor 12:9 makes this 'physical' interpretation of the apostle's words startlingly clear. For Paul 'the situations and circumstances of weakness are especially the occasions in which he feels the divine power of Christ streaming into himself and incarnating itself in his own person.'[9]

R. H. Strachan accepts much the same explanation in the *Moffatt New Testament Commentary*, albeit Pelagian implications surface in his remarks. Heavenly help provides an alternative source for the apostle's energy when his own strength fails. 'Grace', Strachan writes, 'indicates not only "favour" but power; exerting its fullest power when human incapacity is at its meanest and weakest. The source of Paul's heroic energy and missionary fervour is found in the "grace of God", which is heavenly strength bestowed on men at those moments when they need it most, and can contribute none of their own.'[10]

This quick glance at some past interpretations leaves us with three important issues. Should we accept the view of Bultmann and others that Paul wishes to formulate a general principle which remains valid for any 'weakness'? Second, what logic controls the connection between 'weakness' and 'power'? Is 'weakness' a cause or pre-condition of 'power'? Third, do Paul's statements about 'power' and 'weakness' concern primarily the order of knowledge or the order of reality? Are they 'epistemological' or 'ontological'? With these questions in mind let us turn to the exegetical details of our passage.

II

Paul refers in v. 7b to his plight ('a thorn in the flesh' given to keep him 'from being too elated by the abundance of revelations'), states how he prayed for deliverance from this affliction (v. 8) and, without explaining how this disclosure took place, records an answer which came from the Lord (v. 9a). This reply (the only words of the risen Christ found in Paul's letters) may include only ἀρκεῖ σοι ἡ χάρις μου. The following words (ἡ γὰρ δύναμις ἐν ἀσθενείᾳ τελεῖται) would then form a comment added by Paul himself to provide the theological justification for the Lord's response. However, it seems more plausible to take v. 9a as a single logion with two parts.[11]

We can conveniently begin with the second half of the logion and the verb τελεῖται ('it is brought to fulfilment', 'it is made perfect'). In 1 Cor 15:43 (σπείρεται ἐν ἀσθενείᾳ, ἐγείρεται ἐν δυνάμει) Paul supposed a two-stage process in which 'power' succeeds 'weakness'. Here the two notions are made simultaneous: 'power' is brought to fulfilment in 'weakness'. He then reformulates the word of the Lord and sharpens the paradox: 'When I am weak, then I asm strong' (v. 10b). Some scholars explain Paul's choice of τελεῖται as deliberate anti-Gnostic polemic. Thus E. Güttgemanns writes:

> The concept of τελείωσις plays a great role in Gnosis. There τέλειος is synonymous with πνευματικός. In τελείωσις the Gnostic becomes wholly πνεῦμα, δόξα, δύναμις. One must recognize that our passage is formulated in sharp antithesis to this Gnostic thesis. The τελείωσις and permeation with divine δύναμις comes about not in the sphere of the heavenly πνεῦμα which is experienced in the visions of vs. 1, but precisely in the sphere of the earthly weakness.[12]

Prior to Güttgemanns, Ulrich Wilckens had detected in the use of τελεῖται 'clearly one of the sharpest anti-Gnostic sallies which we find anywhere in Paul'.[13] In support of his interpretation Güttgemanns draws attention to the use of δύναμις and ἀσθένεια within Gnosis. The terms were opposed both logically and ontologically, the first indicating the heavenly, 'pneumatic' sphere and the second the earthly, 'fleshly' sphere.[14]

This interpretation supposes not only that Paul (1) continues in v. 9f the polemical argumentation which seems present in vv. 1ff., but also that he (2) adopts the terminology of his opponents and (3) does so in a way which enables us to draw conclusions about their position. Moreover, to make anti-Gnostic polemic our assured point of entry for the exegesis of v. 9f. would be to ignore the serious alternative which Dieter Georgi and others have offered in arguing that Paul's opponents in 2 Corinthians were Jewish-Christian missionaries.[15] In any case there is no need to credit supposed Gnostics with having monopolized the insight that δύναμις and ἀσθένεια seem mutually exclusive. We hardly weaken the paradox which Paul wishes to assert if we take ordinary usage – and not more or less elaborate Gnostic hypotheses – as the background to his statement.

Clearly ἡ δύναμις (v. 9a), as well as 'the power of Christ' (v. 9b), is used here synonymously with ἡ χάρις μου (which according to v. 9a is already communicated to Paul). The 'grace' or 'power' of Christ reaches fulfilment 'in weakness'. Paul almost personifies 'power' here. One recalls his name for Christ as the Θεοῦ δύναμις (1 Cor 1:24). Does Paul mean that 'the powerful (risen) Christ' reaches fulfilment in 'the weak apostle'? Windisch refers us to Galatians 2:20 where Christ is said to 'live in Paul'.[16] But that assertion of Christ's existence 'in' the apostle remains highly unusual. Normally Paul speaks of believers existing 'in Christ', who functions as an inclusive personality into whom they are incorporated.[17]

The notion of 'weakness' in noun or verb form occurs four times in vv. 9 and 10. In v. 10 Paul lists four classes of 'weaknesses' which he experiences ('insults, hardships, persecutions and calamities'). He has already mentioned the 'thorn in the flesh' which afflicted him (v. 7), apparently some physical ailment known to the Corinthians, the nature of which his description leaves obscure.[18] Without question, Paul understands his 'weakness' Christologically; its various forms are endured 'for

Christ's sake' (v. 10a). The apostle professes himself perfectly willing to 'boast' of his 'weaknesses,' so that the power of Christ (perhaps 'the powerful Christ') may shelter him (v. 9; cf. v. 5).

In 2 Corinthians (where the problem of weakness and power bulks large)[19] Paul lists in a unique series the 'weaknesses' which characterize his apostolic existence (4:8ff., 6:4ff., 11:23ff., 12:10). Dieter Georgi has drawn attention to the fact that apart from 12:10 all these lists include the notion of διαϰονία. (In the case of 4:8ff. the idea is carried over from 4:1)[20] . 'Weakness' constitutes a special mark of apostolic 'service'. Paul's work of preaching the gospel must not, of course, be interpreted apart from his Christology. The understanding of the crucifixion as the event in which Christ proved radically 'weak' forms the background to Paul's whole discussion.[21] In the case of the crucifixion and resurrection, weakness and power constitute an inseparable unity. By raising Christ, God's power was effective and manifested in the face of that ultimate 'weakness' which the crucifixion meant. In its turn the apostolic ministry undertaken on Christ's behalf involves participation in this weakness and power of Calvary and Easter.

Paul is far from wishing to compose a treatise on his apostolic office. His remarks occur in a letter in which among other things he confronts the self-portrayals of opponents. Apparently these men proclaimed their 'spiritual' power and boasted of their ecstatic experiences (5:12f.). Paul reluctantly takes up the theme of visions and revelations and lays claim to a high degree of such experiences (12:1ff., even though he declines to justify his apostolic authority on that basis. In chs. 10, 11 and 12 he explains his view of 'boasting'. He himself is ready – paradoxically – to boast of that 'weakness' which, by aligning him with Christ's death, brings him to experience the power of the resurrection. The 'thorn in his flesh' and further 'weaknesses' (whether physical or otherwise) fail then to serve as evidence that he is powerlessly under the dominion of Satan's angel (v. 7) and does not count as a true apostle.[22]

Some words of summary are now in order. Our passage may be paraphrased as follows: The power which is both effective and manifested in the resurrection of the crucified Christ reaches its fulfilment for the apostle (not in ecstatic experiences but) in diverse 'weaknesses'. When in this sense the apostle becomes and appears weak, he is in fact strong, effective in his ministry (cf. 10:4).

III

We are now in a position to take up the three questions posed at the beginning of this chapter. If we plan to arrive at conclusions by counting noses, then we can agree with Bultmann that Paul intends to state a general principle in the words 'power is made perfect in weakness'. According to Wilckens the apostle formulates here a 'thesis' which expresses the experience of 'the Christian' as such.[23] Schmithals suggests that in 2 Cor 12:5ff. Paul 'wants to be understood only as a type of correct Christian existence'.[24] Windisch speaks of 'the law' by which 'divine power, if it is to enjoy its greatest effect requires an organ afflicted by weakness'.[25] Karl Prümm describes as a 'universally valid law' the statement that 'power passes only through weakness'.[26] H. D. Wendland agrees,[27] as does Käsemann who writes: 'Every kind of service to Christ is governed by the law formulated by Paul in II Cor 12:9, namely, that God's power manifests itself only in the experience of temptation and in those who undergo it.'[28] In the face of this widespread agreement it may appear brave or perhaps foolhardy to deny that Paul wishes to enunciate a general principle of divine law valid for all Christians. But the following reasons convince me that his affirmation of power in weakness bears first and foremost on his own situation. The primary meaning intended is: 'My power is made perfect in your (second-person singular) weakness.' (This is not, of course, to deny our right to *apply* the apostle's words to the lives of other Christians.)

In 12:1–10 and 11ff. Paul is consistently speaking of himself – his visions, his 'thorn in the flesh', his prayer to the Lord, the reply he received, his 'boasting' about the 'weaknesses' which he endures, his being forced to play the fool (v. 11) and the signs that accompanied his stay in Corinth (v. 12). The 'general law' view supposes that in the midst of such autobiographical reflections Paul throws in a principle about the life of Christians as such, a principle which he (confusingly) repeats in the first-person singular ('when I am weak, then I am strong'). Windisch, who explains these words as well the previous enunciation ('power is brought to fulfillment in weakness') as generally valid gnomic principles, points to the use of 'the present tense as well as the lack of a μου (with δύναμις)'.[29] There is, however, no real cause to read some 'gnomic' value into the present tense of τελεῖται. It would be surprising to find another tense in the explanatory statement which follows the words 'my grace is sufficient for you'. The absence of a μου with δύναμις (at least in the better reading) can scarcely prove significant, as 'power' functions here synonymously with 'my grace' and will be used personally in the second half of the verse ('that the power of Christ may rest upon me'). Furthermore, v. 9a exhibits a chiastic structure (ABC, CBA) which presumably operates to tie in the second half more closely with the first half and thus render its meaning personal.

A	ἀρκεῖ	C	ἡ γὰρ δύναμις
B	σοι	B	ἐν ἀσθενείᾳ
C	ἡ χάρις μου.	A	τελεῖται.

'My grace' and hence 'power' must be understood with respect to Paul's own person, if we accept Käsemann's suggestion that χάρις is here used in the particular sense of Paul's χάρισμα as an apostle, that specific grace calling Paul to his ministry.[30] What concerns Paul in 12:9a is his own apostleship, not other χαρίσματα. Elsewhere he lists and reflects on various χαρίσματα; in 2 Corinthians he lists the 'weaknesses' which mark his own apostolic existence.

Finally, we can appeal to H. D. Betz's conclusion that in 12:9a we find not 'an oracle' directed to a community but 'an oracle of healing directed to his [sc. Paul's] person'.[31] This conclusion would seem to rule out the 'general law' interpretation of the verse. But if we move out of the immediate context in ch. 12, does this interpretation find support elsewhere in the Corinthian correspondence? Windisch refers us to 2 Cor 4:7 and 1 Cor 1:25ff.[32] When setting out in 2 Cor 4:7ff. the forms of 'weakness' which affect his apostolic ministry, Paul opposes himself to other Christians. 'Death works' in him to the spiritual gain of the community (4:12). In 1 Cor 1:25ff. those who believed at Paul's preaching are styled the 'weak in the world' (v. 27), but not in the sense of 'weakness' in 2 Cor 12 (the sufferings of the apostolic ministry). In 1 Cor 1 'weakness' indicates the social unimportance that attaches to lowly-born, ignorant nobodies (vv. 26ff.). Power belongs to God's (apparent) 'weakness' (v. 25) and to Paul's message delivered in 'weakness' (2:3f.). In 1 Cor 1:25ff. we do not find Paul stating: 'When you were (are) weak, you were (are) strong.'

Our second question touches the link which Paul supposes to exist between weakness and power. What kind of logic governs this connection? Some exegetes join Windisch in maintaining that the existence of weakness along with the humble confession of this weakness provides the necessary *condition* for the bestowal of divine strength. Thus Plummer comments on v. 9: 'The Lord's reply convinced the Apostle that this grievous affliction would not hinder his work; he may even have been convinced that it was a condition of success.'[33] Hans Lietzmann's paraphrase shows close agreement with this interpretation: 'Through this word of the Lord I have received the comforting assurance that my weaknesses are a pre-condition for my success.'[34] R. C. Tannehill explains that the weakness contributes by preventing man from confusing the divine strength with his own strength and attempting to rely on his own resources. 'The continuing weakness is necessary so that man might not confuse the power of God with his own power and lose God's power by attempting to rely on himself. Through 12, 7–10 we see that Paul views the participation in Christ's weakness mentioned in 13,4 not only as contrasting with participation in the power of his resurrection, but also as contributing to participation in that power.'[35] Those who favour such an explanation of apostolic weakness almost inevitably slip into psychological considerations and the theme of Paul's moral education. He is taught by experience and learns the lesson of patience. Windisch reflects that 'according to v. 10a being strong is the patience with which he [sc. Paul] bears all suffering, the energy with which in spite of all obstacles he performs his work.'[36]

How do we evaluate this view that Paul is in effect saying: 'When I am weak, that is the pre-condition of my becoming strong'? This view may command some respect, but it merits

dissent. Paul's words both in 2 Cor 12:9f. and elsewhere indicate the *simultaneity* of weakness and power. When he was
with the Corinthians 'in weakness and in much fear and trem-
bling' his 'message' was characterized by 'the Spirit and
power' (1 Cor 2:3f.). As his statements stand, Paul simply
asserts the coincidence of weakness and power, not that one
element occurs as a precondition to the other. The psychological trend in interpretation can distract us from the
Christological setting in which Paul sees his ministry. Far
more important than any moral education he undergoes is the
fact that his apostolic activity involves participation in the
weakness and power of Calvary and Easter.

Lastly we reach the question: Do Paul's statements about
power and weakness concern primarily the order of 'ontological' reality? Or perhaps he wishes first to assert something
about the revelatory function of 'weakness': 'When I am
weak, then I am aware of being strong and others are aware
of my being strong.' We have already noted that Plummer and
Bultmann favour such a 'revelatory' explanation for 2 Cor
12:9f. So too does Güttgemanns who repeatedly chooses the
word 'epiphany' in his reflections on this passage. The 'apostolic weakness', he explains, should be understood as the
'epiphany of the divine power of the Crucified One.'
Commenting on ἐπισκηνώσῃ Güttgemanns declares: 'The
motif conveyed by this rare word has its origin in the Jewish
language of revelation and meant there the epiphany of the
divine glory.'[37] H. D. Betz likewise describes Paul's 'weakness' as 'an epiphany of the crucified *Kyrios*'.[38]

However, it seems to me that such an interpretation of
our passage can be reached only by tampering with the
text. Various 'weaknesses' intervene to cause suffering in
his apostolic activity. The risen Christ reassures his servant
that his triumphant power reaches its perfection in the situation of 'weakness.' Power is given (in fullness) even as 'a
thorn in the flesh' comes to change Paul's situation. The
upshot is something in the order of revelation. The divine
coming with power leads to the 'epiphany' of this powerful
presence. This point emerges clearly in ch. 4 where Paul
explains that his sufferings occur 'so that the life of Jesus
may also be manifested in our bodies' (v. 10). The apos-

tle's 'boasting' serves to bring to men's notice the victorious power at work in his sufferings: 'On my own behalf I will not boast, except of my weaknesses' (12:5; cf. 11:30). Ultimately what I am suggesting is the reverse of W. G. Kümmel's position: 'Human weakness is precisely the place where Christ's glory reveals itself, and where it alone is visible and effective.'[39] Paul's 'weakness' remains first of all a transaction between himself and his risen Lord and then plays a role in the apostolic transmission of revelation. Christ's triumphant power is 'effective' in the concrete circumstances of Paul's life, and hence it is visibly revealed.

19

St Paul and the language of reconciliation

The realms of religious discourse and theological discourse are often characterized by the extraordinary use of ordinary words, and nowhere is this situation more clearly exhibited than in the letters of St Paul. The apostle continually tries – sometimes subtly, sometimes with alarming casualness and naiveté – to express the message of the Gospel in language which, while adequate for ordinary human affairs, remains quite incapable of handling the dealings of God with men. As a result, he is required again and again to force expressions that have their grounding in the world of men to do substitute service for the unsayable. An inevitable consequence of this situation is that, if we wish to understand him rightly, we need to introduce important qualifications into the rules which govern the use of these expressions – to the point where we continually hang precariously on the edge of paradox, if not outright contradiction.

The concept of reconciliation occurs in a particularly prominent way in Romans 5:8–11 and 2 Corinthians 5:18–21. Before investigating Paul's employment of the concept and the limitations imposed on our adopting his expressions, however, we must first examine the use of the term on its home ground in ordinary discourse situations. Only then will we be able to see why Paul might have thought the term an appropriate one for his purposes, and how far we can accept the consequences of his usage without landing ourselves in absurdities. If it is proper to characterize theology as the activity of paying attention to the religious uses of language, then theology – no less than philosophy – is bound by Wittgenstein's charge to 'battle against the bewitchment of our intelligence by means of language'.[1]

There are three main uses of the words 'reconcile' and 'reconciliation' that could be relevant to our purposes here, and we shall examine each of them briefly. They have to do, respectively, with (1) the acceptance of situations or facts; (2) the removal of contradictions or incompatibilities; (3) the removal of enmity or conflict.

(1) An accident victim may become reconciled to the fact that he will never walk again, or a diabetic may become reconciled to the necessity of taking daily insulin injections. It must be noticed here that what is involved is not just the acceptance of situations, but of *limitations*. A man does not become reconciled to winning a million dollars in the lottery. The element of struggle needs to be present: a medical student does not become reconciled to discontinuing his studies if he has not previously struggled against adverse circumstances and failed to overcome them. At the same time, there is also an irreducibly positive aura about the use of the term in these situations. Becoming reconciled to the facts is a very different thing from giving up.

(2) It may be the task of an insurance investigator to reconcile the descriptions of an accident given by several witnesses. A doctor can be asked to reconcile his position on the dangers of cigarette smoking with his own heavy smoking. An accountant may reconcile the statement produced by a bank with the different figures shown on some company's books. In all these cases there is a perceived incompatibility that must be resolved, a conflict that must be removed, but *there need be no personal conflict* in such situations. In fact, there can be amicable personal relationships even where differences exist that cannot be reconciled. Two politicians may be close personal friends, in spite of the fact that they hold irreconcilable positions on a number of issues.

(3)   A husband and wife can be reconciled after a separation
      that might have ended in divorce. (This is Paul's secular
      sense of *katallasso* ('reconcile') in 1 Corinthians 7:11:
      'Let her (sc. the wife) be reconciled to her husband.')
      Two families might be reconciled after years of enmity
      and dispute. A wayward or headstrong son can be rec-
      onciled with his father after a long period of mutual ani-
      mosity and rejection. The differences that are reconciled
      in this situation are often related to those of type two,
      except that here there exists *personal* involvement on a
      deep level. Reconciliation in these cases can take place if
      (a) one party in the dispute admits error and acknowl-
      edges the rightness of the other's position. A son may
      give up his dissolute life-style and admit that his father's
      disapproval was justified. Reconciliation can also take
      place, however, if (b) both parties compromise, or even
      if they come to recognize a transcendent value which can
      unite them in spite of continuing to hold tenaciously to
      deeply-felt incompatible opinions. This occurs when the
      parties agree not to allow their differences to continue to
      permeate and poison their whole relationship.

It is impossible to be reconciled (in this third sense) with a
stranger, or with one to whom I am related only superficially.
A man is not reconciled with someone whom he has angered
by colliding with him on a crowded sidewalk. Further, it
would be odd to talk of the reconciliation of corporations or
states (although not of families), because the dimension of personal involvement is lacking in such cases. It would be proper
to speak of the reconciliation of the *positions* taken by two
nations (for instance at peace talks), but this is reconciliation
in sense (2) above. In cases where such talk of reconciliation
seems less odd, the nations in question tend to take on the
aspects of families and become personified, as is often the
case in accounts of the current Arab–Israeli conflict.

A clear presupposition behind this third sense of reconciliation is that (i) there exist some sort of significant personal
relationship between the parties involved, and (ii) that there be
some sort of conflict or dissonance to be resolved. It is in this
latter feature that sense (3) of reconciliation enjoys its simi-

larities to the previous two senses. It is also presupposed that some sort of interaction takes place between the agents involved; it is not possible that one party to the dispute remains simply passive. A one-sided argument, in which one of the parties refuses to engage the other and remains indifferent to him both in dispute and resolution, has no element of real conflict. The resolution, therefore, can be called reconciliation only in a pickwickian sense.

What is *not* presupposed by this third sense of reconciliation is that the parties to be reconciled necesssarily enjoyed a relationship of close friendship *prior* to their state of conflict, although this *may* be so. In the examples given above the husband and wife were, presumably, joined in loving intimacy before their separation took place. The estranged families once stood on good terms with each other. The father and his wayward son loved one another prior to the onset of mutual rejection and animosity. What precedes the state of conflict, however, may be simply no personal relationship at all. Two officers who were previously unknown to each other could join the same army unit and take an instant dislike to one another. Their deep personal animosity might so disrupt the life of the unit that a superior officer could be forced to intervene to settle their differences and so reconcile these warring parties. Reconciliation, then, need not always imply the following three stages: (i) that the parties were previously on terms of close intimacy and friendship; (ii) that a serious breach led to their becoming more or less totally estranged; and (iii) that the good relationship was restored by the resolution of the conflict. Even where stage (i) is absent, we can still speak of reconciliation taking place, although Gordon Kaufman, for example, ignores this possibility when he simply assumes that these three stages are always involved: 'Reconcilation is the bringing together of parties who had become alienated and reuniting them; relations which had become strained and distorted are brought back to the harmony and peace and fulfilment of friendship and love.'[2] One could multiply almost indefinitely examples of this unwarranted assumption on the part of systematic theologians.

Let us turn now to examine Paul's use of the language of reconciliation. In Romans 5:8–11 (RSV translation), we read:

But God shows his love for us in that while we were yet sinners Christ died for us. Since, therefore, we are now justified by his blood, much more shall we be saved by him from the wrath of God. For, if while we were enemies we were reconciled to God by the death of his Son, much more, now that we are reconciled, shall we be saved by his life. Not only so, but we also rejoice in God through our Lord Jesus Christ, through whom we have now received our reconciliation.

2 Corinthians 5:18-20 runs as follows:

All this is from God, who through Christ reconciled us to himself and gave us the ministry of reconciliation; that is, God was in Christ reconciling the world to himself, not counting their trespasses against them, and entrusting to us the message of reconciliation. So we are ambassadors for Christ, God making his appeal through us. We beseech you on behalf of Christ, be reconciled to God.

Both passages clearly presuppose an antecedently-existing enmity between God and man in which man is the enemy of God. Clearly, however, the relationship is not symmetrical. While Paul seems to conceive the situation as that of man seeing God as enemy, God does not see man so, else he would not take the initiative, despite his standing as the aggrieved party in the conflict.

What these passages do *not* presuppose is that man *fell* from a situation of friendship with God into one of conflict and enmity. J. A. Fitzmyer is simply reading this sense into Paul's words by speaking of 'the *return* of man to God's favour and intimacy after a period of estrangement and rebellion through sin and transgression'.[3] Two stages suffice to account for Paul's language, (i) a situation of hostility, followed by (ii) a resolution of this conflict and a state of friendship. Romans 5:12ff. may deal with so-called original sin, but such a doctrine does not necessarily imply a fall from a state of original justice and friendship with God. If we wish to find support for a doctrine of the fall, we need to look beyond Paul's language of reconciliation.

A parenthetical comment about the concept of 'cosmic' reconcilition is in order here. In Colossians 1:19-20, for example, we read: 'For in him all the fulness of God was pleased to dwell, and through him to reconcile to himself all things, whether on earth or in heaven, making peace by the blood of his cross.' Käsemann sees this as a result of Christ's assumption of lordship over the world, resulting in a sort of cosmic peace.[4] It must be recalled, however, that only *agents* can be at enmity, so only agents can be at peace in the primary sense of those words. 'All things', on the other hand, must refer to more than agents, unless we are to attribute to the community that produced this hymn an animistic world-view far too primitive for the time. It makes much more sense to assimilate this use of 'reconcile' to sense (2) above, so that Christ is seen as making 'all things' *conform* to the divine plan.

There are two rather odd aspects to Paul's thought in Romans. First, he pictures our reconciliation as (i) having already been accomplished, and (ii) as effected by a third party. As regards (i), if our reconciliation has already been accomplished, it seems that the individual man need not do anything. As regards (ii), we must ask how Christ accomplishes *our* reconciliation with the Father. One can readily understand how reconciliation can be brought about through the 'good offices' of a third party, but it seems clear that the status of this third party must be acknowledged by both sides. If our reconciliation has already been accomplished, however, before we are even able to acknowledge the status of Christ, in what sense is he representing our interests in this matter? One might presume that since man is the guilty party in the conflict, he has no interests to represent, but even if that were so it would still be necessary that man be in some way actively involved in the process of reconciliation. If man continues to be passive while his 'reconciliation' with the Father is accomplished, indeed if he remains ignorant of the event until *after* Christ's intervention, then 'reconciliation' is here being used in a logically extended sense. Even if Christ enjoys an ontological status as the 'universal man' and does not need to be commissioned by mankind as its representative, it would still seem to be necessary that individual men make some acknowledgment of Christ's status in order for each individual to be existentially reconciled with the Father. The 'reconciliation' here spoken of by Paul as having already been accomplished, is then reconciliation in potentiality only.

These problems are compounded in the passage from 2 Corinthians, since Christ is not acknowledged to be a separate agent at all. It is the Father who emerges as the sole agent in the matter, and it is he (*in* Christ) who accomplishes our reconciliation. Once again man remains excluded from active participation. Even the concept of vicarious participation through Christ is here excluded, since it is the Father, not Christ, who is active.

Two further problems need to be mentioned. In 2 Corinthians 5:19 the phrase occurs 'not counting their trespasses against them'. Clearly 'trespasses' is used in an extended sense, since the vast majority of mankind lacked the kind of clear knowledge required for the malevolent purpose which is involved in really culpable action. For most, what was involved could only have been 'missing the mark' in the Socratic sense.[5] If this is the case, however, then 'reconciliation' as used here has an aura of 'as-ifness' about it that shows the usage to be at best metaphorical. One might think that this is an example of reconciliation for the sake of a higher value, as in the case of two men who decide not to let their differences of opinion stand in the way of friendship, which they perceive as a higher value. Someone might even overlook a serious offence for the sake of such a friendship, since friendship might be perceived as transcending the requirements of justice in such a situation. This ploy will not quite work here, however, for there seems to be an absolute (logical) incompatibility between the goodness of God and (moral) evil in the world, and one is hard put to come up with a value that can reasonably be thought of as transcending God's goodness.

Finally, in 2 Corinthians 5:20, Paul pleads with the Corinthians to 'be reconciled to God'. This almost sounds as though God were the guilty party and it was man who was being asked for mercy. It is likely, however, that the reconciliation spoken of here is meant in sense (1) above, at least partially. God has saved man, and man is being requested to be reconciled to this fact and to order his life accordingly. If reconciliation is meant in sense (3), then there seems to be an incompatibility between this verse and the passage from Romans, in which reconciliation has *already* taken place.

In one sense, it is easy to bring up problems *ad infinitum* concerning Paul's use of nearly every significant concept found in the letters. That this is to be expected seems obvious from the subject matter he deals with. It remains important, however, to realize what these problems are, for acknowledgment of their appropriateness in no way excuses us if we fall into the traps they lay for us. The *New American Bible, New English Bible, Revised Standard Version,* and other widely-used versions render Paul's *katallage* and *katallasso* 'reconciliation' and 'reconcile', but we need to recognize that Paul uses this language in a logically extended fashion. His problems with the concepts were not the same as ours, because his purpose was to communicate rather than to analyse. We must be open to this communication, and this means paying attention to the fringes of the concepts used. By realizing how the concepts may lead us astray we can come to appreciate better Paul's purposes in using the expressions in question. In this sense, some insight into the inadequacies of Paul's language of redemption may tell us more about God's work of salvation for man than the literal meaning of that passage.

20

On not neglecting hatred

In 1918, on the very day the First World War ended, Karl Barth (1886–1968) wrote of doing theology with the Bible in one hand and the newspapers in the other.[1] The Scriptures and the daily papers converge in presenting one real, if highly unpleasant, feature of our human existence: hatred.

The daily press constantly reports episodes of cruel hatred that affect individuals, ethnic and religious groups, and even whole nations. Genocidal hatred flourishes in almost every continent. Government agencies, lawyers and social workers gather statistics on hate crimes, and struggle with strategies to curb this absurd and self-destructive violence. Any current library search will turn up books with such titles as *Free to Hate*, *The Tyranny of Hate*, *The Hate Virus*, *The Dark Side of Love*, and *Bigotry, Prejudice and Hatred*. In his article on *miseō* for Kittel's *Theological Dictionary of the New Testament*, Otto Michel spent ten pages in reporting what the Scriptures have to say about hatred.[2] The Old Testament repeatedly shows how God hates evil, idolatry and other manifestations of false religion. Along with other biblical books, the Psalms bear witness to the ways in which the wicked show their hatred for the righteous. The gospels write of hatred in the present (Luke and John) and the future (in particular, Mark and Matthew) towards God's new community. The disciples of Jesus are destined to be hated (Luke 6:22, 27); the future, especially as the end approaches, will see hatred dramatically flaring up against them on their mission (Matt 10:22; 24:9–10). The opposition between love and hatred plays a key role in Johannine theology, with its series of symbolic polarities. Whoever does evil hates the (divine) light and refuses to 'come to the light' (John 3:20). The (evil) world hates Jesus (John 7:7; 15:18), God (John 15:23–24) and the disciples (John 15:18; 17:14). The cost of discipleship is clear: whoever lives in the (divine) sphere of light and love will be hated by the forces of darkness.[3]

Beyond question, hatred satisfies Barth's dictum and qualifies for theological treatment by featuring solidly both in the daily press and in the Bible. (1) But have theologians done their duty and reflected on hatred as a way of 'illuminating', for example, the love and light Christ has brought? What can we find on this theme in the writings of Barth, Paul Tillich, Karl Rahner, and other prominent twentieth-century theologians? (2) Are there useful entries on 'hatred' in the major dictionaries of theology and similar works in collaboration? (3) In any case, how might we analyse hatred? What would be the theological value of such an analysis?

(1) It may be astonishing but it seems true that the great modern theologians, by and large, have ignored the theme of hatred. The subject index to Barth's *Church Dogmatics* has no entry under 'hatred'.[4] That classic work of our century, which ran to over 9,000 pages, appeared from 1932 to 1967 and thus coincided with appalling events of hatred in Stalin's reign of terror, the Nazi rise to power, the Second World War and the opening decades of the Cold War. Surprisingly, as regards our theme, Barth failed to take his own advice.

His contemporary, Paul Tillich (1886–1965), did not align himself with Barth's dialectical and subsequent neo-orthodox theology, but came to follow a more existentialist line. His *Systematic Theology* appeared shortly after the Second World War, first in three volumes (1951–64) and then in a single volume. The subject index for Tillich's major work has nothing to report on 'hatred'.[5] The yield from Karl Rahner (1904–84) is similarly negative. The sixteen volumes of his *Schriften* (1954–84) have been translated into twenty-three volumes

(1974–92) as *Theological Investigations.*[6] 'Hatred' makes no appearance, either in the tables of content or in the indices.

(2) If we turn to dictionaries and similar collaborative works, we come across very little on hatred. The *Theologische Realenzyklopädie* (1976–) offers no article on '*Hass*' and the 1990 index for the first seventeen volumes does not list any reference to this topic. The third edition of *Die Religion in Geschichte und Gegenwart* includes no entry on '*Hass*' nor any reference to the theme in its *Registerband.*[7] The second edition (in eleven volumes) of the *Lexikon für Theologie und Kirche* (1957–67) has less than two columns on '*Hass*'. The entry remains solidly non-theological, being concerned with biblical and psychological points.[8] The brief article on 'Hatred' in the *New Catholic Encyclopedia* (eighteen volumes, 1967–89) remains similarly brief (only one column) and is mainly biblical.[9]

The yield from standard, one-volume dictionaries turns out to be equally negative. *A New Dictionary of Christian Theology* (1983)[10] and *The New Dictionary of Theology* (1987)[11] both have substantial entries on 'love' but nothing on 'hatred'. The *Lexikon der katholischen Dogmatik* (1987), edited by Wolfgang Beinert,[12] contains no entry on '*Hass*'; the subject index directs the reader to one solitary reference: the Old Testament's view of salvation means, among other things, the 'absence of hatred' (p. 236).

The third volume of a six-volume work in collaboration, *Sacramentum Mundi*, passed straight from 'habitus' to 'health'; the general index provided by the sixth volume fails to mention hatred.[13] A few years later all five volumes of *Mysterium Salutis* were published. Its 1981 supplementary volume offered a subject index for the complete work; the index did not list '*Hass*'.[14]

Some major encyclopedias and dictionaries from the earlier part of this century pay attention to hatred. The *Encyclopedia of Religion and Ethics*, edited by James Hastings, allowed 'hatred' just over two pages and discusses some of its psychological, religious and ethical aspects.[15] This contrasts with *The Encyclopedia of Religions* (1987), edited in sixteen volumes by Mircea Eliade, which has neither an entry on hatred nor even any reference to hatred in its index.

The persistent absence of 'hatred' from current theological dictionaries, encyclopedias of religion and similar volumes in collaboration is only to be expected. Since individual theologians have written practically nothing on the topic, it is not going to turn up in reference works. We can document its absence; yet one should try to fill the gap. How would we propose analysing hatred – from a theological point of view?

(3) In producing systematic analyses, many theologians have quite consciously drawn help from their philosophical contemporaries or predecessors. The difficulty with regard to our topic, however, is that philosophy has little to offer. The six volumes of the *Handbuch Philosophischen Grundbegriffe*, edited by Hermann Krings and others, contains no entry on '*Hass*' nor any reference to '*Hass*' in its '*Sachregister*'.[16] The *Historisches Wörterbuch der Philosophie*, edited by Joachim Ritter and Karlfried Gründer, which has reached the letter 'S', includes no entry on '*Hass*'.[17] The eight volumes of *The Encyclopedia of Philosophy*, edited by Paul Edwards, contains no entry on 'hate or 'hatred'; under 'hate' its index has two references: one to Empedocles and the other to the philosophy of education.[18] The *Enciclopedia Filosofica* in eight volumes, edited by Carlo Giacon and others, offers the reader half a column on '*Odio*' by Enrico Cattanaro. In the course of that very brief treatment, Cattanaro refers only to Empedocles, Tommaso Campanella, and the work of Sigmund Freud and other psychologists.[19]

It seems surprising that these major encyclopedias, which – incidentally – all have substantial articles on 'love', should yield so little on hatred and the history of its philosophical treatment. Thomas Aquinas drew partly on Aristotle to develop a treatise on the emotions or *passiones animae* in the *Prima Secundae* of his *Summa Theologiae*.[20] Associating love with hatred as its contrary, he examined both dispositions as belonging to the eleven species of the *passiones animae*. In Question 29 Aquinas devoted six articles specifically to '*odium*', reflecting on hatred also in other questions. In particular, he did so when considering anger. In the *Secunda Secundae*, which considers the vices opposed to love, Aquinas spent Question 34 (six articles) discussing the sinfulness of hatred – appealing to Scripture and the Fathers rather more than to Aristotle. The considerations on hatred proposed by Aquinas in (partial) dependence on Aristotle make it somewhat puzzling that the standard philosophical encyclopedias listed above both remain practically silent on the topic; if they do have something say about hatred (the *Enciclopedia Filosofica* and *The Encyclopedia of Philosophy*), they fail to mention either Aquinas or Aristotle.

What would our experience of the human condition, reflected at the popular level in Barth's daily newspapers, indicate about hatred? At least eight points call for attention.

First of all, hatred means deeply felt disapproval or antipathy towards someone or something that is experienced as disagreeable, fearful, unpleasant, loathsome or downright repugnant. The intensity with which someone or some group is unconditionally feared, loathed and despised can amount to saying, 'I wish that you do not exist but simply die'. Where love, according to Gabriel Marcel,[21] signifies desiring the immortality of the beloved, hatred wishes people ill to the point of desiring their speedy annihilation.

Second, hatred, especially intense hatred, entails a mysterious choice which cannot be accounted for rationally. Undoubtedly, motives arise for hating (and fearing) others: cruel and repeated victimization can prompt deep hatred of one's oppressors. But hatred is not simply to be explained that way. Many victims have freely chosen to act otherwise by deliberately following Jesus' call to forgive and love their enemies (Luke 6:27). A mysterious exercise of freedom is involved in the decision to hate. More than that, hatred often comes across as quite irrational and self-destructive. Here it differs strikingly from the contrary disposition of love. Where love goes *beyond* merely reasonable motivation in its choices, hatred goes *against* reason in its option for evil – something that Aquinas repeatedly grapples with in his discussion of hatred.

To hate someone is to desire that he or she suffers evil. Intending evil as such for enemies and *actively* seeking to harm, injure, or simply destroy them constitute a third feature of hatred. In willing and inflicting evil, hatred can be insatiable and implacable. As Aquinas remarks, 'no amount of evil will satisfy it'.[22] Unlike anger, hatred is not short-lived. Closely linked to this third feature of hatred is its fourth: those who hate can be ready to sacrifice much, at times very much, to inflict harm on those they consider their enemies. Experience shows how hatred can be prepared to pay a price and even suffer a great deal in pursuit of its objective: bringing harm and evil to the enemy.

Fifth, where its contrary, love, brings dialogue, and works to reconcile, welcome and unite, hatred brings division, separation and absence. It means moving away from something or someone who is perceived as repugnant and evil. Those who love make a gift of themselves to the people they love. Those who hate want to remove themselves from the presence of those they find utterly unpleasant and antipathetic.

Almost paradoxically in the light of the deep separation it effects, hatred seems of its nature to 'require' reciprocity. Experience leads us to accept this sixth point: hatred is not complete unless and until it is returned. Unilateral hatred 'lacks' something. Those who hate can feel outraged when their victims offer forgiveness and love. The disposition or passion of hatred almost seems to obtain a perverse pleasure from being reciprocated and so 'perfected'.

Two final characteristics of hatred are its sadness and ugliness. Where love celebrates with joy, there is something bleakly sad about hatred. The vicious enjoyment it takes when its victims suffer and die differs from the laughing happiness of love, in the way that evil differs from good. Hatred is triggered by feeling its objects to be ugly and repulsive. But there is something revolting and sickening about the way those who hate pursue their aims of harming and destroying those they deem to be enemies.

To conclude: we are well aware that hatred is not a pretty topic, yet the Bible and daily experience bring it solidly to our notice. Reflection on eight characteristics of hatred can help to fill out some aspects of redemption. The coming of Christ means salvation from hatred (Luke 1:71) and victory over it (Luke 6:22-23, 27-29). John's gospel and first letter present the symbolic polarities of hatred/darkness and love/light; in Johannine usage the opposite of loving is hating. Aquinas associated love and hatred as a pair of contraries within the eleven species of *passiones animae*. Philosophically one can speak of hatred and love as ethical opposites. However we care to relate hatred and love, serious reflection on the former can have the happy theological and philosophical result of not only putting the latter into sharper focus, but also of articulating the ultimate scope of redemption: Christ's loving victory over darkness and hatred.

21

Questions about Christ

A handy way into contemporary discussions about the person of Jesus Christ (Christology) and his saving mission (Soteriology) is provided by the post-Vatican II document of the International Theological Commission: *Select Questions on Christology*.[1] This Commission, whose members are appointed by the Pope to serve for five years, was established as an adjunct to the Congregation for the Doctrine of the Faith in 1969. Its purpose is to provide that Congregation and the Holy See with the consultative and advisory services of theologians, exegetes and liturgical experts representative of various schools of thought. Among those serving on the Commission when it produced *Select Questions on Christology* were such well-known theologians as Juan Alfaro, Hans Urs von Balthasar, Walter Burghardt, Yves Congar, Edouard Hamel, Karl Lehmann, John Mahoney, Gustave Martelet, Cardinal Joseph Ratzinger, Jean-Marie Tillard and Jan Walgrave.

In its latest document the Commission clearly announced that it did 'not intend to expound and explicate a complete Christology' (p. 13). Nevertheless, it did indicate many current issues and hence serves as well as any other contemporary statement to inform us about the state of the question in Christology and Soteriology. Without pretending to offer anything like a complete commentary on the document, I want to single out and discuss some major themes to be found in *Select Questions on Christology*.

Jesus and history

Right from the outset the Commission recognizes that 'historical research concerning Jesus Christ is demanded by the Christian faith itself' (p. 1). This was always true, inasmuch as Christianity is an historical religion which from its beginning has recalled and lived by what the God of Abraham, Isaac and Jacob did and revealed in the particular life, death and resurrection of Jesus of Nazareth. Nevertheless, from the end of the eighteenth century Christology began to be deeply affected by the rise of scientific history and, in particular, by critical methods in biblical research. Debates about the earthly history of Jesus have often occupied centre stage. Scientific history has emerged as Christology's most prominent dialogue partner in modern times.

Along with this special concern for historical issues, Christology has undergone a certain proper *humanizing*. From the Middle Ages professional Catholic theology tended to present Christ largely in terms of his divinity, and it was left to popular devotions to defend his genuinely human existence and experience. Thus the devotions to the Christmas crib, the stations of the cross and the devotion to the Sacred Heart witnessed to the ordinary faithful's instinctive attachment to the authentic humanity of Jesus. Since the Second Vatican Council the Christologies of Walter Kasper (*Jesus the Christ*, 1974), Jon Sobrino (*Christology at the Crossroads*, 1976) and other Catholic scholars have incorporated 'a return to the earthly Jesus' which the Theological Commission considers not only 'beneficial' but 'indispensable today in the field of dogmatic theology'. Our document frankly admits past deficiencies in this matter: 'The untold riches of Jesus' humanity need to be brought to light more effectively than was done by the Christologies of the past' (p. 4).

How far can historical scholarship take us in reconstructing the ministry and message of the earthly Jesus? The

Commission first recalls the *intention* of our basic sources, the gospels. They offer an amalgam of believing witness and historical reminiscence with the aim of eliciting or at least developing the faith of their readers. They cannot be treated as if they were ordinary, disinterested historical sources from ancient times. Further, the gospels do not provide sufficient data to write a biography 'in the modern sense of this word'. Nevertheless, 'we should not draw from this fact excessively pessimistic conclusions as to the possibility of coming to know the historical life of Jesus' (p. 2).

Essentially the Commission is making a double point here. On the one hand, we would not be justified in renewing the nineteenth-century attempts to write a life of Jesus. But, on the other hand, historical research can use the gospels to establish a good deal about the activity, message, claim and impact of Jesus during the last period of his life. Scholarly principles can vindicate the following conclusions. Jesus came from Nazareth, was baptized by John, and began a wandering ministry in which he proclaimed that 'the Kingdom of God is at hand', associated with sinners and outcasts, called disciples to follow him, worked miracles and taught some memorable parables. His violation of certain sabbath laws, cleansing of the temple and other 'offences' aroused the antagonism of some influential Jewish leaders. In Jerusalem (where he had come for the Passover celebration) he was arrested, interrogated by members of the Sanhedrin, tried by Roman authorities, and then executed as a messianic pretender on a cross which bore an inscription giving the charge against Jesus as 'King of the Jews'. This is not anything like a complete list of items about the earthly Jesus which scientific methods can validate. But it should illustrate the kind of material the Theological Commission has in mind when it notes how scholarly research can verify 'the historicity of certain facts relative to the historical existence of Jesus' (p. 2).

Ever so much more could be said about the necessity and the limits of historical enquiry. Let me content myself with singling out two items from *Select Questions on Christology*.

In the first place, the document insists on the unity between the earthly Jesus and the glorified Christ. Because of his 'substantive and radical unity', any Christological inquiry which limited itself to the Jesus of history 'would be incompatible with the essence and structure of the New Testament' (p. 2). The Commission rightly sees how this 'original and primitive synthesis of the earthly Jesus with the risen Christ' implies an ecclesial setting for anyone's theology at this point: 'We cannot secure a *full* knowledge of Jesus unless we take into account the living faith of the Christian community' (p. 2ff; italics mine). Our document goes on to state this even more strongly:

> The Church continues to be the place where the *true* knowledge of the person and work of Jesus Christ is to be found. Apart from the assistance provided by the mediation of ecclesial faith, the knowledge of Jesus Christ is *no more possible* today than in New Testament times (p. 4; italics mine).

At the same time, the Commission acknowledges the primacy of Christology over ecclesiology, the priority of Jesus Christ over his Church. Even though we will fully and truly know him only in 'the ecclesial context', 'Our Lord always preserves vis-à-vis the Church the priority of his position and his primacy' (p. 4).

So much then for the unity between the Jesus of history and the glorified Christ whom the Christian community confessed and confesses in faith. My second point is a tiny doubt about what our document envisages when it speaks of 'mere historical information', 'a purely historical image of Jesus', 'a purely historical kind of research', 'pure history' and 'a mere historical evocation' (p. 2f.). Is the document forgetting that historians deal with 'the remembered *and interpreted* past', and weave their own evaluations into the work of recovering data from the past? My doubts here are fed by the Commission's reference to 'the modern notion of history ... according to which history is the bare and objective presentation of a reality now past' (p. 3). This 'modern notion of history' in fact sounds all too like the approach of Leopold von Ranke and other *nineteenth*-century theologians who fondly imagined that they could describe with 'scientific', objective neutrality what had actually happened. More recently this positivist understanding of history has been widely abandoned and at least some proper role of *subjective* appropriation and interpretation has been acknowledged. Perhaps Willi Marxsen in his weaker moments exemplifies 'the modern notion of history' which the Commission speaks of and objects to.

Perhaps I am being unduly sensitive on this issue. But when dealing with the earthly Jesus (and, for that matter, other persons and events in past history), I certainly want to fight shy of language which could suggest anything like a separation between the bare facts, on the one hand, and someone's vision or interpretation of these facts, on the other. Right from the stage of sense experience a totally uninterpreted grasp of anyone or anything is impossible. From their earliest contacts with Jesus the first disciples were interpreting him. The Church traditions and then the Gospel-writers (rightly and inevitably) carried on this process of interpretation. There never was mere historical information about Jesus in the sense of some set of objective, uninterpreted facts about him.

Nicaea, Chalcedon and beyond

The Commission recalls the work of the early Church Councils which aimed to state the double reality of Christ's being 'true God and true man', so that one aspect would not prevail at the expense of the other.

Our document correctly argues that the doctrine of Christ's divinity developed from the biblical revelation and, so far from being a product of Greek philosophy, was an affront to major philosophical schools. With their strong sense of divine transcendence the Platonists regarded a divine incarnation as 'unthinkable' (p. 5; cf. p. 7). The Stoics with their doctrine of divine immanence could accept the hypostatic union but not that distinction between Christ's two natures which was entailed by the divine transcendence (pp. 5, 6f.).

There are several important points recalled by the Commission when it endorses the Christological teachings of the early Councils. It notes, for example, the 'in-depth interaction between lived experience and the process whereby theological clarification was achieved' (p. 5). Theological reflection and doctrines sprang from the immediacy of a personal relationship with the Son of God, and were intended in their turn to clarify and promote the faith which constituted that relationship. Then and now teachings *about* Christ come from a living experience *of* him and should feed back into that experience.

Select Questions on Christology also recognizes not only that the Chalcedonian definition about the two natures in one person did 'not pretend to offer an exhaustive answer' to the question of the union of humanity and divinity in Christ (p. 7), but also that the Council's formula needs to be enriched 'through more soteriological perspectives' (p. 11). Explicitly as such the definition gave only a passing nod to human redemption (when it spoke of Jesus Christ as being 'begotten for us men and for our salvation'). To put matters in an extreme form: everything that Chalcedon affirmed could still be valid if Jesus had been miraculously snatched away from this world and never died on Calvary to save us. At best, his death is only hinted at in phrases like 'truly man' and 'like us in all respects, apart from sin'. Chalcedon's formula passes over in silence the resurrection which took place 'for our justification' (Rom. 4:25). The Theological Commission helpfully observes that the Chalcedonian Christology must be supplemented by an adequate Soteriology. I will return to this issue shortly.

A final point which concerns Chalcedon's terminology: *Select Questions on Christology* makes the astonishing claim that 'terms such as "nature" and "person" which the Fathers of the Council use undoubtedly retain the same meaning in today's parlance'. Yet then at once the Commission goes on to summarize what is very often denoted today by 'human nature' and 'person' (p. 9). Perhaps I am missing something here. But the meaning shifts noted in the second half of the paragraph undercut the claim that 'nature' and 'person' retain 'the same meaning in today's parlance'. Doubtless there is a healthy family resemblance between the fifth century's use and meaning of these terms and what we find today, but hardly an identity.[2]

Soteriology

One of the best passages in our document is that which lists the severe difficulties which many people experience in understanding what salvation through Christ is about. Let me quote it in full.

Today many ... recoil from any notion of salvation which would imply a heteronomy in the project of life. They take exception to what they regard as the purely individualistic character of Christian salvation. The promise of blessedness to come seems to them a utopia which distracts people away from their genuine obligations which, in their view, are all confined to this world. They want to know what it is that mankind had to be redeemed from, and to whom the price of salvation had to be paid. They grow indignant at the idea that God could have exacted the blood of an innocent person, a notion in which they detect a streak of sadism. They argue against what is known as 'vicarious satisfaction' (that is, through a mediator) by saying that this mode of satisfaction is ethically impossible. If it is true that every conscience is autonomous, they argue, no conscience can be freed by another. Finally, some of our contemporaries lament the fact that they cannot find in the life of the Church and of the faithful the lived expression of the mystery of liberation which is proclaimed (pp. 9–10; translation corrected).

Given the scope of its document, the Theological Commission could not (and could not be expected to) respond in detail to all of these difficulties. But it was good to see a frank and fair account of the genuine problems which any treatment of Soteriology must confront.

What does our document have to say about Soteriology?[3] It opens its section on 'Christology and Soteriology' with the clear affirmation that 'the person of Jesus Christ cannot be separated from the deed of redemption. The benefits of salvation are inseparable from the divinity of Jesus Christ.' No one could quarrel with the mild verdict on the past: 'Some theological speculations have failed adequately to preserve this intimate connection between Christology and Soteriology' (p. 12). Some Protestant theologians from Philipp Melanchthon (1497–1560) to Rudolf Bultmann (1884–1976) could be so preoccupied with what Christ did and does 'for us' that they practically reduced Christology to Soteriology. On the Catholic side the opposite situation often prevailed. Christology took pride of place and Soteriology got treated subsequently – sometimes very briefly.

The Theological Commission develops its own brief sketch of Soteriology on the basis of the human intentions of Jesus when faced with his passion and death. Our document tackles the issue on two levels: that of principle and that of the ascertainable facts. In principle, if Jesus 'lost hope in his own mission' and saw his passion simply as 'a failure and a shipwreck', then

> his death could not be construed then, and cannot be construed now, as the definitive act in the economy of salvation. A death undergone in a purely passive manner could not be a 'Christological' saving event. It must be the consequence, the willed consequence, of the obedience and love of Jesus making a gift of himself. It must be taken up in a complex act, at once active and passive (p. 13).

At the level of the ascertainable facts the Commission points to items in the gospel record which indicate how Jesus interpreted his coming death. Our document speaks of Jesus' 'fundamental attitude' of 'existence-for-others' which was given 'more vitality and concreteness' as questions emerged for Jesus and events unfolded. Among the questions which came to confront him were these:

> Would the Father want to establish his reign, if Jesus should meet with failure, with death, nay, with the cruel death of martyrdom? Would the Father, in the end, ensure the saving efficacy of what Jesus would have suffered by 'dying for others'?

Jesus 'gathered affirmative answers to these questions', and hence went to death confidently reasserting at the Last Supper 'the promise and presence of the eschatological salvation' (p. 14).

To put matters bluntly, this approach – very correctly, I believe – appears to acknowledge a certain shift in perspective on the part of the earthly Jesus. Historically his fundamental attitude of self-giving led Jesus from an awareness that through his preaching, actions and personal presence he was establishing God's final salvation to a subsequent acceptance of his victim-role. The Jesus who began by proclaiming the eschatological reign of God ended by obediently agreeing to be a victim whose death and vindication would bring salvation. At least on pp. 13–15 (section IV B) our document seems to allow for some shift or at least clarification in Jesus' mind about the specific shape of his vocation and destiny. This section which suggested some influence from Heinz Schürmann is followed by a section (pp. 15–19, IV C) in which I could not fail to detect the hand of Hans Urs von Balthasar and which contained several themes that invite a little scrutiny.

To begin with, this section maintains that 'Jesus knows that he is to die for all, for our sins; in this perspective he lives out his *entire* earthly life' (p. 16f.; italics mine). At the very least this statement stands in a certain tension with what we have just seen.

Second, although I welcomed the document's readiness to defend one of the basic models for redemption, vicarious expiation – which is better called representative expiation – I was sorry to see it expounded as if it amounted to expiatory *substitution*. Space does not permit me to discuss matters in detail.[4] Let me pick out only two points in the treatment of this interpretation of redemption as expiatory substitution.

The earthly Jesus is credited with 'the will to take on himself as a proxy the sufferings (cf. Gal. 3:13) and the sin of the human kind (cf. John 1:29; 2 Cor 5:21)' (p. 16). There are several questionable items here. The two texts from St Paul indicate nothing about the intentions of the earthly Jesus. It is a bold man indeed who would use the statement in John's gospel ('Behold, the Lamb of God, who takes away the sin of the world') to support a claim about the historical intentions of the earthly Jesus. Further, the 'for us' of Galatians 3:13 points not to a proxy suffering 'in our place' but to a representative suffering for our sake and to our advantage. John 1:29 speaks of Christ not as assuming or as 'taking *on*' the sin of the world but as taking it *away*. Paul's dense statement in 2 Corinthians 5:21 ('For our sake he [God] made him [Christ] to be sin who knew no sin') demands unpacking, and we can do so in any of the following ways: 'God made the innocent Christ a sin-offering for us'; 'God sent the sinless Christ into a sinful world'; 'God submitted the innocent Christ to the regime of law which was the regime of sin.' The apostle is not maintaining something that in any case seems impossible – that the innocent Christ literally 'took on the sin of the human kind'. A guiltless person cannot carry the moral guilt of others. Another point which comes across as thoroughly questionable is the document's claim that

no matter how great be the sinner's estrangement from God, it is not as deep as the sense of distance which the Son experiences vis-à-vis the Father in the kenotic emptying of himself (Phil 2:7) and in the anguish of 'abandonment' (Matt 27:46), (p. 18).

This is a latterday example of a cherished theme of Christian rhetoric. But in Philippians Paul is not employing early Christian hymnic language to speak of a deeply experienced 'sense of distance'. The cry of abandonment in Matthew's account of the passion is a quotation from a psalm which does not allow us to compare Jesus' interior state with the sinner's feeling of estrangement from God.

Conclusion

The Theological Commission's document on Christology, if here and there needing some tightening, covers many of the important current issues. Besides themes which have already been mentioned, the document recalls the pneumatological and cosmic dimensions of Christology (pp. 19–22). It refers to two other extremely important questions: (a) Christ's consciousness and knowledge, and (b) ways of expressing 'the absolute and universal value of the redemption effected by Christ for all and once for all' (p. 11). Echoing the Second Vatican Council's Constitution on the Church in the Modern World (n. 58), the Commission acknowledges 'the originality and value of various cultures', which entail the need to set forth the mystery of Christ through the 'particular riches and charisms' of all cultures (p. 12).

Personally I would like to have seen more detailed treatment of two themes: (a) Christ and non-Christians, and (b) the relationship between Christ's roles in creation and redemption.

Then nothing was really said in the document about the genesis and nature of belief in Christ as *risen* from the dead. Perhaps current issues on Christ's resurrection will be taken up in the next document from the Commission. Nevertheless, all in all, as a kind of an official position paper *Select Questions on Christology* serves extremely well to direct Catholic and Christian reflection in that field.

Notes

INTRODUCTION

1. Gerald O'Collins, *Interpreting Jesus* (London: Geoffrey Chapman, 1983); *Christology* (Oxford: Oxford University Press, 1995).

1 WHAT THEY ARE SAYING ABOUT JESUS NOW

1. James Dunn, *Christology in the Making* (London: SCM Press, 2nd ed., 1989).
2. On Eleonore Stump and Norman Kretzmann, see B. Leftow *Time and Eternity* (Ithaca, NY: Cornell University Press, 1991).
3. Karl-Joseph Kuschel, *Born Before All Time?* (London: SCM Press, 1992).
4. John Hick, *The Metaphor of God Incarnate* (London: SCM Press, 1993)
5. *Catechism of the Catholic Church* (London: Geoffrey Chapman, 1994).
6. (The Jesus Seminar) *The Five Gospels: What Did Jesus Really Say?* (New York: Macmillan, 1993).
7. (The Jesus Seminar) *The Gospel of Mark: Red Letter Edition* (Sonoma, CA: Polebridge, 1991).
8. Burton Mack, *The Lost Gospel* (San Francisco: Harper San Francisco, 1993).
9. Luke Timothy Johnson, *Commonweal,* 3 December 1993, p. 21.
10. John Dominic Crossan, *The Historical Jesus* (San Francisco: Harper San Francisco, 1991); *Jesus: A Revolutionary Biography* (San Francisco: Harper San Francisco, 1993).
11. Gerald O'Collins, *Christology* (Oxford: Oxford University Press, 1995), pp. 268–71.
12. Raymond E. Brown, *The Death of the Messiah* (London: Geoffrey Chapman, 1994).
13. Gerald O'Collins, *Interpreting Jesus* (London: Geoffrey

Chapman, 1983)

14. Bernard Sesboüé, *Jésus-Christ l'unique médiateur* 2 vols.
    (Paris: Descleé, 1988–91).
15. Stephen Davis, *Risen Indeed. Making Sense of the
    Resurrection* (London: SPCK, 1993).

2 Christ today

1. Composed by Sister Elizabeth Mary Strub, Superior General
   of the Society of the Holy Child Jesus, and her community at
   the *Casa Cornelia* in Rome, as a greeting for Christmastide
   1979–80, and cited here with her permission.

3 The Incarnation under fire

1. For further details and bibliographies on Adoptionism,
   Arianism, Arius, the Ebionites and Socinianism see the
   relevant entries in *Encyclopedia of the Early Church*, ed.
   A. di Berardino, 2 vols. (New York: Oxford University
   Press, 1992); *The Oxford Dictionary of the Christian
   Church*, ed. F. L. Cross and E. A. Livingstone, 3rd edn
   (Oxford: Oxford University Press, 1996). On the
   Enlightenment and liberal theology, see various articles in
   The Blackwell Encyclopedia of Modern Christian Thought,
   ed. A. E. McGrath (Oxford: Blackwell, 1993).
2. John Hick, *The Metaphor of God Incarnate* (London: SCM
   Press, 1993); hereafter references to this book will be given
   intertextually.
3. See K. H. Neufeld, *Adolf Harnacks Konflict mit der Kirche*
   (Innsbruck: Tyrolia, 1979), and *Adolf von Harnack.
   Theologie als Suche nach der Kirche* (Paderborn:
   Bonifacius, 1988).
4. Although he is never mentioned in *The Metaphor of God
   Incarnate*, there is an echo here of Alfred Loisy's famous
   remark in his 1902 debate with Harnack ('Jesus preached
   the kingdom and what came was the church') – a remark
   that Loisy did not then intend to carry the meaning often
   attributed to it later: namely, the Church is a weak, even

false surrogate for the rule of God preached by Jesus.
5. Hick slides from various uses of the 'Son of God' title in Judaism to talk about 'divinizing' (pp. 40–42). Because of his election to a function, royal installation and new relationship to God, Jews gave the 'son of God' title to their king. But this was not to 'divinize' him, even in a 'soft' sense. What the Greco-Roman world and, in particular, official Roman society and religion tried to do for their living and dead heroes and rulers can, however, be called 'divinizing'. See Jarl Fossum, 'Son of God', *Anchor Bible Dictionary*, ed. D. N. Freedman (New York: Doubleday, 1992), 6:128–37, at 132–33.
6. See H. D. Betz, 'Jesus and the Cynics: Survey and Analysis of an Hypothesis', *Journal of Religion* 74 (1994), pp 453–75. This is a devastating critique of the hypothesis about Jesus as a Cynic-style sage.
7. At the end of a learned article on 'Son of Man' in the *Anchor Bible Dictionary*, 6:137–150, at 149, G. W. E. Nickelsburg finds it 'problematic' to maintain that 'any of the sayings which identify Jesus as the son of man are genuine sayings of Jesus. To accept them as genuine more or less in their present form, one must posit that Jesus ... believed that his vindication from death would result in his exaltation to the unique role of eschatological judge.' Nickelsburg has the merit of indicating here how theological motivation firmly influences the conclusions he is willing to entertain.
8. See H. Hübner, *Biblische Theologie des Neuen Testaments*, vol. 2 (Göttingen: Vandenhoeck & Ruprecht, 1993), p. 325.
9. On the basis of the Synoptic gospels, Hick holds that the historical Jesus would probably have regarded talk of his incarnation as 'blasphemous' (p. 161). While the earthly Jesus was not aware of himself in terms of the later, partly philosophical language of Nicaea and Chalcedon, he did, however, make various startling claims to a more-than-human, personal authority (see chapters 3 and 5 of my *Christology* (Oxford: Oxford University Press, 1995). His sense of sonship emerges from Matt 11:27, a key passage not considered by Hick. Jesus was humanly conscious of his divine Father AND of himself in a unique relationship to the

Father; see my *Interpreting Jesus* (London: Geoffrey Chapman, 1983), pp. 183–190. Hick chides me for affirming 'a self-consciousness and self-presence in which he [Jesus] was intuitively aware of his divine identity' (p. 30).

10. See N. T. Wright, *The Climax of the Covenant* (Edinburgh: T. & T. Clark, 1991), pp. 120–36.

11. In dealing with Acts 2:36 ('God has made him Lord and Christ, this Jesus whom you crucified'), Hick likewise thinks of God adopting Jesus at the end (p. 28), overlooking the fact that Luke names Jesus as 'Lord' and 'Christ' right from the beginning of his two-volume work (Luke 2:11).

12. See J. A. Fitzmyer, 'Pauline Theology', *New Jerome Biblical Commentary*, ed. R. E. Brown et al. (Englewood Cliffs NJ: Prentice Hall, 1990), pp. 1389–90 and 1393–94.

13. For Eastern theology on deification, see J. Gross, *La divinization du chrétien d'après les Pères grecs* (Paris: Gabalda, 1938).

14. On not preferring Acts to 1 Cor 15 (and other Pauline letters) as the primary source for information about Paul, see J. A. Fitzmyer, 'Paul', *New Jerome Biblical Commentary*, 1329–37, p. 1330.

15. The self-indulgent and non-scientific use of evidence by many authors who write on near-death experiences has been widely criticized.

16. See I. R. Nerken, 'Grief and the Reflective Self: Toward a Clearer Model of Loss Resolution and Growth', *Death Studies* 17 (Washington, DC, Hemisphere Publishing Co., 1993), pp. 1–26, especially the bibliographical items on bereavement at pp. 24–6.

17. See G. O'Collins, 'Crucifixion', *Anchor Bible Dictionary*, 1:1207–10.

18. See R. Swinburne, *Revelation: from Metaphor to Analogy* (Oxford: Clarendon Press, 1992).

19. On the way experience is always interpreted experience, see E. Schillebeeckx, *Christ: The Experience of Jesus as Lord* (New York: Seabury, 1980).

20. See J. Hick, *An Interpretation of Religion* (New Haven: Yale University Press, 1989); G. D'Costa, 'Other Faiths and Christianity', *Blackwell Encyclopedia of Modern Christian Thought*, ed. A. McGrath, pp. 412–13.

21. See my review of D. Cupitt, *Jesus and the Gospel of God* (London: Lutterworth Press, 1979) in *Heythrop Journal* 21 (1980), pp. 190–93.

8 The founder of Christianity

1. See, for example, A. Anton, *La Iglesia de Cristo* (Madrid: Biblioteca de Autores Christianos, 1977), pp. 337ff, 400ff.; R. J. Braus, *Jesus as Founder of the Church according to Joachim Jeremias* (Rome: Gregorian University Press, 1970, dissertation abstract); H. Küng, *On Being a Christian* (London: Collins, 1977), pp. 283–86; J. Reumann, *Jesus in the Church's Gospels* (Philadelphia: Fortress Press, 1968), pp. 296, 306–14, 447 n. 84.
2. New York: Macmillan, 1970.
3. Ibid., p. 1.
4. Ibid., p. 4.
5. Ibid., p. 16.
6. On this use of scriptural evidence see B. F. Meyer, *The Aims of Jesus* (London: SCM Press, 1979), pp. 154, 157, 166f., 192, 201, 294, 297.
7. We have multiple attestation for the fact that at some point during the ministry Jesus chose a core-group of twelve from the wider ranks of his disciples. The Marcan narrative includes a story of such a call (3:13–19) and a subsequent mission of the Twelve (6:7–13). The logia or Q tradition from which Matthew and Luke draw also attests the existence of this core-group: 'Jesus said to them, "Truly I say to you, in the new world, when the Son of man shall sit on his glorious throne, you who have followed me will also sit on twelve thrones, judging the twelve tribes of Israel"' (Matt 19:28 par.). Finally, a faith formula quoted by St Paul confirms that such a group existed before Jesus' death and hence could receive an appearance of the risen Lord: 'He appeared to Cephas [Peter], and then to the twelve' (1 Cor 15:5).
8. On this see Meyer, *Aims of Jesus*, pp. 134, 150, 178, 180f, 182, 189, 192f., 205, 209.
9. I wish to avoid calling Christianity a new religion. It shares

a strong spiritual patrimony with Judaism, and looks at itself as the logical and necessary extension of the Law and the Prophets. Indeed, although the Church looks at herself as the new people of God, she acknowledges all that God is and has been doing for and through Judaism. To bring this point out, it might be helpful to speak of 'the Jewish-Christian religion'.

10. See W. Kasper, *Jesus the Christ* (London: Burns and Oates, 1976), pp. 114ff.; H. Küng, *On Being a Christian*, pp. 319ff.

11. *Jesus and the Constraints of History* (Oxford: 1982), p. 94.

12. On *'archēgos'* see H. Bietenhard, 'Beginning, Origin, Rule, Ruler, Originator', *Dictionary of New Testament Theology*, ed. C. Brown, I, (Grand Rapids, MI: Zondervan, 1975-78) pp. 1 64-69, especially p. 168.

13. In what follows I am *not* concerned with the arguments for Mark 12:10-11 containing an authentic saying of Jesus, the authorship of Ephesians, historical connections between 1 Peter and the Pauline letters, and the detailed exegesis of the passages cited. My point is simply to note the fact that a number of important New Testament works use the *image* of Christ as corner-stone or foundation-stone.

14. See Rahner's 'The Theology of the Symbol', *Theological Investigations* 4, pp. 221-52.

15. On the signs of the times see Gerald O'Collins, *Fundamental Theology* (London: Darton, Longman and Todd, 1981), pp. 102-107.

16. Pp. 101-102; see also Gerald O'Collins, *Theology and Revelation* (Cork: Mercier Press, 1968), pp. 45-7, 49-50.

17. The opening words of verse 20 could also be translated as follows: 'You are built upon the foundation laid by the apostles and prophets ...' (*New English Bible*). On this whole passage see M. Barth, *Ephesians* 1-3 (Anchor Bible, Garden City, NY: Doubleday, 1974), pp. 268-74, 314-22.

18. See M. H. Shepherd, 'Apostle', *Interpreter's Dictionary of the Bible* 1, pp. 170-72. For the language which has been traditionally used of apostles as founders see M. L. Held and F. Klostermann, 'Apostle', *New Catholic Encyclopedia* 1, pp. 679-82.

19. *On Being a Christian*, pp. 212–13.
20. Ibid., pp. 344–45.
21. James Mackey, *Jesus the Man and the Myth* (London: SCM Press, 1979), pp. 206–10.
22. See Gerald O'Collins, *What Are They Saying about Jesus?* (2nd edn, Ramsey NJ: Paulist Press, 1983), pp. 40–53.
23. James Mackey, *Jesus the Man and the Myth*, pp. 2–3.

9 Our peace and reconciliation

1. *Jesus the Man and the Myth* (London: SCM Press, 1979), p. 74.
2. *Christology at the Crossroads* (London: SCM Press, 1978), p. 189.
3. *Dictionnaire de Théologie Catholique*, vol XIV (Paris: Libraire Letouzey et Ané, 1939).
4. Cf Dennis McCarthy SJ, in *Journal of Biblical Literature* 88 (1969), pp 166–76: 92 (1973), pp. 205–10.
5. *The Crucified is no Stranger* (New York: Paulist Press, 1977), p. 8.
6. *The Crucified God* (London: SCM Press, 1974) pp. 148–53.
7. *Love Alone* (New York: Herder and Herder, 1969), pp. 76 and 120.
8. For assistance in writing this chapter, I wish to thank Bernard Carman SAC, Sr Cosima Resta SASC, George Sullivan, and two religious communities in Australia: the Jesuits of Parkville and the Good Samaritan Sisters of Belgrave.

10 Did Joseph of Arimathea exist?

1. R. Bultmann, *The History of the Synoptic Tradition* (New York: Harper & Row, 1963), p. 274.
2. J. A. Fitzmyer, *The Gospel According to Luke* (X–XXIV) (Garden City, NY: Doubleday, 1985), p. 1526.
3. S. E. Porter, 'Joseph of Arimathea', *ABD* III, pp. 971–2.
4. See, for example, J. Gnilka, *Das Evangelium nach Markus*, II (Zürich-Einsiedeln-Köln: 1979), p. 336; M. Hooker, *The*

Gospel According to St. Mark (London: A & C Black, 1991), p. 380.

5. J. D. Crossan, *Four Other Gospels* (Minneapolis, MN: Winston Press, 1985), pp. 152–7; *The Cross That Spoke: the Origins of the Passion Narrative* (San Francisco: Harper & Row, 1988), pp. 234–8; *The Historical Jesus: the Life of a Mediterranean Jewish Peasant* (San Francisco: Harper San Francisco 1991), pp. 391–4.

6. *Four Other Gospels*, pp. 160–1, sec. 16A.

7. *The Cross That Spoke*, p. 248.

8. R. E. Brown, 'The *Gospel of Peter* and Canonical Gospel Priority', *NTS* 33 (1987), pp. 321–3.

9. See P. A. Mirecki, 'Peter, Gospel of', *ABD* V, 278–81, at p. 280.

10. On the dubious existence of a 'primitive passion narrative in written form in the pre-Marcan stage' see Fitzmyer, *Luke*, pp. 1359–91, especially pp. 1361–2. It is notable that neither this 1985 commentary nor any of the forty items in its bibliography (pp. 1370–71) except for one work (by J. R. Donahue) appear in Crossan's *The Cross That Spoke*.

11. *Four Other Gospels*, p. 147; in general see the section 'Prophecy and Passion', pp. 137–148.

12. Ibid., pp. 156, 161. See *The Cross That Spoke*, pp. 237–48; *The Historical Jesus*, pp. 393–4.

13. *The Cross That Spoke*, pp. 238–9.

14. Mark's language about Joseph (εὐσχημων βουλευτής) does not make it quite clear that he belonged to the Jerusalem Sanhedrin (as Luke seems to suppose); it may indicate a rich property owner and member of some local council. Hence Matthew may be simply interpreting Mark's text rather than redactionally changing it.

15. See Fitzmyer, *Luke*, pp. 1523–30; Porter, 'Joseph of Arimathea', p. 972.

16. *The Cross That Spoke*, pp. 17–20.

17. *Horizons* 16 (1989), p. 379.

18. *The Historical Jesus*, p. 393. Crossan goes on to exaggerate here when describing Joseph of Arimathea as enjoying a 'powerful foot in both camps'. He obviously lacked power needed in the Jewish court to prevent the condemnation of Jesus. His lack of 'power' in the Christian camp may be

gauged by the fact that, outside the burial story in the gospels, the New Testament nowhere mentions him.

11 The resurrection of Jesus: some current questions

1. Paul Winter, *On the Trial of Jesus* (Berlin: Gruyter 1961).
2. Edward Schillebeeckx, *Jesus* (London: Collins, 1979).
3. Edward Schillebeeckx, *Interim Report on the Books 'Jesus' and 'Christ'* (New York: Crossroad, 1982), p.147, n.43.
4. Paul Knitter, *No Other Name? A Critical Survey of Christian Attitudes Towards World Religions* (Maryknoll, NY: Orbis, 1985).

12 The uniqueness of the Easter appearances

1. Edward Schillebeeckx, for instance, underplays the unique nature of the Easter encounters, presenting them as hardly more than the first instance of experiences (of forgiveness and conversion) available to all later Christians (*Jesus: an Experiment in Christology* (London: Collins, 1979), pp. 354–90, 674; idem, *Interim Report on the Books 'Jesus' and 'Christ'* (New York: Crossroad, 1982), pp. 78, 80, 81. The consequence, drawn by Schillebeeckx himself, is that the experience of the apostles ceases to be truly normative for later Christians (*Interim Report*, p. 7).
2. See Gerald O'Collins, *Interpreting the Resurrection*, (Mahwah, NJ: Paulist Press, 1988), pp. 5–21.
3. Reginald H. Fuller, *The Formation of the Resurrection Narratives* (Philadelphia: Fortress Press, 1980), p. 48.
4. For the thesis of luminous experiences see James M. Robinson, 'Jesus: From Easter to Valentinus (or to the Apostles' Creed)', *JBL* 101 (1982) pp. 5–37. Schillebeeckx has argued the case for the appearances being events of conversion and forgiveness.
5. Wilhelm Michaelis, 'Horaō', *TDNT*, 5, pp. 315–82.
6. Ibid., p. 330.
7. Ibid., p. 327.
8. Ibid., p. 330.

9. Ibid., p. 333.
10. Ibid., pp. 355–61.
11. Ibid., p. 359.
12. Ibid., p. 359, n. 212.
13. Ibid., p. 360.
14. Hans Kessler, *Sucht den Lebenden nicht bei den Toten: Die Auferstehung Jesu Christi in biblischer, fundamentaltheologischer und systematischer Sicht* (Düsseldorf: Patmos, 1985), pp. 150–51.
15. Ibid., p. 149. At the same time, one should insist on identifying in their context the particular kind of appearance indicated by *ōphthē*. The range of events and subjects covered by this term in the LXX and NT is so broad that the mere use of the term is not decisive.
16. R. J. Sider, 'St. Paul's Understanding of the Nature and Significance of the Resurrection in 1 Cor 15:1–29', *NovT* 19 (1977), p. 140.
17. Hans Conzelmann, *1 Corinthians* (Hermeneia: Philadelphia: Fortress Press, 1975), p. 257, n. 74.
18. Kessler, *Sucht den Lebenden*, p. 231.
19. As we saw above, Michaelis finds support for his case in Galatians 1. Hans Dieter Betz *Galatians* (Hermeneia: Philadelphia: Fortress Press, 1979), pp. 64, 71), while allowing that Gal 1:1, 11–16 points to 'a verbal revelation', does not rule out identifying the same event as also involving 'a visionary experience', an internal vision of which Paul speaks elsewhere in language that suggests an external vision (1 Cor 9:1; 15:8). Apparently for the apostle, Betz remarks, 'the two forms of visions (external and internal) are not as distinct as they may be for some commentators.'
20. Karl Dahn, 'See, Vision, Eye', *The New International Dictionary of New Testament Theology* (3 vols. ed. Colin Brown, Grand Rapids: Zondervan, 1975–78), vol. 3. p. 518. The Easter narratives in the Gospels prefer the active form of *horaō* which as such emphasizes the activity of the witnesses in seeing the risen Christ. The usage predominates from the promise 'you will see him' (Mark 16:7) through Mary Magdalene's 'I have seen the Lord' (John 20:18; see also Matt 28:7, 17; Luke 24:39; John 20:20, 25, 27, 29). Other verbs occur sporadically in the Easter narra-

tives and indicate a visible perception of the risen Christ: *deiknymi* (John 20:20), *phaneroō* (John 21:1, 14, *theaomai* (Acts 1:11) and *theōreō* (Luke 24:37; John 20:14). See also Luke 24:16, 31; Acts 1:9; 10:40 for further use of the language of sight in the Easter context.

21. Michaelis, 'Horaō', p. 357.

22. Betz, *Galatians*, p. 71. In *Resurrection: New Testament Witness and Contemporary Reflection* (Garden City, NY: Doubleday, 1984), Pheme Perkins holds a similar view, accepting that Paul had 'some sort of external vision' but arguing that it was an 'ecstatic experience' (p. 198). For a discussion of Perkins' position, see O'Collins, *Interpreting*, pp. 11–17.

23. Joachim Jeremias, *New Testament Theology: Vol 1, The Proclamation of Jesus* (London: SCM Press, 1971), pp. 307–8. This identification of these two traditions has been widely rejected; see William Lang Craig, *Assessing the New Testament Evidence for the Historicity of the Resurrection of Jesus*, Studies in the Bible and Early Christianity 16 (Lewiston, NY: Edwin Mellen, 1989), pp. 58–9.

24. Ibid., p. 308.

25. For further details, see O'Collins, *Interpreting*, pp. 9–10.

26. Ibid., pp. 7–9.

27. For further details, see O'Collins, *Jesus Risen* (Mahwah, NJ: Paulist Press, 1987) pp. 210–16.

28. For further details, see O'Collins, *Interpreting*, pp. 13–15. In *I Corinthians* (Garden City, NY: Doubleday, 1976), William Orr and James Walther warn readers of 1 Cor 15:3–8 to remember that Paul never equates the reception of the Spirit with witnessing an appearance of the risen Lord (p. 322).

29. See, e.g., Raymond E. Brown, 'John 21 and the First Appearance of the Risen Jesus to Peter,' *Resurrexit: Actes du Symposium international sur la Résurrection de Jésus (Rome 1970)*, ed. Edouard Dhanis (Vatican City: Editrice Vaticana, 1974), p. 250. Craig, *Assessing the New Testament Evidence*, p. 52.

30. Béda Rigaux (*Dieu l'a ressuscité: Exégèse et théologie biblique*, Studii Biblici Franciscani Analecta 4; Gembloux, Duculot, 1973, p. 123) is one of the few authors to note the

significance if the difference between the aorist tense of 'he died', 'he was buried', and 'he appeared' (four times) and the perfect tense of 'he has been raised' (1 Cor 15:4). The perfect indicates the beginning but not the completion of an act. The aorist tense, however, locates an event in the sphere of past history, among things that happened, so as to be over and done with.

31. C. F. Evans, *Resurrection and the New Testament* (Naperville, IL: Allenson, 1970), p. 46.
32. Ibid., p. 50.
33. Conzelmann, *1 Corinthians*, p. 258.
34. Fuller, *The Formation*, pp. 42-3.
35. Ibid., p. 49.
36. Jacob Kremer, *Das älteste Zeugnis von der Auferstehung Christi: Eine bibeltheologische Studie zur Aussage und Bedeutung von 1 Kor 15, 1-11* (Stuttgart: KBW, 1967), p. 78.
37. C. K. Barrett, *A Commentary on the First Epistle to the Corinthians* (New York: Harper & Row, 1971), pp. 343-4: 'The last of the witnesses of the risen Christ was Paul himself. It is true that "last of all" could be taken to mean "least in importance", and would agree with verse 9; but at the end of a list punctuated by *then ... then ... then*, the other meaning of the word must be accepted.'
38. F. W. Grosheide, *Commentary on the First Epistle to the Corinthians* (Grand Rapids: Eerdmans, 1968), p. 352.
39. Leon Morris, *The First Epistle of Paul to the Corinthians* (Tyndale NT Commentaries, Grand Rapids: Eerdmans, 1966), p. 207.
40. J. W. C. Wand, *What St. Paul Really Said* (New York: Schocken, 1969), p. 85.
41. K. H. Rengstorf, *Die Auferstehung Jesu: Form, Art und Sinn der urchristlichen Osterbotschaft* (Witten: Luther V., 1967), p. 47. See also Jean Héring, *The First Epistle of Saint Paul to the Corinthians* (London: Epworth, 1962), p. 162.
42. Gordon Fee, *The First Epistle to the Corinthians* (Grand Rapids: Eerdmans, 1987), p. 733.
43. J. Moffatt (*The General Epistles: James, Peter and Jude* (London: Hodder & Stoughton, 1963), p. 98 is practically alone in reading here 'without having known' (*eidotes*) in

place of the much better attested 'seen' (*idontes*). Nevertheless, he sums up well the point of the passage: 'Out of sight but not out of reach: such is Peter's description of Christ.'

44. H. Balz and W. Schrage (*Die 'Katholischen' Briefe* (Göttingen: Vandenhoeck und Ruprecht, 1973), p. 70) gratuitously qualify the seeing as 'ecstatic': 'This love and this faith do not ... rest on personal knowledge or ecstatic vision.'

45. So F. W. Beare, *The First Epistle of Peter* (Oxford: Blackwell, 1961), p. 62; J. N. D. Kelly, *A Commentary on the Epistles of Peter and of Jude* (New York: Harper & Row, 1969), pp. 56-7; Moffatt, *The General Epistles*, p. 98.

46. Beare, *The First Epistle of Peter*, p. 62.

47. E. Best, *1 Peter* (London: Oliphants, 1971), p. 79.

48. Since the explicit notion of an apostle is found only in 1 Pet 1:1, Balz and Schrage find it hard to define exactly the 'meaning of this self-characterization'. They are inclined to interpret 'apostle' here in terms of being authorized through Jesus Christ (*Die 'Katholischen' Briefe*, p. 66). In the author's self-identification as 'apostle of Jesus Christ', J. Ramsey Michaels finds a 'consciousness of a unique status and authority' (*1 Peter* (Waco, TX: Word, 1988)), pp. 5-6.

49. Unlike Beare (*The First Epistle of Peter*, p. 72), several other commentators deny that 1 Pet 5:1 constitutes a claim to have been an eyewitness but simply 'one who testifies to the truth without having literally witnessed the event behind that truth'. An example of this viewpoint is N. Brox (*Der Erste Petrusbrief* (Zürich: Benziger, 1974) 229) who argues that 'witness' can mean 'witness in deed' – one in whose sufferings the passion of Christ continues, and who doubts that 1 Pet. 1:8 indicates a contrast between the apostolic generation (who saw Jesus) and those who believe in and love him without having seen him (*Der Erste Petrusbrief*, p. 16, n. 223)

50. So Moffatt, *The General Epistles*, p. 38; and Selwyn, *The First Epistle*, p. 131. Michaels, however, denies that the writer even implies 'You have not seen him – but I have, as an apostle and witness' (*1 Peter*, p. 32).

51. Kelly, *A Commentary*, p. 56. On the case for Petrine

authorship see William J. Dalton, *Christ's Proclamation to the Spirits: A Study of 1 Peter 3:18—4:6* (Rome: Pontifical Biblical Institute, 1965, 2nd edn 1989), pp. 77–91.

52. On the ascension see Gerhard Schneider, *Die Apostelgeschichte* (Freiburg: Herder, 1980), pp. 209–11, and Joseph A. Fitzmyer, *The Gospel According to Luke* (Garden City, NY: Doubleday, 1981–85), pp. 1586–89.

53. On the twelve apostles as witnesses, see Fitzmyer, *Luke*, pp. 253–5, 294, 613–16; Joseph Plevnik 'The Eyewitnesses of the Risen Jesus in Luke 24', *CBQ* 49 (1987), pp. 90–103, especially pp. 100–103.

54. In the light of 1 Cor 15:5–7, Schneider lists among the prior elements used in the making of the ascension story in Acts 'the concept of the closed nature of the Risen One's appearances' (*Die Apostelgeschichte*, p. 210).

55. Here we follow the general lines of Conzelmann's thesis about the three periods that make up Luke's historical perspective: the period of Israel (from creation up to John the Baptist), the period of Jesus (from the start of his ministry to his ascension), and the period of the Church (from the ascension to the *parousia*) see H. Conzelmann, *Theology of St. Luke* (New York: Harper and Row, 1960), pp. 16–17. 'The description of the threefold division of Lucan salvation-history presented by Conzelmann is correct. Some modifications of it are necessary, but by and large it is still valid' (Fitzmyer, *Luke*, 18; see pp. 18–22, 181–7). At the same time, we must insist that Jesus is in no way confined to the second period (from his baptism to his ascension). Through his Spirit he is, for example, the moving force behind the whole story of Acts that ends with Paul in Rome 'teaching about the Lord Jesus Christ' (Acts 28:31).

56. Schneider, *Die Apostelgeschichte*, p. 210.

57. Schneider comments (ibid., p. 211): 'The apostles are ear-witnesses of Jesus' last promise (Acts 1:8) and eye-witnesses of his earthly activity right up to the ascension. It is precisely in the story of the ascension that they are portrayed as those who guarantee the continuity between Jesus and the time of the church.'

58. The twelve apostles are 'witnesses not only because of their association with the earthly Jesus and not yet even through

their post-Easter contact with the Risen One. To exercise their function as witnesses they need the power of the Spirit' (ibid., p. 224).

59. See Victor P. Furnish, *II Corinthians* (Garden City, NY: Doubleday, 1984), pp. 528–31, 547–51.

60. In Luke's first and second version of the Damascus road encounter the disciple Ananias plays a significant role. Only in the first version does Ananias experience the Lord (Jesus) 'in a vision' (Acts 9:10–19). The emphasis in this pericope, however, is on what the 'Lord *said* to him in a vision'. Likewise the men travelling with Paul on the Damascus road hear the voice (of Jesus) but see no one (Acts 9:7). In the second account they see the 'great light from heaven' but do not hear the voice speaking to Paul (Acts 22:6, 9). In the third account the apostle's companions are not said to see the light or hear the voice. None of the three accounts reports that the risen Jesus 'appeared' to those others or that they 'saw' him. Their case provides no exception to the Lucan scheme of no Christophanies after the ascension. Luke presents Stephen, just before his martyrdom, as seeing Jesus 'standing at the right hand of God' (Acts 7:55–56). Here Luke wishes to explain why Stephen's face shone like that of an angel (Acts 6:15 is intelligible because Stephen reflected the glory of God). In no way does Luke put Stephen's vision on a par with the appearances of Jesus to his original disciples (up to the time of the ascension) or with Paul's Damascus road encounter. The doomed martyr's vision really does not break the pattern of no post-ascension Christophanies. The solitary real exception to this Lucan pattern is the special case of Paul, whose encounter with the risen Jesus turned him into the apostle to the Gentiles (Acts 9:15, 13:46–47; 22:21).

61. Raymond Brown, *The Gospel According to John* (Garden City, NY: Doubleday, 1964 (2nd edn 1966), 1970), pp. 1050–51.

62. Ibid. See R. Bultmann (*The Gospel of John* (Philadelphia: Westminster, 1971), pp. 695–6). According to Brown, however, proper belief 'does not discard the sign or the appearance of the risen Jesus, for the use of the visible is an indispensable condition of the Word's having become flesh.

As long as Jesus stood among men, one had to come to faith through the visible. Now, at the end of the Gospel, another attitude becomes possible and necessary. This is the era of the Spirit or the invisible presence of Jesus (xiv 17), and the era of signs or appearances is passing away. The transition from 29a to 29b is not merely that one era precedes the other, but that one leads to the other.'

63. C. K. Barrett, *The Gospel according to St. John* (Philadelphia: Westminster Press, 2nd edn, 1978), p. 573.
64. Rudolf Schnackenburg (*The Gospel According to St. John*, (New York: Crossroad, 1982), vol. 3. p. 334) similarly argues that the special experience of Thomas can be summed up in 'seeing'. 'Thomas is the exponent of that experience by a disciple, of Jesus' "appearances", which is denied to later believers.'
65. Raymond Brown, *The Epistles of John* (Garden City, NY: Doubleday, 1982), pp. 154, 158, 167.
66. Ibid., p. 182.
67. A. E. Brooke, *Johannine Epistles* (Edinburgh: T. & T. Clark, 1912), p. 2. Brooke agrees with Westcott when he says, 'What the writer and his contemporaries have heard and seen remains with them, so that they can make it known to others who have not themselves had the same privileges.'
68. I. Howard Marshall, *The Epistles of John* (Grand Rapids: Eerdmans, 1978), p. 101.
69. B. F. Westcott, *The Epistles of John* (Grand Rapids: Eerdmans, 1952 (originally published 1886)), p. 5.
70. Brown, *The Epistles of John*, pp. 160–63, 170–72, 182.
71. Rudolf Bultmann, *The Johannine Epistles* (Hermeneia, Philadelphia: Fortress Press, 1973), pp. 9–11.
72. Pheme Perkins, *The Johannine Epistles* (Wilmington: Michael Glazier, 1979), pp. 9–10.

14 Newman's seven notes: the case of the resurrection

1. This chapter uses the second edition of Newman's *Essays* (London: 1878) rather than the first edition of 1845. All page references inserted in my text itself are to the 1878 edition of the *Essay*.

2. See *Lectures on the Doctrine of Justification* (uniform edition of Longmans, London), pp. 202-22.
3. Schillebeeckx, *Jesus* (London: Collins, 1979).
4. Ibid., pp. 346-97.
5. Schillebeeckx, *Interim Report on the Books 'Jesus' and 'Christ'* (New York: Crossroad, 1982).
6. Ibid., p. 147, n. 43; see p. 148, n. 46.
7. Ibid., p. 75.
8. H. Küng, *On Being a Christian* (London: Collins, 1976).
9. Ibid., pp. 363-6.
10. Ibid., p. 366.
11. In *From Bossuet to Newman: The Idea of Doctrinal Development* (Cambridge: 1957) Owen Chadwick contends that Newman's tests 'convinced no one' and were 'rather pegs on which to hang a historical thesis than solid supports for a doctrinal explanation, (pp. 143, 155); on p. 236 Chadwick provides a list of the first Anglican criticisms of Newman's *Essay*. Nicholas Lash interprets Newman's notes more benignly; see his *Newman on Development* (London: Sheed and Ward 1975), esp. pp. 114-45.
12. Among the exegetes who criticized Schillebeeckx's *Jesus* see e.g. R. E. Brown, *CBQ* 42 (1980), pp. 420-23; A. L. Descamps, *Rev. théol. de Louvain*, 6 (1975), pp. 212-23; R. H. Fuller, *Interpretation*, 34 (1980), pp. 293-6.
13. Schillebeeckx, *Jesus*, p. 645.
14. Ibid., p. 710, n. 119.
15. On the appearances as 'very evident signs' of Jesus' resurrection, see Aquinas, *Summa Theologiae* IIIa, Q. 55, a. 5.
16. Schillebeeckx, *Jesus*, p. 710, n.119.
17. Ibid.
18. Ibid., p. 390.
19. Yet one should not ignore here the gospels which come later and, at least in the case of Matthew, Luke, and John, include appearance stories. Moreover, it is understandable that (brief) kerygmatic, credal, or liturgical material like Rom 1:4 and 10:9 normally would not make reference to post-resurrection appearances.
20. See J. N. D. Kelly, *Early Christian Creeds* (1950, 3rd edn London: Longman 1976), p.
21. Schillebeeckx, *Jesus*, p. 710, n. 119.

22. Ibid., p. 647.
23. Schillebeeckx, *Interim Report*, p. 7.
24. Ibid., pp. 78, 80.
25. Ibid., p. 7.
26. Perkins, *Resurrection* (London: Geoffrey Chapman, 1985).
27. H. Kessler, *Sucht den Lebenden nicht bei den Toten* (Düsseldorf: Patmos, 1985).
28. Schillebeeckx, *Christ: The Experience of Jesus as Lord* (New York: Seabury, 1980), p. 529.
29. Schillebeeckx, *Interim Report*, p. 75.
30. Ibid., p. 147, n. 43.
31. Küng, *On Being a Christian*, p. 352.
32. Ibid., pp. 348–9, 373–9.
33. Ibid., p. 366.
34. Küng, *On Being a Christian*, p. 366.
35. Ibid., p. 365. For a long list of such exegetes see my *Jesus Risen* (London and Mahwah: 1987), p. 123.
36. See W. Pannenberg, *Jesus: God and Man* (Philadelphia: 1968), pp. 100–108; Xavier Léon-Dufour, *Resurrection and the Message of Easter* (London: 1974), pp. 105–24.
37. Küng, *On Being a Christian*, pp. 346–5.
38. Perkins, *Resurrection*, pp. 84, 90, 94.
39. Küng, *On Being a Christian*, p. 365.
40. One should add that for the beloved disciple in John's story the sign included the grave cloths which had been tidily separated (John 20:5–7).
41. Küng, *On Being a Christian*, p. 365.
42. See e.g. Kessler, *Sucht den Lebenden*, pp. 121, 322.
43. See J. A. Fitzmyer, *A Christological Catechism: New Testament Answers* (Ramsey, NJ: 1982), pp. 76, 77, 79. R. E. Brown rightly concludes that 'while there may be debate about the nature of the transformed resurrected body, Catholic teaching does not permit one to maintain that the body of Jesus corrupted in the tomb' (Brown, *Biblical Exegesis and Church Doctrine* (London: 1986), p. 38).

16 On reissuing Venturini

1. For details see Pheme Perkins, *The Gnostic Dialogue: The*

Early Church and the Crisis of Gnosticism (New York/Ramsey: Paulist Press, 1980), pp. 114, 118, 121, 146, 180, 186.

2. There are many translations of this passage (S.4 A. 157). One by Muhammed Marmaduke Pickthall (*The Glorious Koran* (London: George Allen and Unwin, 1976), p. 129) renders it thus: 'And because of their saying: We slew the Messiah, Jesus son of Mary, Allah's messenger – They slew him not nor crucified him, but it appear so unto them; and lo! Those who disagree concerning it are in doubt thereof; they have no knowledge thereof save pursuit of a conjecture, they slew him not for certain.'

3. Albert Schweitzer, *The Quest of the Historical Jesus* (New York, Macmillan, 1961 (German original, 1906)), pp. 38–47.

4. For Schleiermacher's version of what happened to Jesus after burial see his *The Life of Jesus*, ed. Jack C. Verheyden (Philadelphia: Fortress Press, 1975), pp. 431–81. Verheyden (p. 456, note 60) argues that Schweitzer was mistaken in understanding Schleiermacher to hold that Jesus suffered only an apparent death and through his strong God-consciousness was able to recover. Verheyden's work does not convince us that Schweitzer misunderstood Schleiermacher over this point.

5. Barbara Thiering, *Jesus and the Riddle of the Dead Sea Scrolls* (San Francisco: Harper, 1992; London: Doubleday).

6. George Moore, *The Brook Kerith: a Syrian Story* (New York, Macmillan, 1916).

7. D. H. Lawrence, *The Man Who Died* (New York: A. Knopf, 1931).

8. Ibid., p. 13.

9. Ibid., p. 24.

10. Ibid., p. 25.

11. Ibid., pp. 26–7.

12. Margaret Mitchell, *Gone with the Wind,* (New York: Macmillan, 1936), p. 1037.

13. Basil Davenport, *Saturday Review of Literature*, 1 August 1931, p. 20.

14. *The Times Literary Supplement*, 2 April 1931, p. 267.

15. Robert Graves and John Podro, *Jesus in Rome* (London:

Cassell, 1957), pp. 12–13; see also their earlier work, *The Nazarene Gospel Restored* (London: Cassell, 1953).

16. C. F. Nesbitt, 'Misguided Ingenuity', *Interpretation* 9 (1955), p. 102.

17. Ibid., p. 105.

18. H. H. Hoskins, 'The Gospel Challenged', *Church Quarterly Review* 159 (1958), pp. 123–5.

19. Ibid., p. 125.

20. Hugh J. Schonfield, *The Passover Plot* (New York: Bernard Geis Associates, 1966).

21. Ibid., p. 12

22. Ibid., p. 21.

23. Samuel Sandmel, *The Saturday Review*, 3 December 1966, p. 42.

24. The original review was by John M. T. Barton, *Tablet*, 30 October 1965, p. 1212; Schonfield replied at once in a letter printed in the 13 November issue, p. 1278; Barton answered the letter in the 20 November issue, p. 1307.

25. Herbert Musurillo, *America*, 10 September 1966, p. 258.

26. John L. McKenzie, *The Critic*, October–November 1966, p. 106.

27. Updike's short story appeared on 25 December 1971 in the *New Yorker* (47:29–30). It was later reprinted in a collection of his short stories, retaining the title 'Jesus on Honshu', *Museums and Women* (New York: Alfred A. Knopf, 1972), pp. 213–17.

28. Ibid., pp. 215–16.

29. Ibid., p. 217.

30. Donovan Joyce, *The Jesus Scroll* (New York: Dial Press, 1973).

31. Ibid., pp. 2–3.

32. *Time*, 24 December, 1973, p. 55.

33. *Publishers Weekly*, 1 October 1973, p. 70.

34. John B. Breslin, *America*, 6 October 1973, p. 250.

35. Michael Baigent, Richard Leigh and Henry Lincoln, *Holy Blood, Holy Grail* (London: Delacorte Press, 1982). A decade later Baigent and Leigh produced *The Dead Sea Scrolls Deception* (New York: Summit, 1991). As Joseph A. Fitzmyer remarked in his review for *America*, 15

February 1992, p. 119, 'If there is a deception connected with the Dead Sea Scrolls, this book is it.'
36. Ibid., p. 289.
37. Ibid.
38. Ibid., p. 342. Our three authors introduce this claim by assuring us that none of the extant NT manuscripts predate the fourth century. So much for the second and third century Bodmer and Chester Beatty papyri! This and many other inaccuracies (e.g. turning Matthew's magi into kings, ignoring archaeological evidence for the existence of Nazareth since the third century BC, and dating Constantine's victory at the Milvian Bridge to 213) really call for an errata slip in the form of a companion volume.
39. The reference is to: Morton Smith, *The Secret Gospel* (Athlone Press, 1974). This same book was printed in the USA in 1973 by Harper and Row in New York.
40. *Holy Blood, Holy Grail*, p. 331.
41. Ibid., p. 336.
42. Robert Graves, *The Greek Myths* (originally published by Penguin in two volumes in 1955 revised edn, 1978), *King Jesus* (4th edn, London: Cassell, 1960), *The White Goddess* (London: Faber & Faber, 1961). M. J. C. Hodgart ('In the shade of the Golden Bough', *Twentieth Century* 157 (1955), p. 116) argues that Graves was 'unique in combining a great deal of learning with contempt for the normal processes of scholarship'.
43. Ernest Renan, *Life of Jesus*. This was published in English in 1955 by the Modern Library of New York.
44. Michael Holman, in a series for *The Month* (April 1982), p. 140, called the book's central thesis mere 'speculative history'.
45. J. Duncan M. Derrett, *The Anastasis: the Resurrection of Jesus as an Historical Event* (Shipston-on-Stour: P. Drinkwater, 1982).
46. Nicholas Notovitch, *The Unknown Life of Jesus Christ* (Trans. J. H. Connelly and L. Landsberg, New York: G. W. Dillingham, 1894).
47. Günter Grönbold, *Jesus in Indien: das Ende einer Legende* (Munich: Kösel Verlag, 1985).
48. Soami Divyanand, *Jesus Survived Crucifixion* (Herrischried:

Divyanand Verlag, 1987).

49. Holger Kersten, *Jesus Lived in India* (Shaftesbury: Element Books, 1986).

50. For details of this nineteenth-century forgery, see Grönbold, p. 112.

51. See Marvin W. Meyer, 'Mark, Gospel of', *Anchor Bible Dictionary*, vol 4, pp. 558–9.

52. *The Brook Kerith*, p. 270.

53. Sydney: Theological Explorations, 1979.

54. *Journal of Biblical Literature* 101 (1982), 147–8, p. 148. In a long review Jerome Murphy-O'Connor characterized this book, Thiering's 'first venture into paleography' as 'totally implausible'. His detailed critique established (a) 'her uncritical acceptance of any opinion (however subjective) that fits into her theory, (b) her disregard for any known form of logic, and (c) her preference for unjustified assumptions' (*Revue Biblique* 87 (1980), p. 428).

55. 'Teacher of Righteousness', *Anchor Bible Dictionary*, vol. 6, p. 340. In his 'Dead Sea Scrolls', ibid., vol. 2, p. 100, John J. Collins writes: 'Sensational attempts to find direct references to Jesus or John the Baptist in the scrolls have not entirely disappeared but have been thoroughly discredited.'

56. Sydney: Theological Explorations, 1983.

57. Joseph Fitzmyer (*Responses to 101 Questions on the Dead Sea Scrolls* (Mahwah: NJ Paulist Press, 1992), p. 110, explicitly cites Thiering on this point as well as Robert Eisenman (who thinks that James, the brother of the Lord, was the 'Teacher of Righteousness' and that Paul the Apostle was the 'Man of the Lie'). Fitzmyer says, 'Such opinions, however, ride roughshod over the archaeological, palaeographical, and radiocarbon dating of the evidence that pinpoints most of the QS to the pre-Christian centuries. Recently Eisenman has been quoted as objecting to the radiocarbon dating because "neither he nor any outsider was included in the group managing and monitoring the tests" (*BARev* 17/6 (1991), p. 72). By "outsider" he means someone not part of the "consensus" convinced – *a priori*, in his opinion – about the Essene identification of the Qumran sect and the pre-Christian dating of most of the material.'

58. *The Journal of Theological Studies* 34 (1983), 235–37, p. 237. In his review James C. VanderKam wrote of 'the bizarre results of T.'s deciphering the code' (*CBQ* 45 (1983), p. 513).
59. Sydney: Theological Explorations, 1983.
60. *The Expository Times* 95 (1984), p. 284.
61. N. T. Wright, *Who Was Jesus?* (London: SPCK, 1992), p. 23. See also Gerald O'Collins, *Jesus Today*, (Mahwah, NJ: Paulist Press, 1986), pp. 71–3, and O'Collins, review of Wright's book in the *Tablet*, (20 February 1993), p. 245.
62. 'L'auteur a perdu complètement le contact avec toute réalité historique et littéraire. Ce qu'elle nous offre ici n'est que le produit de son imagination, une imagination que, vu les résultats, on n'hésitera pas à qualifier de délirante' (*Journal for the Study of Judaism in the Persian, Hellenistic, and Roman Period* 15 (1984), pp. 210–11).
63. See Gerald O'Collins, 'Selling Jesus', *Tablet*, 26 Sept. 1992, pp. 1184–6.
64. For a scholarly version of the pesher-style commentary from Qumran, see Devorah Dimant, 'Pesharim, Qumran', *Anchor Bible Dictionary*, vol. 5, pp. 244–51. It is relevant to note that Dimant's concluding bibliography (45 entries) does not include anything by Thiering.
65. On this see M. J. D. Hodgart, 'In the Shade of the Golden Bough', pp. 113–19.

17 Why do we need to be saved and who saves us? – a Catholic perspective

1. To prevent a possible misunderstanding, let me point out that I will *not* present the human need for redemption by using a Christian doctrine about original sin that could be unacceptable in mainstream Judaism. What I will say about our human need for redemption can stand up, I hope, without my appealing to any such doctrine.
2. See F. W. Dillistone, 'Redemption', *A New Dictionary of Christian Theology*, ed., A. Richardson and J. Bowden (London: SCM Press, 1983), pp. 487–8; J. C. Fenton, 'Salvation', ibid., pp. 519–21; 'Atonement', *Oxford*

Dictionary of the Christian Church, ed. F. L. Cross and E. A. Livingstone (Oxford: Oxford University Press, 1974), pp. 104-5.

3. See, for example, William Langland (?1330-?1400), 'The Jousting of Jesus', *The Faber Book of Religious Verse*, ed. Helen Gardner (London: Faber & Faber, 1972) pp. 39-48; William Dunbar (?1460-?1520), 'The Lord is Risen', ibid., pp. 70-1.

4. See Gascoyne's poem 'Ecce Homo', ibid., pp. 333-5.

5. Deut 25:5; Exod 3:6; Lev 19:18.

6. In the 'Declaration on the Relation of the Church to Non-Christian Religions' (*Nostra Aetate*) we find this tendency to picture the human condition as involving a bondage and alienation that calls for deliverance and reconciliation through the loving power of God (no. 4). Article 4 ends with a reference to the common guilt of all human beings. Yet more attention is paid to the oppressive bondage and alienation which love must heal.

7. A full account of how the Second Vatican Council views the unredeemed human condition would draw on its other documents like the 'Dogmatic Constitution on the Church' (*Lumen Gentium*), the 'Declaration on Religious Liberty' (*Dignitatis Humanae*) and the 'Decree on the Church's Missionary Activity' (*Ad Gentes Divinitus*).

8. On the human need for salvation see also *Sacrosanctum Concilium* (the 'Constitution on the Sacred Liturgy'), no. 5.

9. On the role of the Church for salvation see Y. Congar, '"Hors de l'Eglise pas de Salut",' *Sainte Eglise* (Paris: Editions du Cerf, 1963), pp. 417-32; J. Ratzinger, *Das neue Volk Gottes* (Dusseldorf: Patmos, 1969), pp. 339-61; J. P. Thiesen, *The Ultimate Church and the Promise of Salvation* (Collegeville: St John's University Press, 1976).

10. Here the healthy 'worldliness' of much in the Jewish tradition could serve as a useful corrective to a passive other-worldliness (wherever it persists in Christianity).

11. On this misrepresentation of a proper model of redemption understood as expiation see further my *Interpreting Jesus* (London: Geoffrey Chapman, 1983), pp. 150-55.

18 Power made perfect in weakness: 2 Corinthians 12:9-10

1. 'Eine Christus-Aretalogie bei Paulus (2 Kor 12, 7-10)', *ZTK* 66 (1969), pp. 288-305.
2. *A Critical And Exegetical Commentary on the Second Epistle of St. Paul to the Corinthians* (Edinburgh: T. & T. Clark, 1915), pp. 354, 356.
3. ET, London: SCM Press, 1952, I, p. 285.
4. Ibid., p. 351.
5. Ibid., p. 349.
6. *Journal for Theology and Church* 1, (1965), p. 104.
7. *Der zweite Korintherbrief* (Göttingen: Vandenhoeck & Ruprecht 1924), p. 392.
8. Leipzig: Hinrichs, 1934, p. 234.
9. Ibid., pp. 192f.
10. *The Second Epistle of Paul to the Corinthians* (London: Hodder & Stoughton, 1965), p. 33.
11. See H. D. Betz, 'Eine Christus-Aretalogie', pp. 293f.
12. *Der leidende Apostel und sein Herr* (Göttingen: Vandenhoeck & Ruprecht, 1966), p. 168.
13. *Weisheit und Torheit. Eine exegetisch-religionsgeschichtliche Untersuchung zu 1 Kor. und 2* (Tübingen: J. C. B Mohr, 1959), p. 218, n. 2; cf. pp. 53ff.
14. *Weisheit*, pp. 150f.
15. See H. D. Betz, 'Eine Christus-Aretalogie', p. 304 for details.
16. *Der zweite Korintherbrief*, p. 393.
17. C. F. D. Moule, *Studies in Biblical Theology*, Second Series, 1, *The Phenomenon of the New Testament* (Naperville: Allenson, 1967), pp. 22ff.
18. Güttgemanns, *Der leidende Apostel*, pp. 162ff.
19. 1:8, 4:7, 6:7, 10:4, 10, etc.
20. *Die Gegner des Paulus im 2 Korintherbrief* (Tübingen: J. C. B. Mohr, 1964), p. 244.
21. See 2 Cor 13:4; U. Wilckens, *Weisheit*, p. 48.
22. Ibid., p. 218.
23. Ibid., p. 218f.
24. W. Schmithals, *Die Gnosis In Korinth*, 2nd edn; Gottingen: Vandenhoeck & Ruprecht, 1965), p. 154.
25. *Der zweite Korintherbrief*, p. 391.

26. *Diakonia Pneumatos* (Freiburg: Herder, 1960), p. 90.
27. *Das Neue Testament deutsch, Die Briefe an die Korinther* (8th edn, Göttingen, Vandenhoeck & Ruprecht, 1962), p. 164.
28. *Studies in Biblical Theology*, 41, *Essays on New Testament Themes* (Naperville: Allenson), p. 84.
29. *Der zweite Korintherbrief*, p. 391.
30. 'In this place "grace" means concretely the power which proves the apostle as representative of Christ. This power is linked to the presupposition of "weakness"', *ZNW* 41 (1942), p. 53.
31. 'Eine Christus-Aretalogie', p. 297.
32. *Der zweite Korintherbrief*, p. 391.
33. *A Critical and Exegetical Commentary*, p. 254.
34. *Handbuch zum NT, Der zweite Korintherbrief* (4th edn, Tübingen, J. C. B. Mohr, 1949), p. 155.
35. *Dying and Rising with Christ* (Berlin: Töpelmann, 1967), p. 100.
36. *Der zweite Korintherbrief*, p. 394.
37. *Der leidende Apostel*, 169.
38. 'Eine Christus-Aretalogie', p. 303.
39. In the *'Anhang'* to H. Lietzmann, *Der zweite Korintherbrief*, p. 212 (on p. 155, line 53).

19 St Paul and the language of reconciliation

1. Ludwig Wittgenstein, *Philosophical Investigations*, 3rd edn, trans. G. E. M. Anscombe (Oxford: Blackwell, 1958), par. 109.
2. Gordon D. Kaufman, *Systematic Theology: A Historicist Perspective* (New York: Scribner's, 1968), p. 389n.
3. Joseph A. Fitzmyer, 'Pauline Theology' in *The Jerome Biblical Commentary*, ed. Raymond E. Brown et al. (London: Geoffrey Chapman, 1968), vol. 2, p. 814.
4. Ernst Käsemann, 'Some Thoughts on the theme "The Doctrine of Reconciliation in the New Testament"', in *The Future of Our Religious Past*, ed. James M. Robinson, trans. Charles E. Carlston and Robert p. Scharlemann (New York: Harper and Row, 1971), pp. 49–64.

5. Plato, *Protagoras*, 355ff.

20 On not neglecting hatred

1. Letter of Karl Barth to Edward Thurneysen dated 11 November 1918 and found in *Karl Barth—Edward Thurneysen Briefwechsel*, bd 1 (Zürich: Theologischer Verlag, 1973), pp. 299–301; this desire to hold together the Bible and the daily newspaper is also cited in John Godsey's *Karl Barth, How I Changed My Mind* (Richmond, VA: John Knox Press, 1966), p. 12.
2. Vol. 4, pp. 683–94; see W. Foerster, *echthros, echthra*, ibid., vol. 2, pp. 811–15. It is worth remarking that the *Anchor Bible Dictionary* has two long articles on 'love' (vol. 4, pp. 375–96) but no entry on 'hatred'. The three volume *Dictionary of New Testament Theology*, ed. Colin Brown (Grand Rapids, MI: Zondervan, 1980) briefly treats 'Enemy, Enmity, Hate': Vol. 1, pp. 553–57.
3. Commenting on John 15:18–21, Raymond Brown explains (*The Gospel According to John* (Garden City, NY: Doubleday, 1966), p. 695) that 'Jesus makes clear that the world's hatred of the Christian is not a passing phenomenon; hate is just as much of the essence of the world as love is of the essence of the Christian. The world is opposed to God and His revelation; it can never have anything but hate from those who recognize that revelation in His Son. In a series of four conditional sentences it is repeated that the world's hatred for Christians is basically a refusal of Jesus himself. Love of Jesus has made the true Christian so much like Jesus that he is treated in the same manner as Jesus.'
4. *Church Dogmatics*, Index Volume, ed. G. W. Bromiley and T. F. Torrance (Edinburgh: T. & T. Clark, 1977), pp. 206–62.
5. Chicago: University of Chicago Press, 1967.
6. London: Darton, Longman & Todd, 1961–92.
7. 7 vols. (Tübingen: J. C. B. Mohr, 1957–75).
8. Vol. 5, col. 24–25; entry contributed by Lorenz Neider and Wilhelm Heinen.
9. Vol. 6, pp. 946–7, entry contributed by J. M. Giannini.

248   *Focus on Jesus*

10. Ed. A. Richardson and J. Bowden (London: SCM Press, 1983).
11. Ed. J. A. Komonchak et al. (Wilmington, Del.: Michael Glazier).
12. Freiburg i. Br.: Herder, 1987.
13. Ed. K. Rahner et al. (London: Burns & Oates, 1968–70).
14. Ed. J. Feiner and M. Löhrer (Zürich/Einsiedeln/Köln: Benzinger, 1965–81).
15. Vol. 6 (New York: Charles Scribner's Sons, 1925) pp. 526–29; entry contributed by William L. Davidson.
16. Munich: Kösel, 1973–74.
17. Basel/Stuttgart: Schwade, 1971–.
18. New York: Macmillan, 1967. Not only the psychological origins of hatred but also social systems which educate children to hate call for much more study and remedy. Melanie Klein, Karl Menninger and their successors must be heard and heeded on the anatomy of hatred and violence.
19. Florence: Editrice Le Lettere, 1982; Cattanaro makes no reference to Aristotle or Aquinas.
20. In 'Aquinas's Construction of a Moral Account of the Passions', *Freiburger Zeitschrift für Philosophie und Theologie* 33 (1986), pp. 71–97, esp. pp. 73–83, Mark D. Jordan provides a very helpful guide to the sources Aquinas used in his study on the passions.
21. G. Marcel, *The Mystery of Being*, trans. G. S. Fraser and R. Hague, vol. 2 (London: Harvill Press, 1951), p. 153.
22. *Summa Theologiae*, Ia IIae, Q. 46, art. 6 ad 1.

21 Questions about Christ

1. Dated 1 September 1980. In this chapter I will use the translation provided by the United States Conference.
2. On this see my *What Are They Saying About Jesus?* (New York: Paulist Press, 1977), pp. 6–8.
3. On what follows see my *What are They Saying About Jesus?*, pp. 10–12, 35–53; *The Calvary Christ* (London: SCM Press, 1977), pp. 55–69; 'Jesus' Concept of His Own Death', *The Way*, 19, (1979), pp. 212–213.
4. See *The Calvary Christ*, pp. 92–114.

Abbrevations

ABD	Anchor Bible Dictionary
CBQ	Catholic Biblical Quarterly
JBL	Journal of Biblical Literature
LXX	The Septuagint (Greek Version of the Old Testament)
NT	New Testament
NovT	Novum Testamentum
NTS	New Testament Studies
OT	Old Testament
RSV	Revised Standard Version
ZNW	Zeitschrift für neutestamentliche Wissenschaft
ZTK	Zeitschrift für Theologie und Kirche
par(r.)	and parallel(s) in other gospels

Index of Names

Sources and acknowledgements

'What are They Saying about Jesus now': *America*, 27 August 1994, pp. 10–14, 32–5; 'Christ Today': *The Way* 21 (1981) pp. 3–13; 'The Incarnation under Fire': *Gregorianum* 76 (1995), pp. 263–80; 'Interpreting Christmas': *America*, 19 December 1987, pp. 470–71; 'Emmanuel': *America*, 17 December 1988, pp. 510–11; 'Jesus between Poetry and Philosophy': *New Blackfriars* 57 (1976), pp. 160–66; 'Jesus the Communicator': *America*, 7 April 1984, pp. 260–61; 'The Founder of Christianity': *Studia Missionalia* 33 (1984), pp. 385–402; 'Our Peace and Reconciliation': *The Way* 22 (1982), pp. 112–21; 'Did Joseph of Arimathea Exist?' *Biblica* 75 (1994), pp. 235–41; 'The Resurrection of Jesus: Some Current Questions': *America*, 14 December 1985, pp. 422–25; 'The Uniqueness of the Easter Appearances': *Catholic Biblical Quarterly*, 54 (1992), pp. 287–307; 'St. Ignatius Loyola on Christ's Resurrection': *America*, 30 March 1991, pp. 346, 359–62; 'Newman's Seven Notes: The Case of the Resurrection': I. Ker and A. G. Hill (eds.) *Newman after a Hundred Years* (Oxford: Clarendon Press, 1990), pp. 337–52 (by permission of Oxford University Press); 'Christ's Resurrection and Ascension': *America*, 25 March 1989, pp. 262–63; 'On Reissuing Venturini': *Gregorianum* 75 (1994), pp. 241–65; 'Why Do We Need to Be Saved and Who Saves Us – A Catholic Perspective': *Face to Face: An Interreligious Bulletin* 14 (1988), pp. 15–20; 'Power Made Perfect in Weakness: 2 Cor 12:9–10: *Catholic Biblical Quarterly*, 33 (1971), pp. 528–37; 'St. Paul and the Language of Reconciliation': *Colloquium* 6 (1973), pp. 3–8 (This article was co-authored by Gerald O'Collins and T. Michael McNulty); 'On Not Neglecting Hatred', *Scottish Journal of Theology* 47 (1994), pp. 511–18.'Questions about Christ' appeared as 'What Are They Saying About Jesus Now?' in *The Furrow* 32 (1981), pp. 203–11.